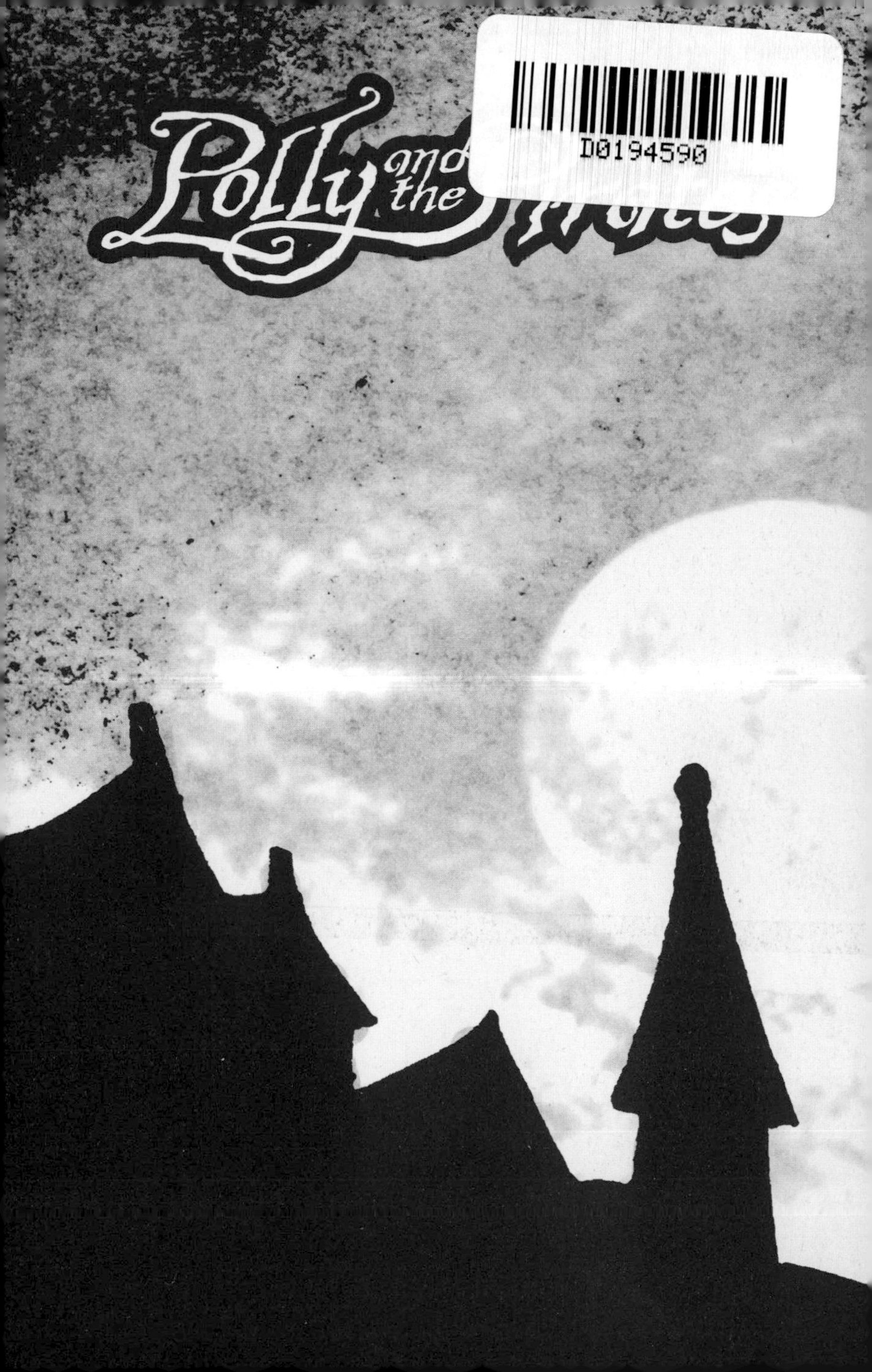
Polly
and the

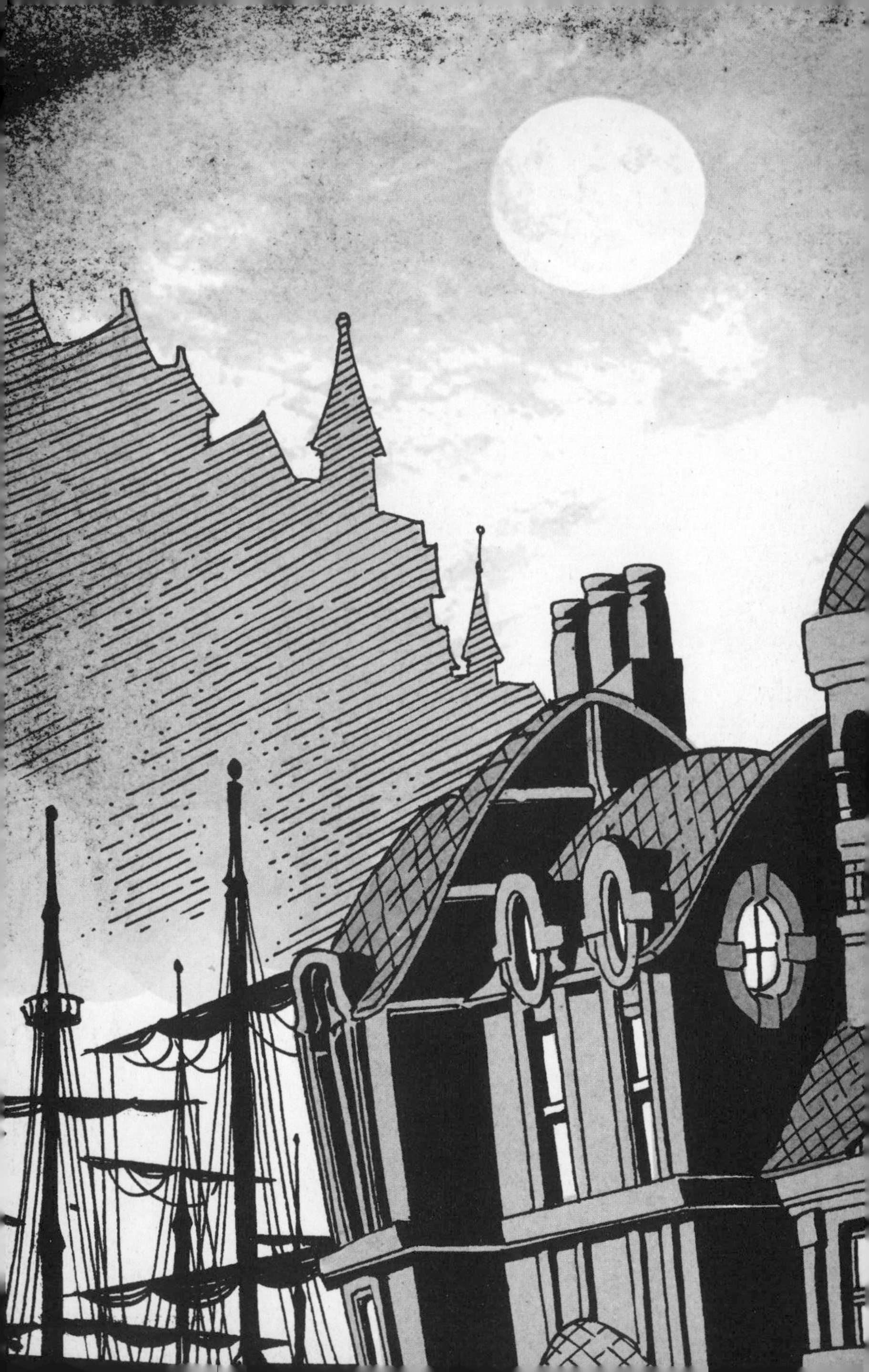

Polly and the Pirates™

Volume One

by
Ted Naifeh

Edited by
James Lucas Jones & Joe Nozemack

Design by
Steven Birch & Ted Naifeh

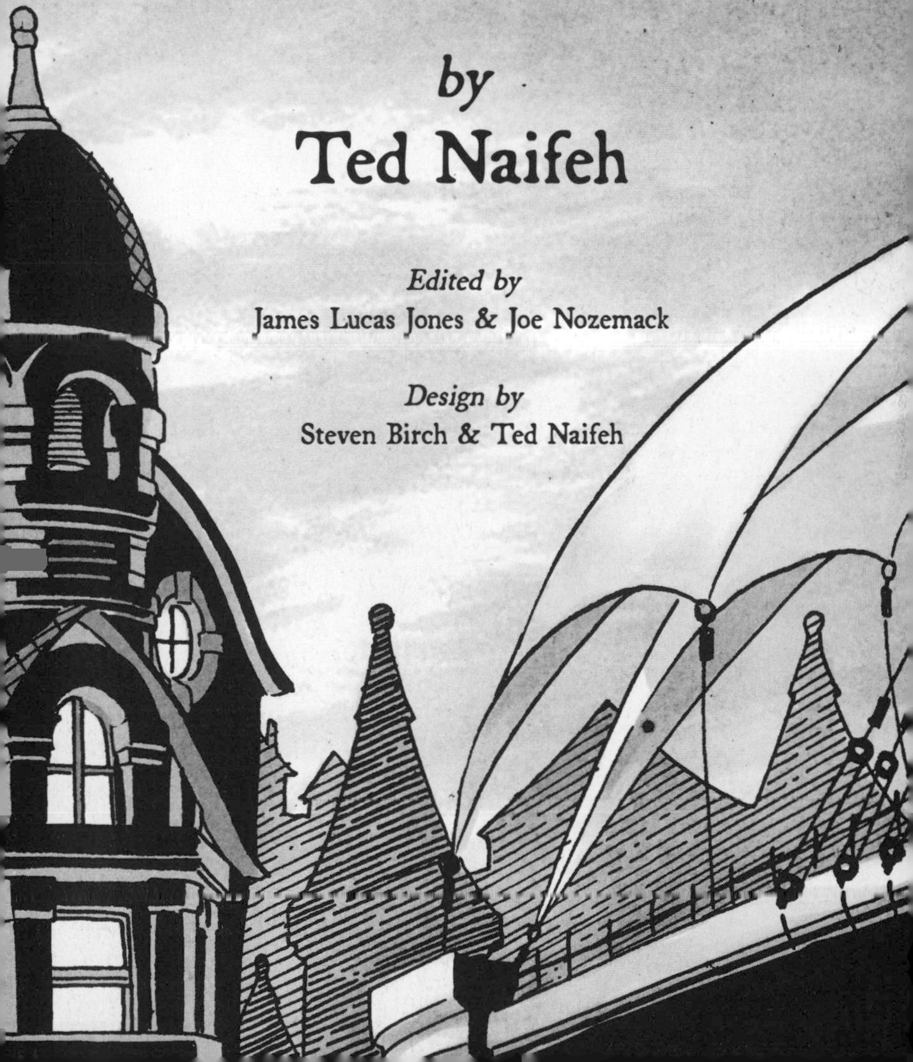

Published by Oni Press, Inc.
Joe Nozemack, publisher
James Lucas Jones, editor in chief
Maryanne Snell, director of marketing & sales
Randal C. Jarrell, managing editor
Douglas E. Sherwood, editorial assistant

Oni Press, Inc.
1305 SE Martin Luther King Jr. Blvd.
Suite A
Portland, OR 97214
USA

www.onipress.com
www.tednaifeh.com

This collects issues 1 — 6 of the Oni Press comics series
Polly and the Pirates

First edition: July 2006
ISBN 1-932664-46-7

1 3 5 7 9 10 8 6 4 2
PRINTED IN CANADA.

Chapter 1

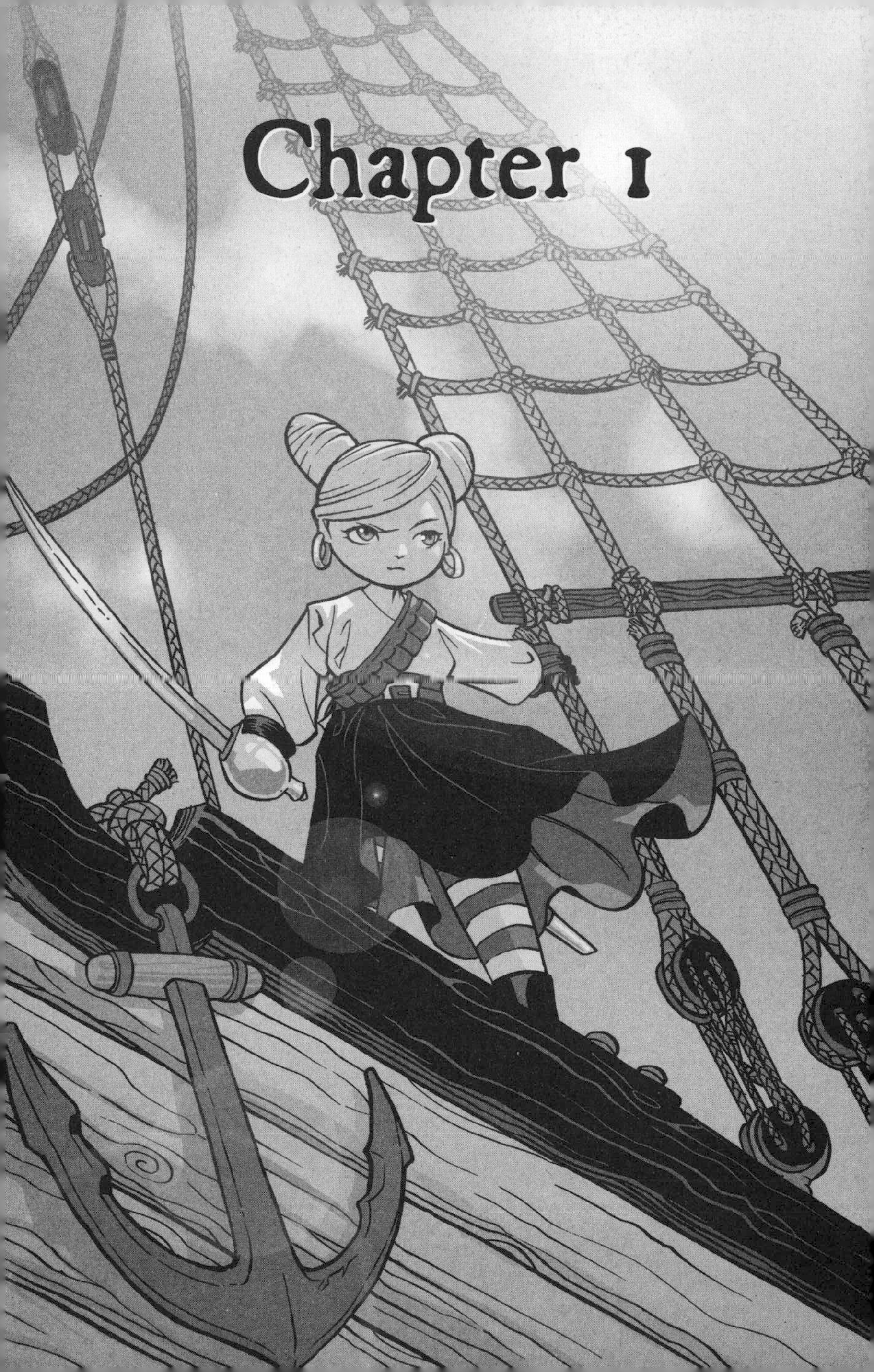

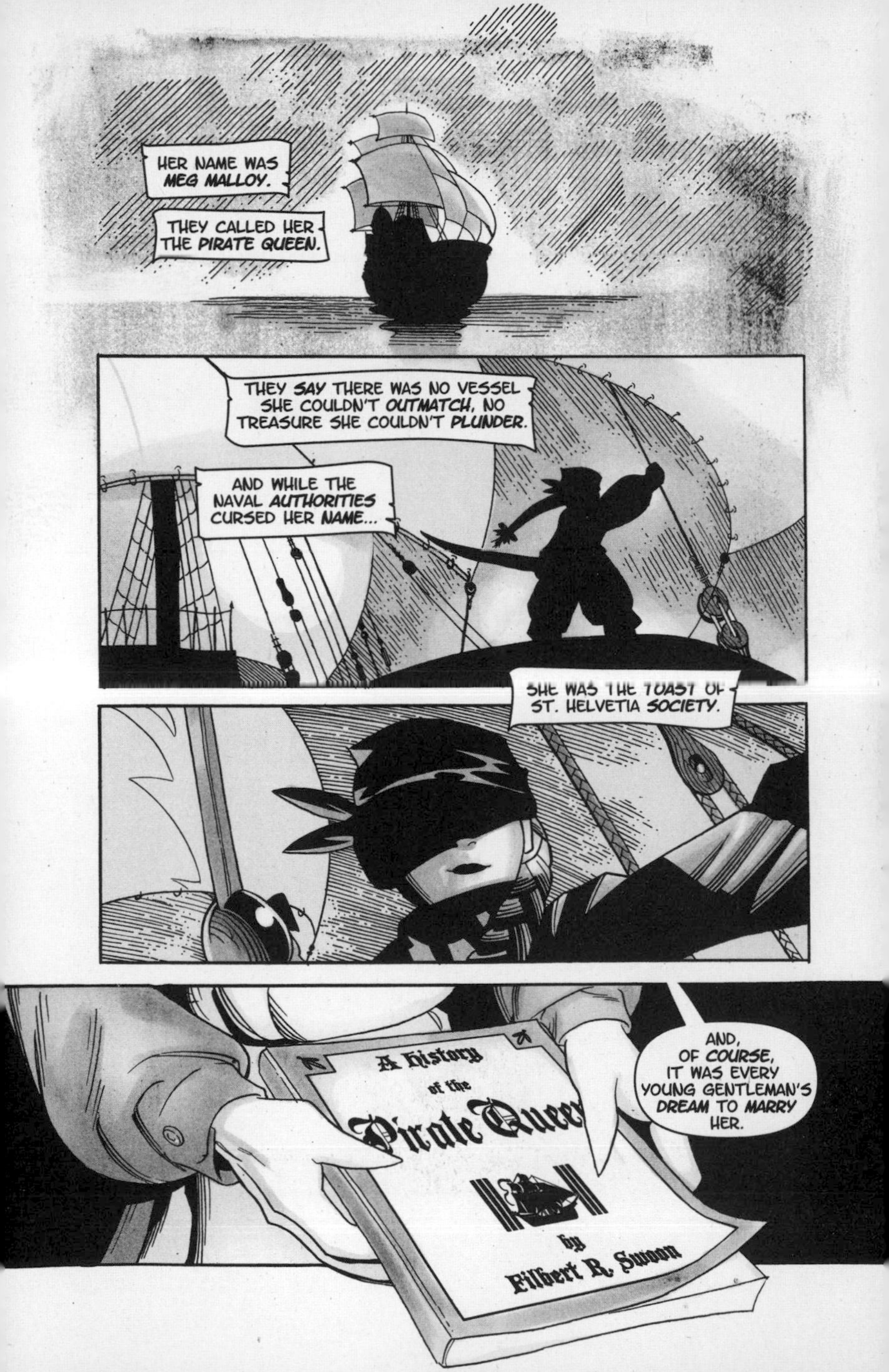
HER NAME WAS MEG MALLOY.
THEY CALLED HER THE PIRATE QUEEN.
THEY SAY THERE WAS NO VESSEL SHE COULDN'T OUTMATCH, NO TREASURE SHE COULDN'T PLUNDER.
AND WHILE THE NAVAL AUTHORITIES CURSED HER NAME...
SHE WAS THE TOAST OF ST. HELVETIA SOCIETY.
A History of the Pirate Queen by Filbert R. Swoon
AND, OF COURSE, IT WAS EVERY YOUNG GENTLEMAN'S DREAM TO MARRY HER.

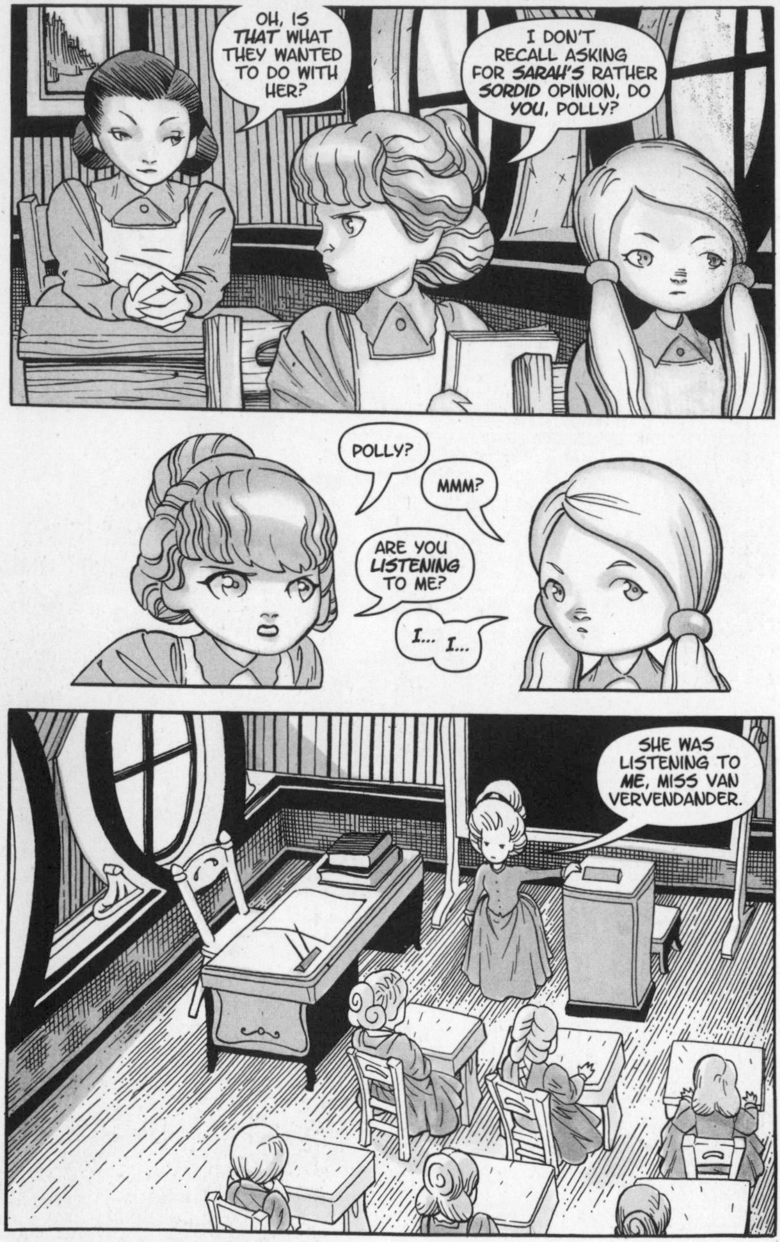
OH, IS THAT WHAT THEY WANTED TO DO WITH HER?
I DON'T RECALL ASKING FOR SARAH'S RATHER SORDID OPINION, DO YOU, POLLY?
POLLY?
MMM?
ARE YOU LISTENING TO ME?
I... I...
SHE WAS LISTENING TO ME, MISS VAN VERVENDANDER.

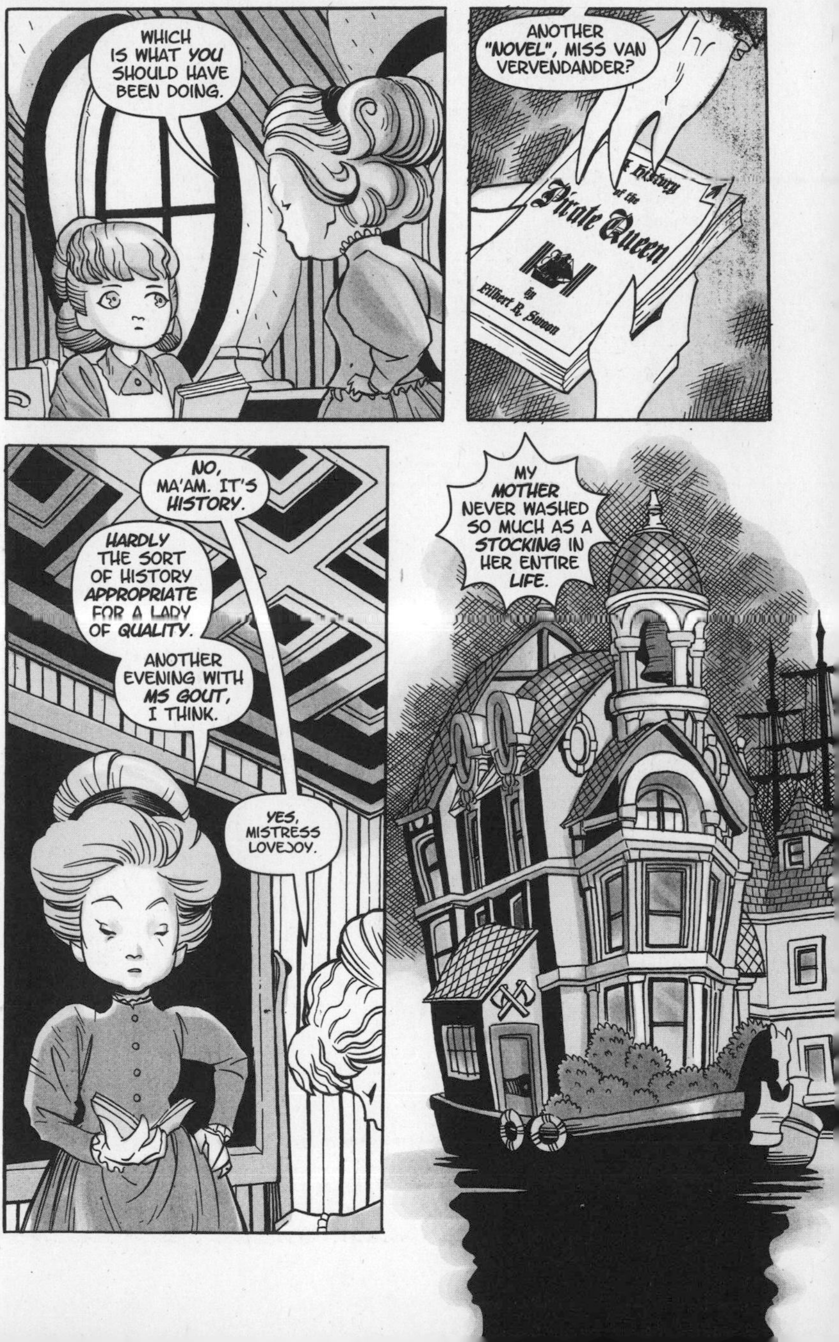
WHICH IS WHAT YOU SHOULD HAVE BEEN DOING.
ANOTHER "NOVEL", MISS VAN VERVENDANDER?
A History of the Pirate Queen by Filbert R. Swoon
NO, MA'AM. IT'S HISTORY.
HARDLY THE SORT OF HISTORY APPROPRIATE FOR A LADY OF QUALITY.
ANOTHER EVENING WITH MS GOUT, I THINK.
YES, MISTRESS LOVEJOY.
MY MOTHER NEVER WASHED SO MUCH AS A STOCKING IN HER ENTIRE LIFE.

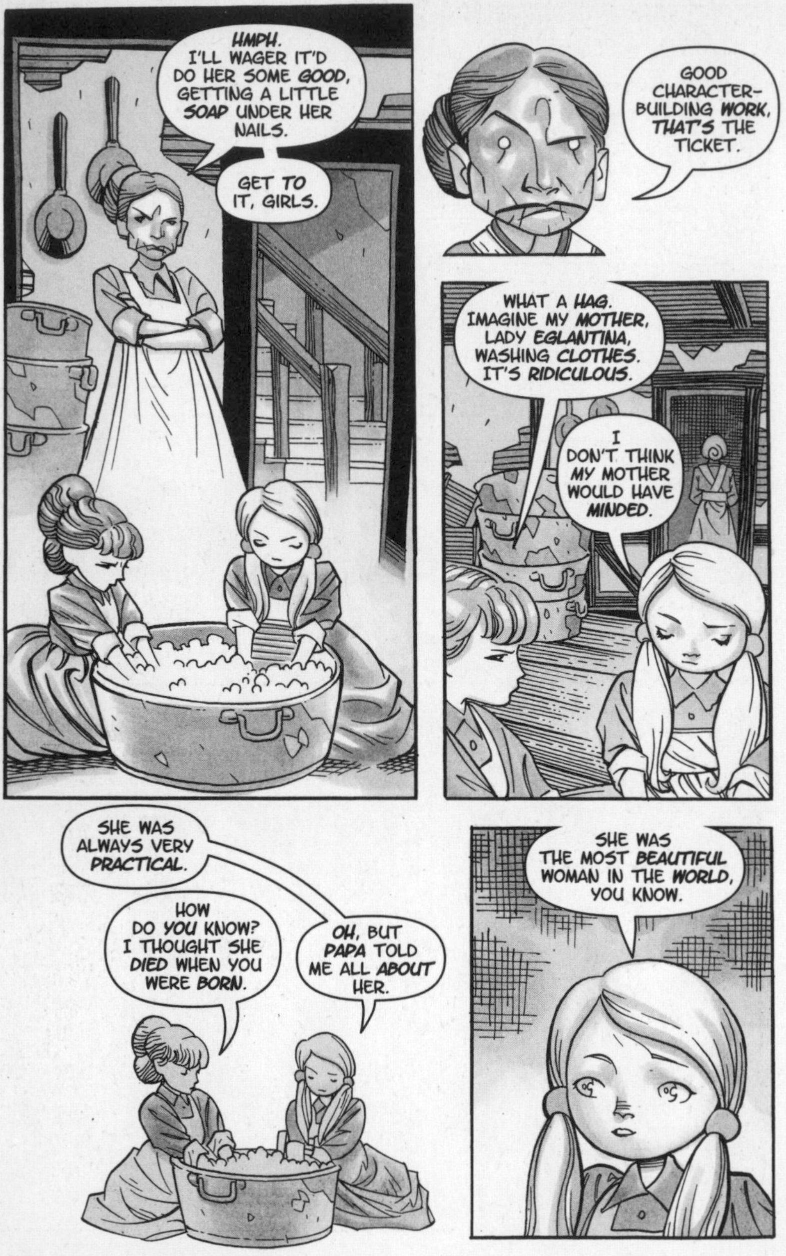
HMPH. I'LL WAGER IT'D DO HER SOME GOOD, GETTING A LITTLE SOAP UNDER HER NAILS.
GET TO IT, GIRLS.
GOOD CHARACTER-BUILDING WORK, THAT'S THE TICKET.
WHAT A HAG. IMAGINE MY MOTHER, LADY EGLANTINA, WASHING CLOTHES. IT'S RIDICULOUS.
I DON'T THINK MY MOTHER WOULD HAVE MINDED.
SHE WAS ALWAYS VERY PRACTICAL.
HOW DO YOU KNOW? I THOUGHT SHE DIED WHEN YOU WERE BORN.
OH, BUT PAPA TOLD ME ALL ABOUT HER.
SHE WAS THE MOST BEAUTIFUL WOMAN IN THE WORLD, YOU KNOW.

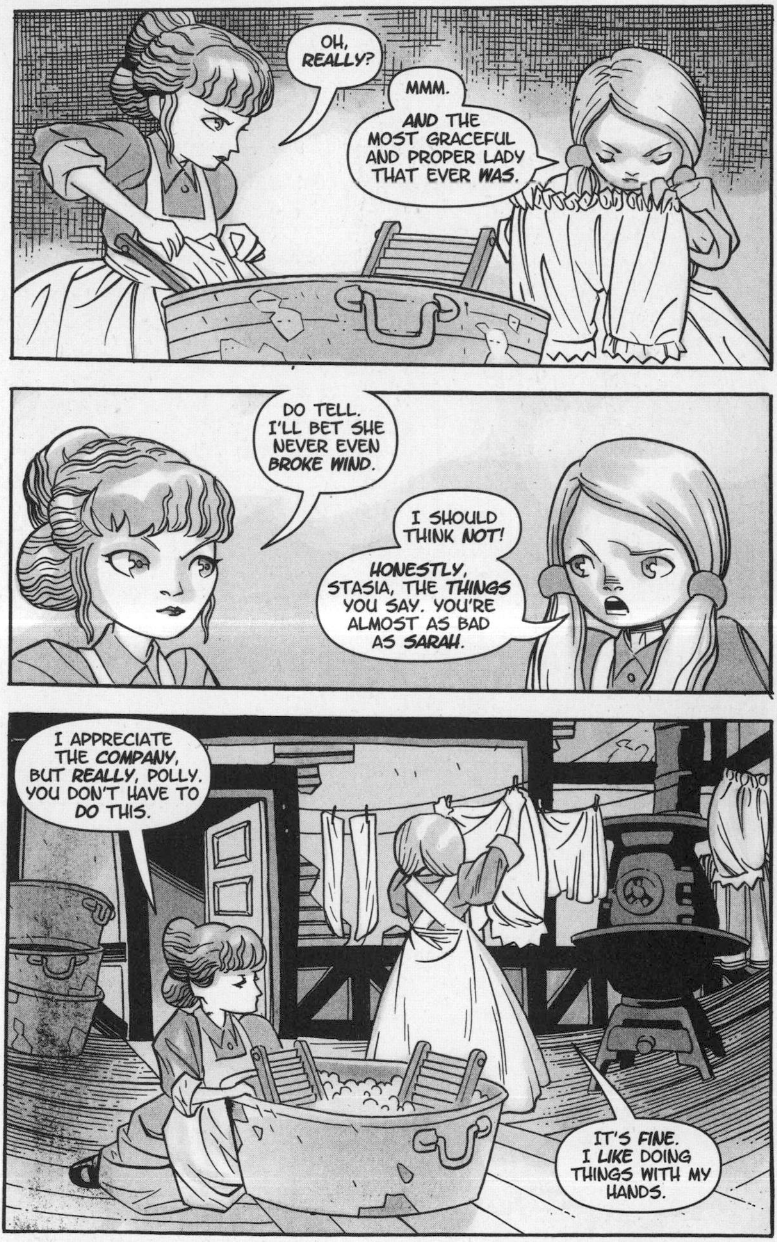
OH, REALLY?
MMM.
AND THE MOST GRACEFUL AND PROPER LADY THAT EVER WAS.
DO TELL. I'LL BET SHE NEVER EVEN BROKE WIND.
I SHOULD THINK NOT!
HONESTLY, STASIA, THE THINGS YOU SAY. YOU'RE ALMOST AS BAD AS SARAH.
I APPRECIATE THE COMPANY, BUT REALLY, POLLY. YOU DON'T HAVE TO DO THIS.
IT'S FINE. I LIKE DOING THINGS WITH MY HANDS.

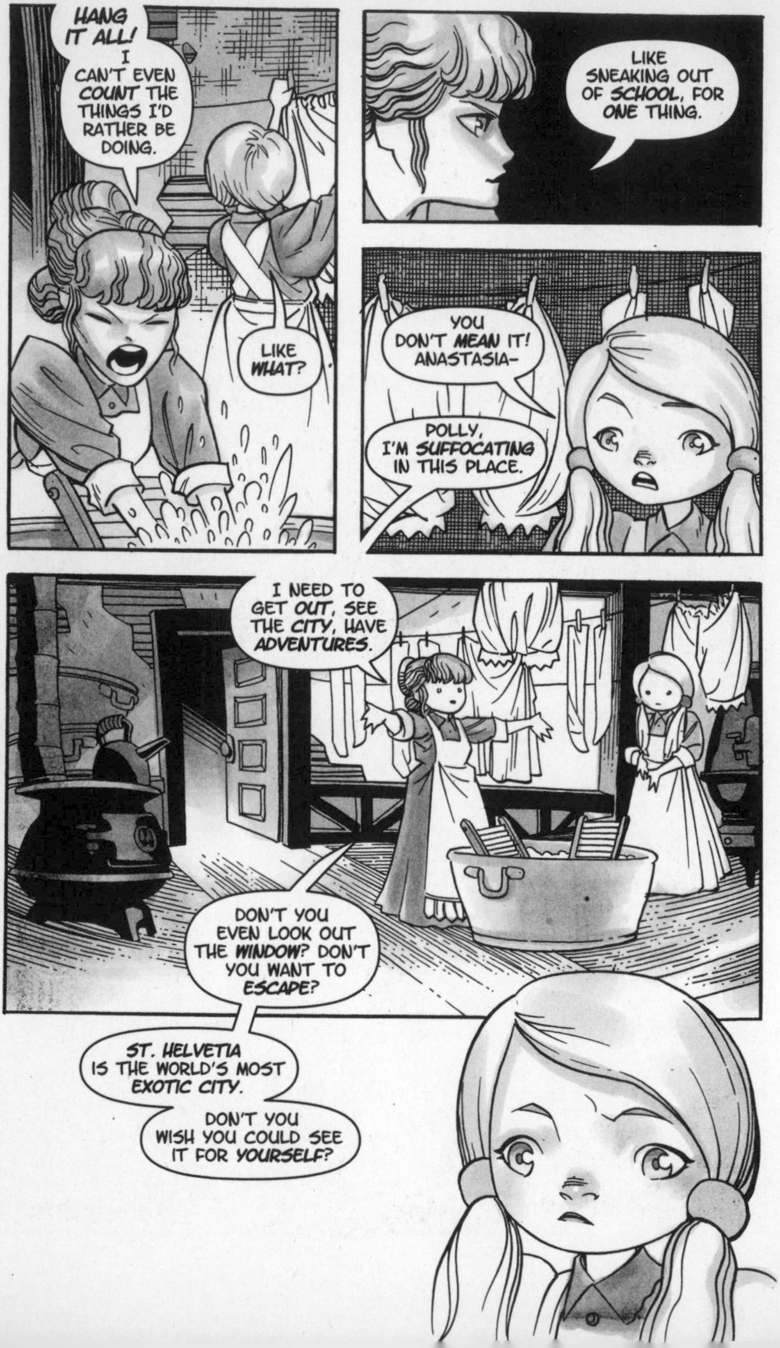

HANG IT ALL! I CAN'T EVEN COUNT THE THINGS I'D RATHER BE DOING.
LIKE WHAT?
LIKE SNEAKING OUT OF SCHOOL, FOR ONE THING.
YOU DON'T MEAN IT! ANASTASIA-
POLLY, I'M SUFFOCATING IN THIS PLACE.
I NEED TO GET OUT, SEE THE CITY, HAVE ADVENTURES.
DON'T YOU EVEN LOOK OUT THE WINDOW? DON'T YOU WANT TO ESCAPE?
ST. HELVETIA IS THE WORLD'S MOST EXOTIC CITY.
DON'T YOU WISH YOU COULD SEE IT FOR YOURSELF?

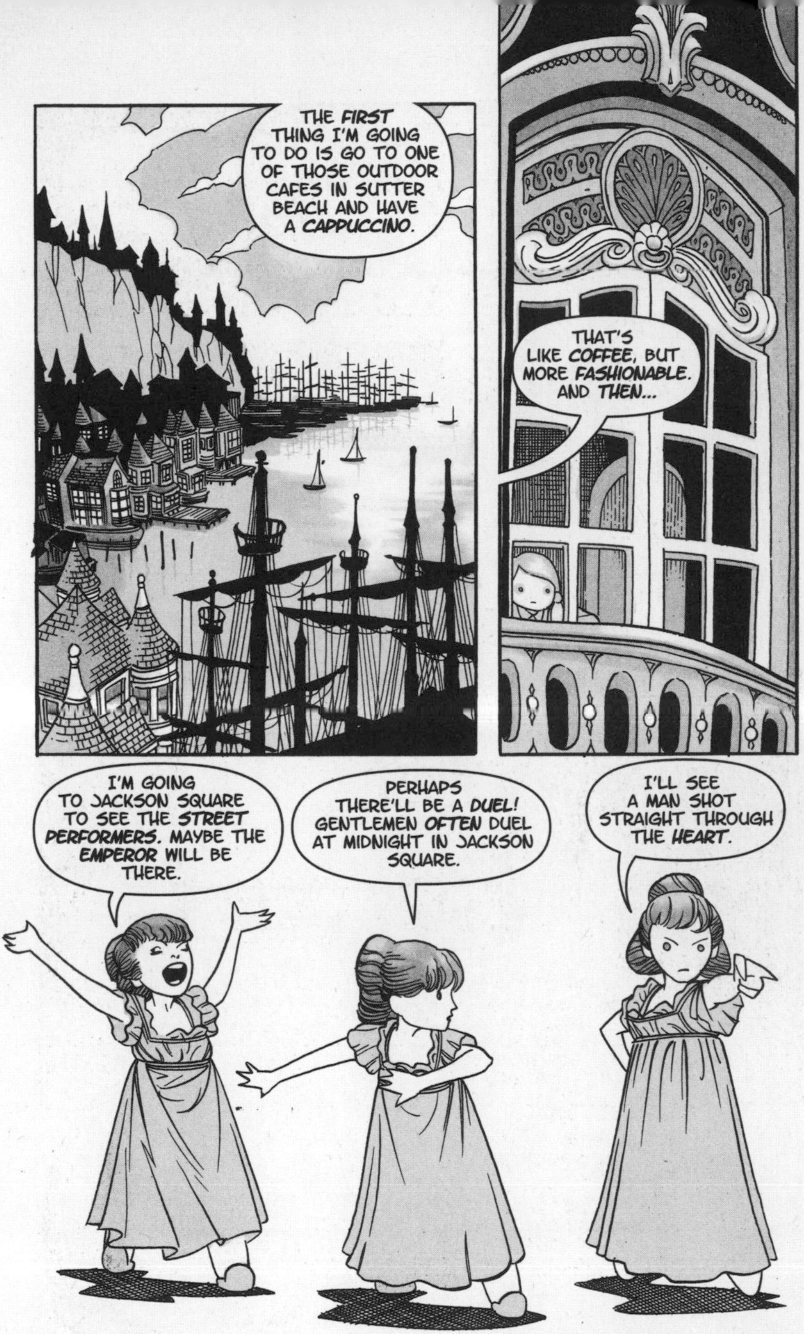
THE FIRST THING I'M GOING TO DO IS GO TO ONE OF THOSE OUTDOOR CAFES IN SUTTER BEACH AND HAVE A CAPPUCCINO.
THAT'S LIKE COFFEE, BUT MORE FASHIONABLE. AND THEN...
I'M GOING TO JACKSON SQUARE TO SEE THE STREET PERFORMERS. MAYBE THE EMPEROR WILL BE THERE.
PERHAPS THERE'LL BE A DUEL! GENTLEMEN OFTEN DUEL AT MIDNIGHT IN JACKSON SQUARE.
I'LL SEE A MAN SHOT STRAIGHT THROUGH THE HEART.

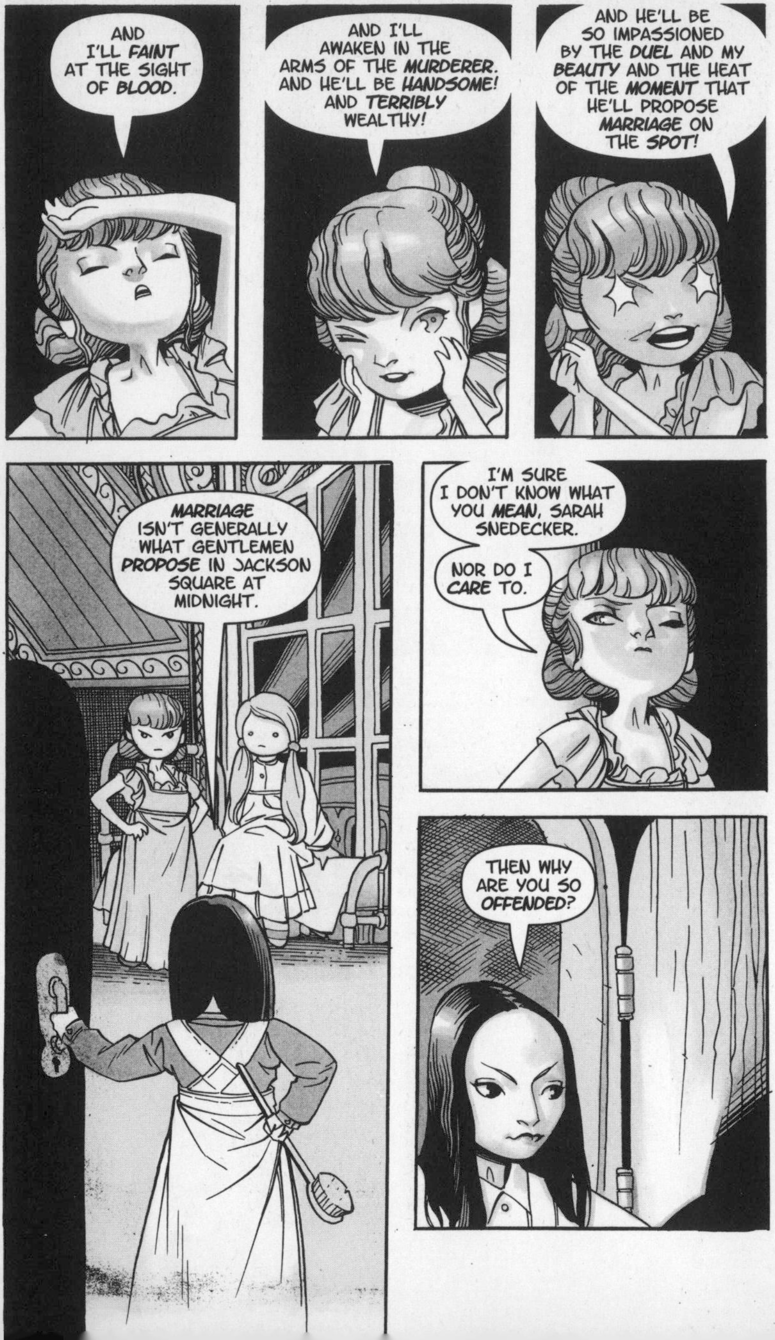
AND I'LL FAINT AT THE SIGHT OF BLOOD.
AND I'LL AWAKEN IN THE ARMS OF THE MURDERER. AND HE'LL BE HANDSOME! AND TERRIBLY WEALTHY!
AND HE'LL BE SO IMPASSIONED BY THE DUEL AND MY BEAUTY AND THE HEAT OF THE MOMENT THAT HE'LL PROPOSE MARRIAGE ON THE SPOT!
MARRIAGE ISN'T GENERALLY WHAT GENTLEMEN PROPOSE IN JACKSON SQUARE AT MIDNIGHT.
I'M SURE I DON'T KNOW WHAT YOU MEAN, SARAH SNEDECKER.
NOR DO I CARE TO.
THEN WHY ARE YOU SO OFFENDED?

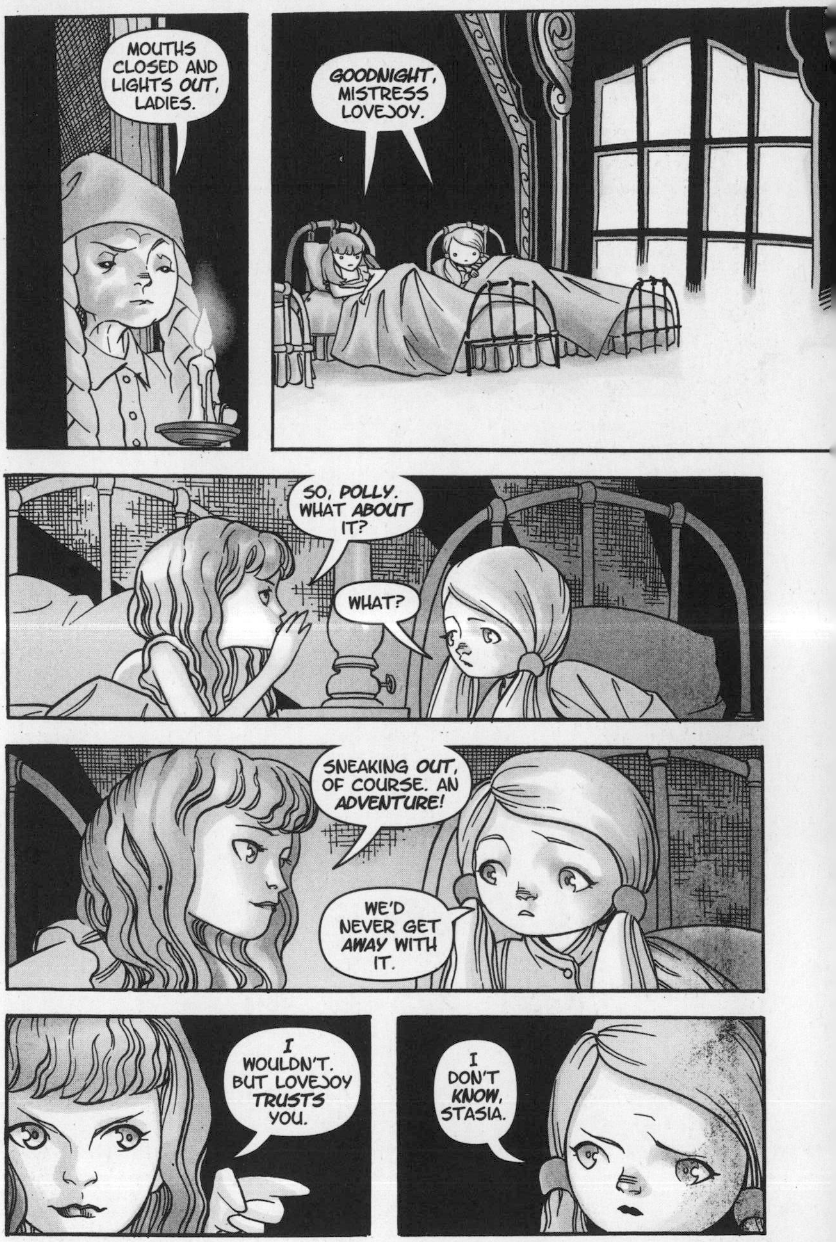
MOUTHS CLOSED AND LIGHTS OUT, LADIES.
GOODNIGHT, MISTRESS LOVEJOY.
SO, POLLY. WHAT ABOUT IT?
WHAT?
SNEAKING OUT, OF COURSE. AN ADVENTURE!
WE'D NEVER GET AWAY WITH IT.
I WOULDN'T. BUT LOVEJOY TRUSTS YOU.
I DON'T KNOW, STASIA.

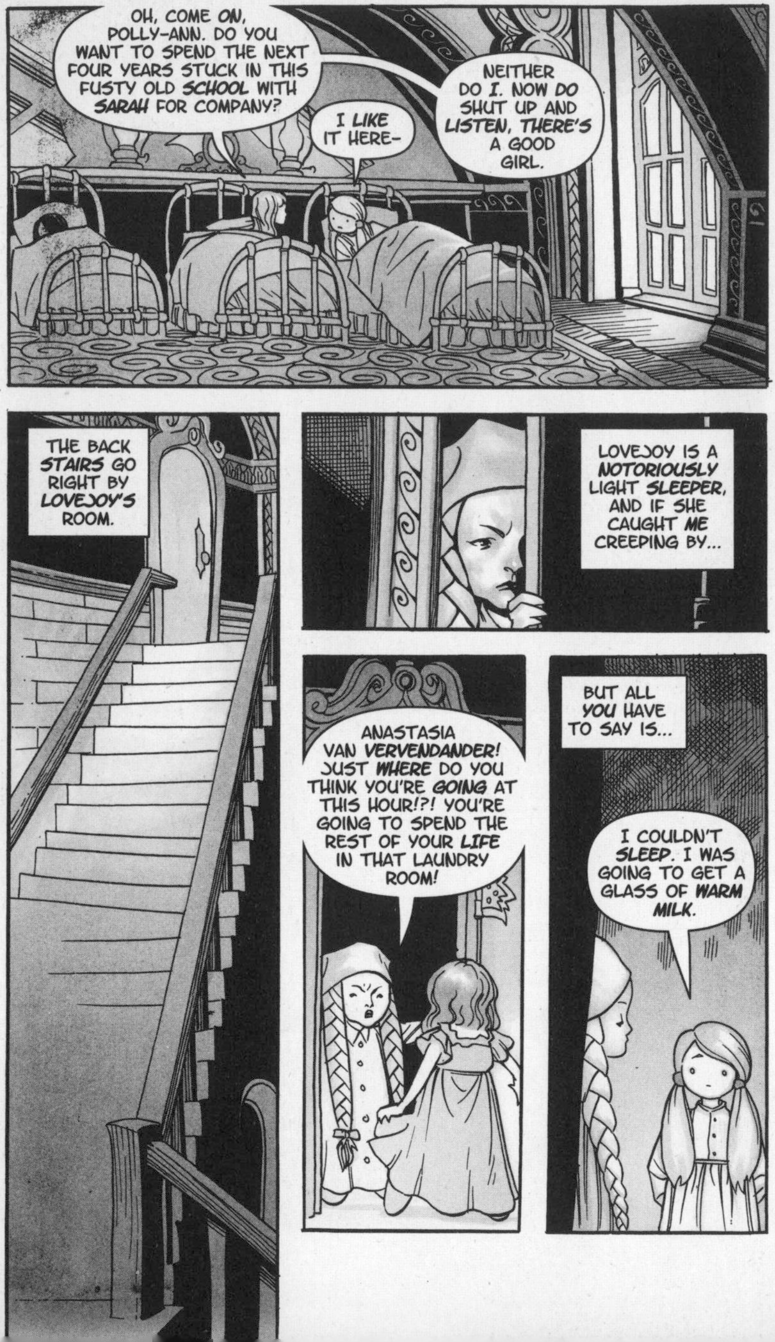
OH, COME ON, POLLY-ANN. DO YOU WANT TO SPEND THE NEXT FOUR YEARS STUCK IN THIS FUSTY OLD SCHOOL WITH SARAH FOR COMPANY?
I LIKE IT HERE-
NEITHER DO I. NOW DO SHUT UP AND LISTEN, THERE'S A GOOD GIRL.
THE BACK STAIRS GO RIGHT BY LOVEJOY'S ROOM.
LOVEJOY IS A NOTORIOUSLY LIGHT SLEEPER, AND IF SHE CAUGHT ME CREEPING BY...
ANASTASIA VAN VERVENDANDER! JUST WHERE DO YOU THINK YOU'RE GOING AT THIS HOUR!?! YOU'RE GOING TO SPEND THE REST OF YOUR LIFE IN THAT LAUNDRY ROOM!
BUT ALL YOU HAVE TO SAY IS...
I COULDN'T SLEEP. I WAS GOING TO GET A GLASS OF WARM MILK.

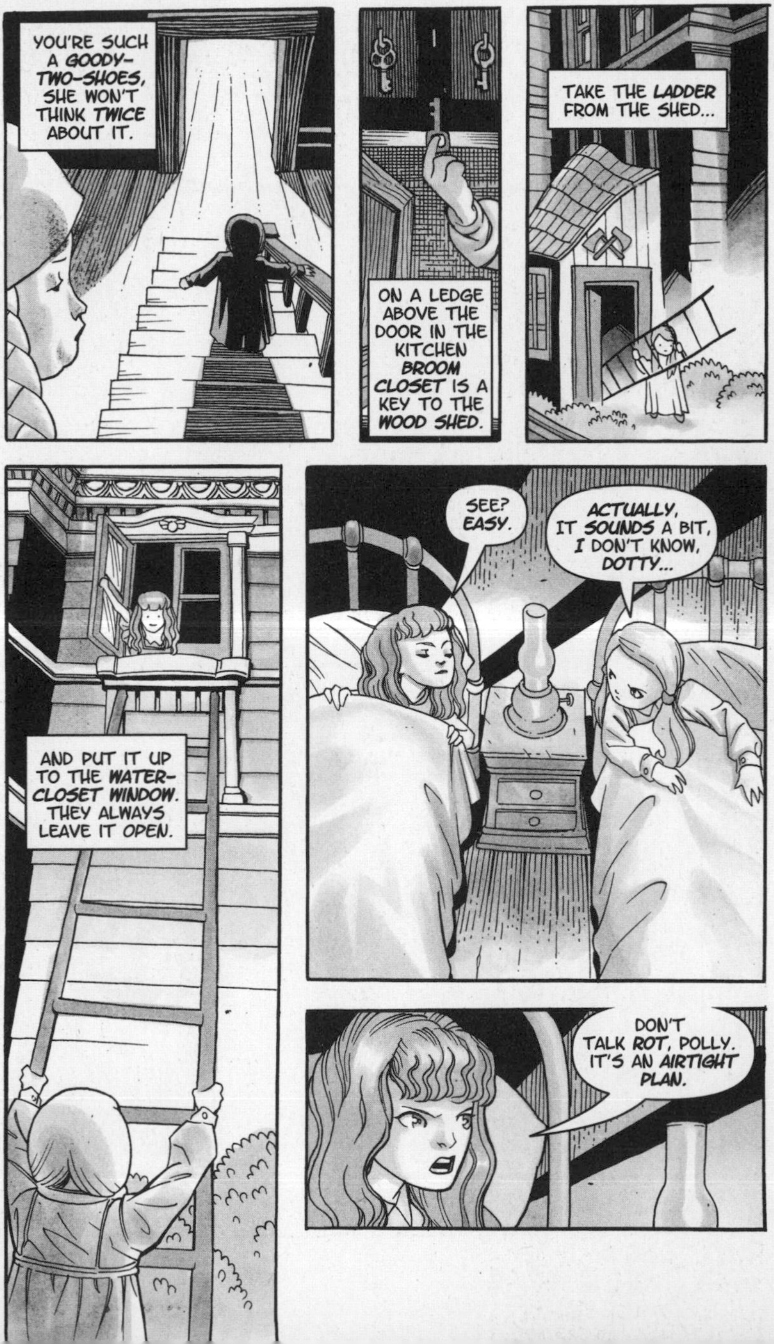
YOU'RE SUCH A GOODY-TWO-SHOES, SHE WON'T THINK TWICE ABOUT IT.
ON A LEDGE ABOVE THE DOOR IN THE KITCHEN BROOM CLOSET IS A KEY TO THE WOOD SHED.
TAKE THE LADDER FROM THE SHED...
AND PUT IT UP TO THE WATER-CLOSET WINDOW. THEY ALWAYS LEAVE IT OPEN.
SEE? EASY.
ACTUALLY, IT SOUNDS A BIT, I DON'T KNOW, DOTTY...
DON'T TALK ROT, POLLY. IT'S AN AIRTIGHT PLAN.

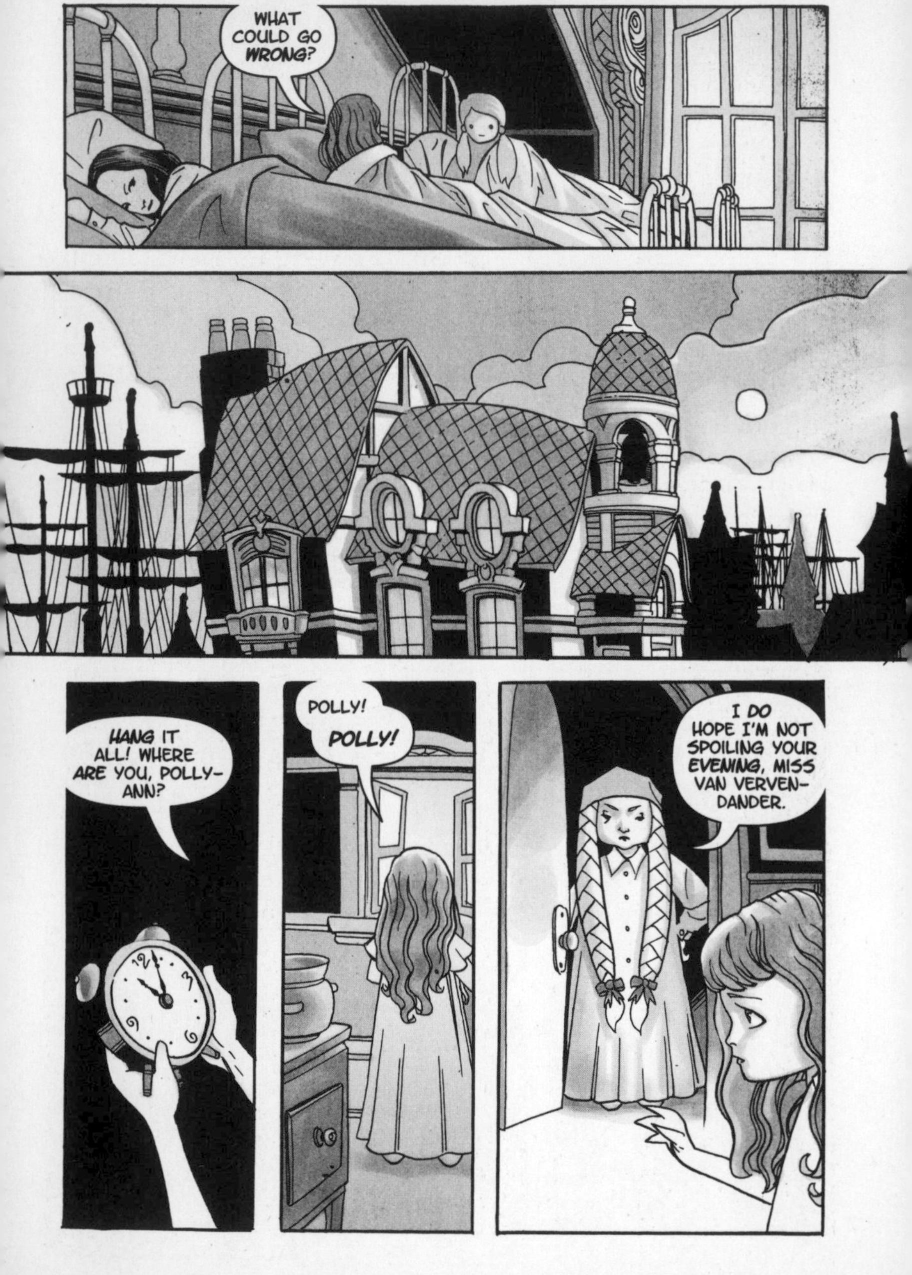
WHAT COULD GO WRONG?
HANG IT ALL! WHERE ARE YOU, POLLY-ANN?
POLLY!
POLLY!
I DO HOPE I'M NOT SPOILING YOUR EVENING, MISS VAN VERVEN-DANDER.

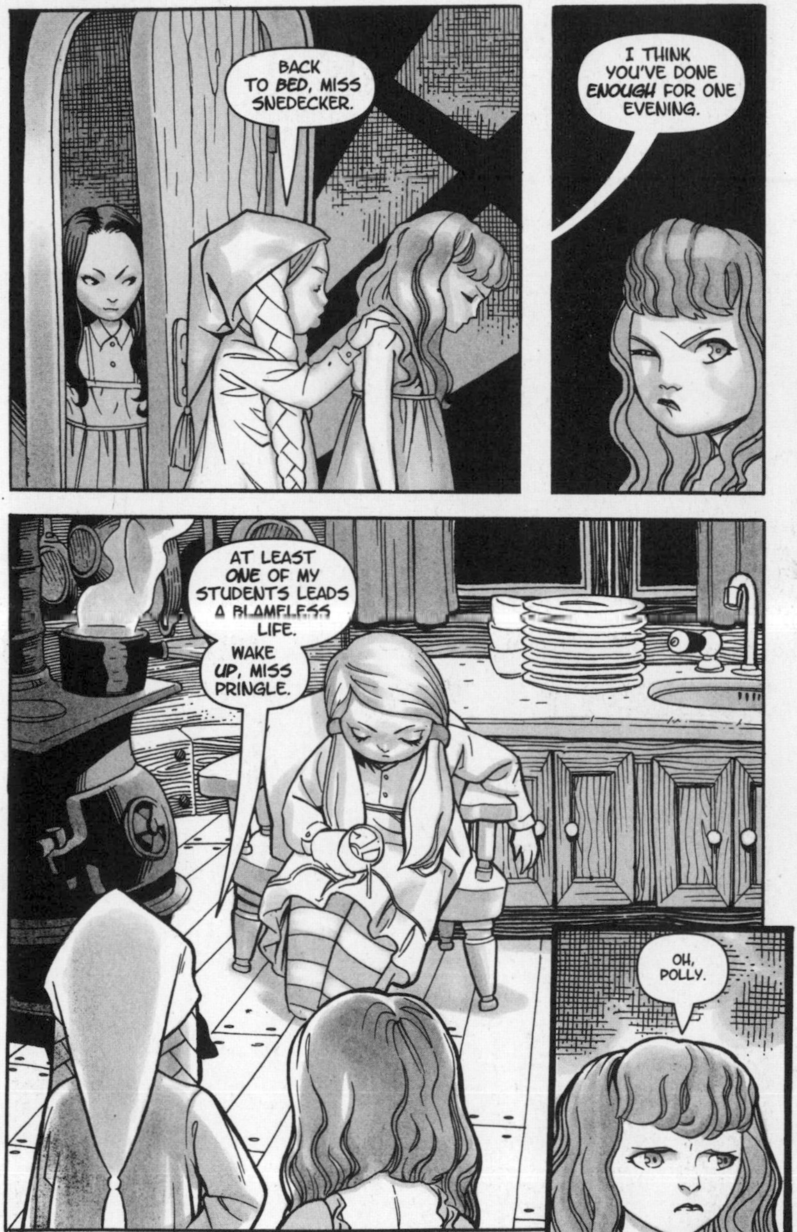
BACK TO BED, MISS SNEDECKER.
I THINK YOU'VE DONE ENOUGH FOR ONE EVENING.
AT LEAST ONE OF MY STUDENTS LEADS A BLAMELESS LIFE.
WAKE UP, MISS PRINGLE.
OH, POLLY.

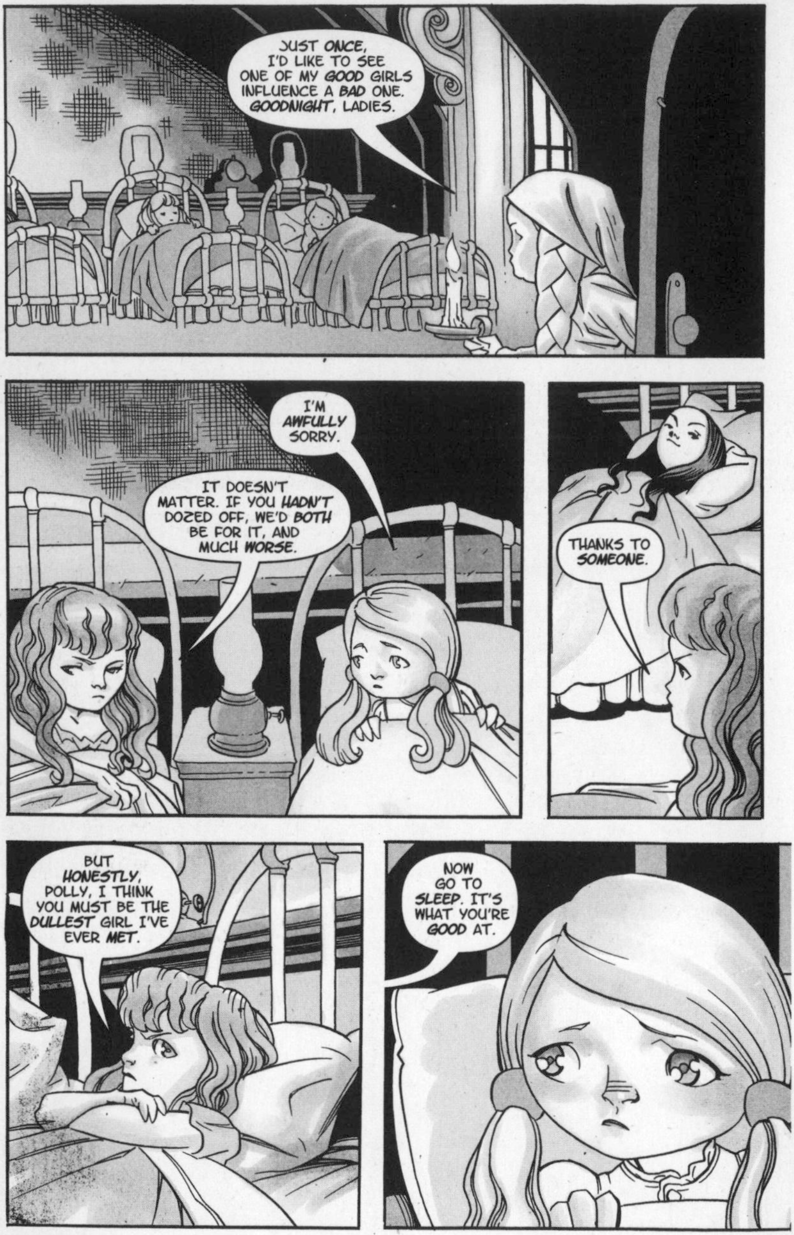
JUST ONCE, I'D LIKE TO SEE ONE OF MY GOOD GIRLS INFLUENCE A BAD ONE. GOODNIGHT, LADIES.
I'M AWFULLY SORRY.
IT DOESN'T MATTER. IF YOU HADN'T DOZED OFF, WE'D BOTH BE FOR IT, AND MUCH WORSE.
THANKS TO SOMEONE.
BUT HONESTLY, POLLY, I THINK YOU MUST BE THE DULLEST GIRL I'VE EVER MET.
NOW GO TO SLEEP. IT'S WHAT YOU'RE GOOD AT.

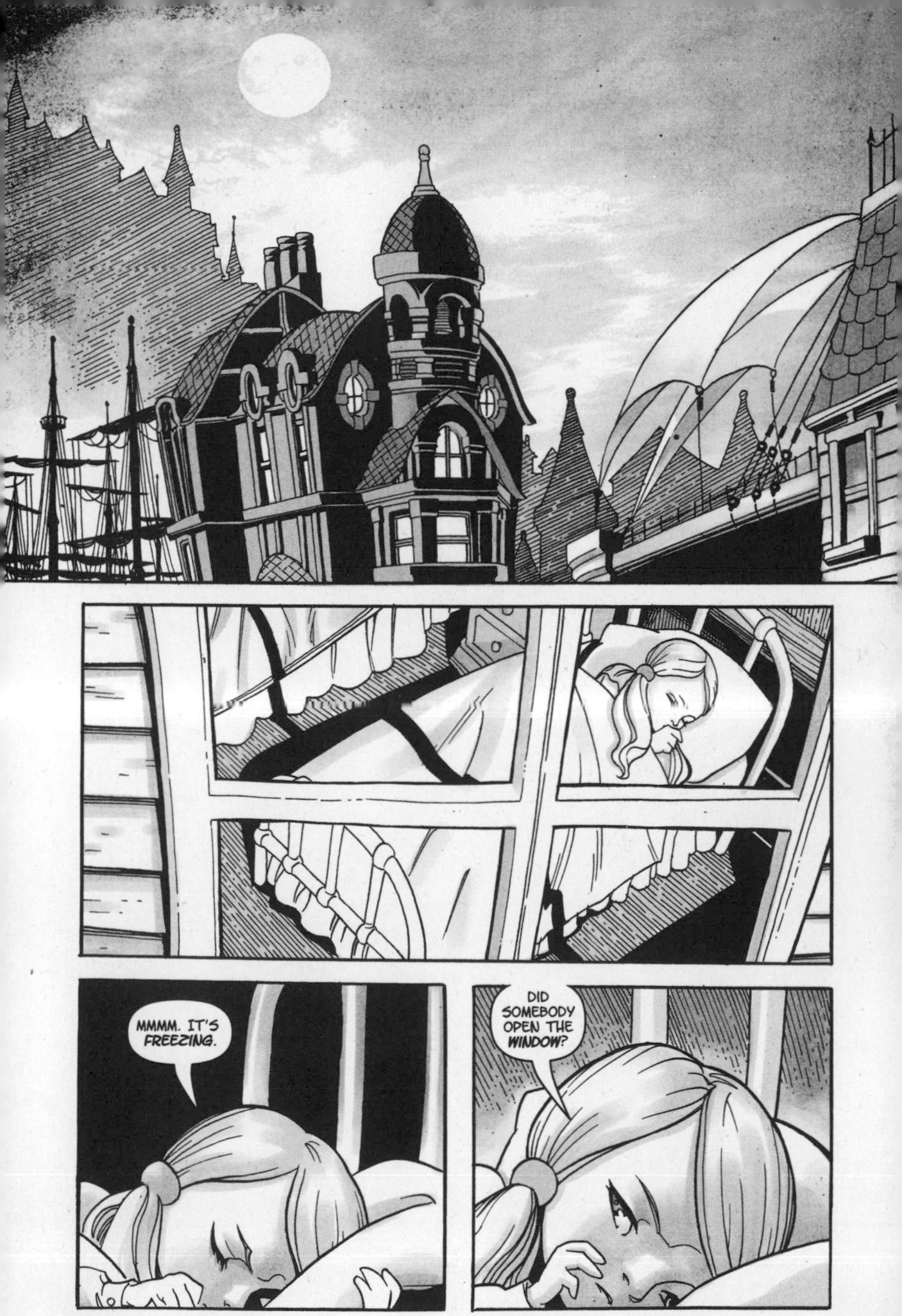
MMMM. IT'S FREEZING.
DID SOMEBODY OPEN THE *WINDOW*?

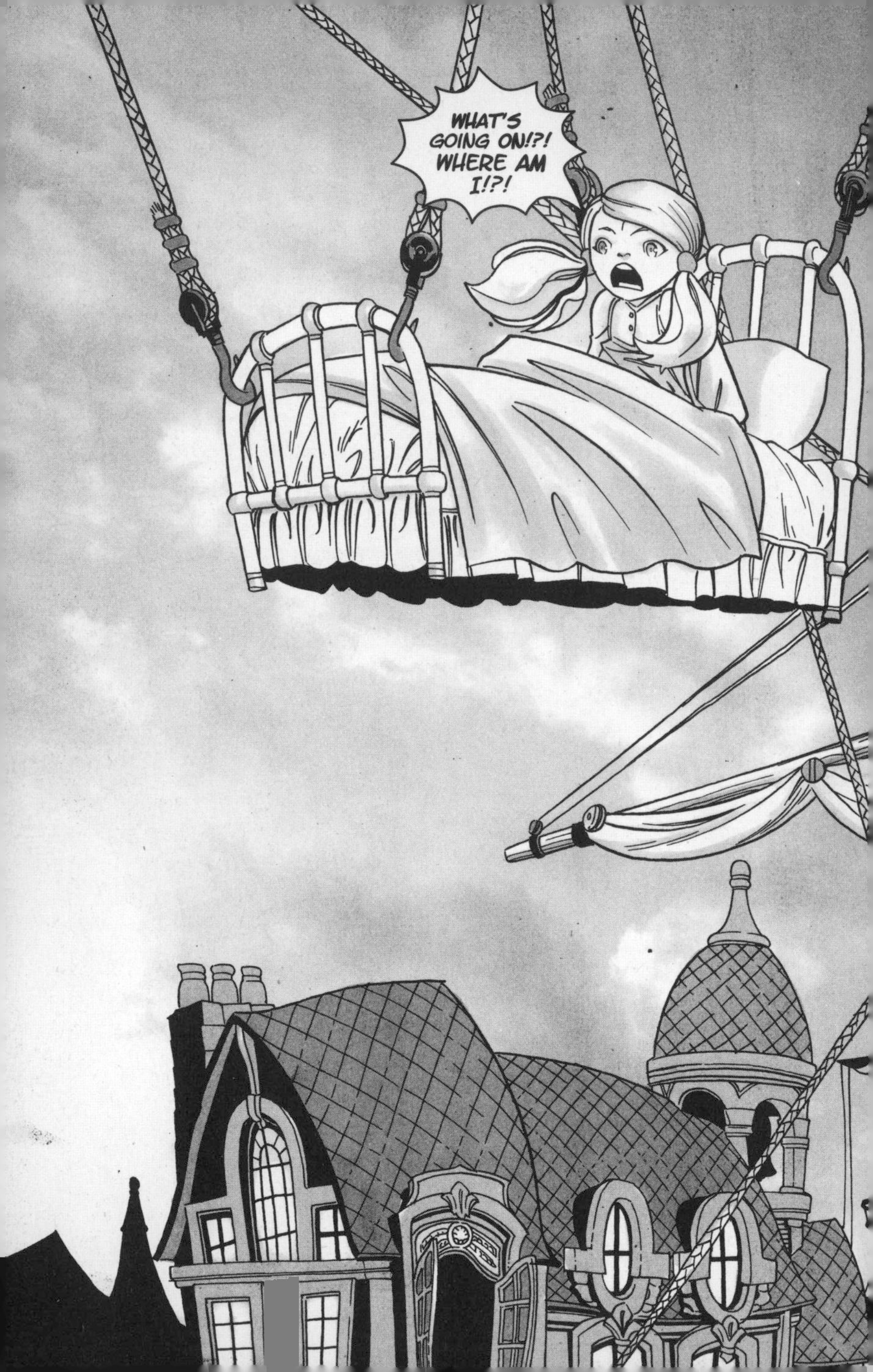
WHAT'S GOING ON!?! WHERE AM I!?!

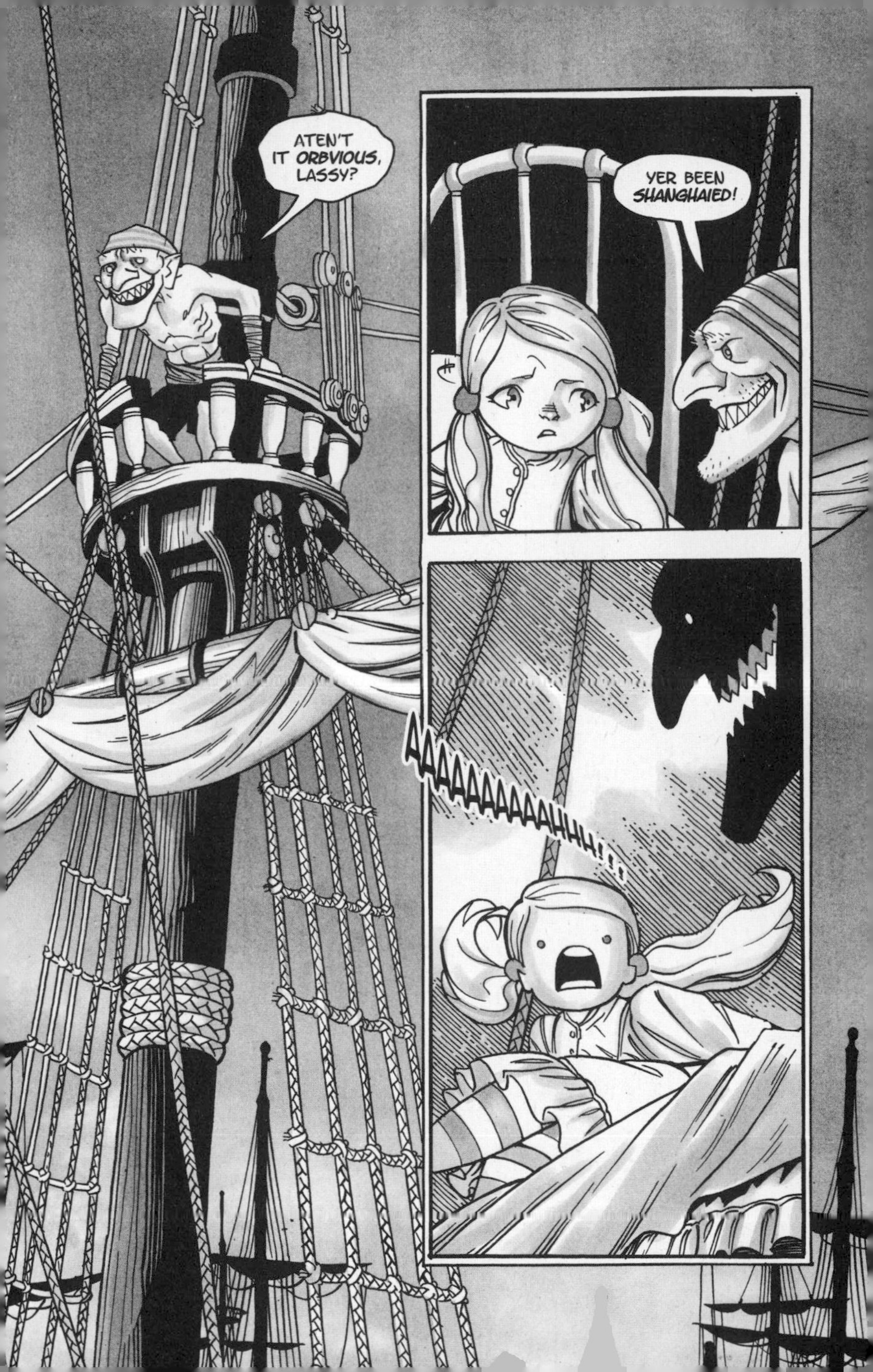
ATEN'T IT ORBVIOUS, LASSY?
YER BEEN SHANGHAIED!
AAAAAAAAAAAHHHH!!!

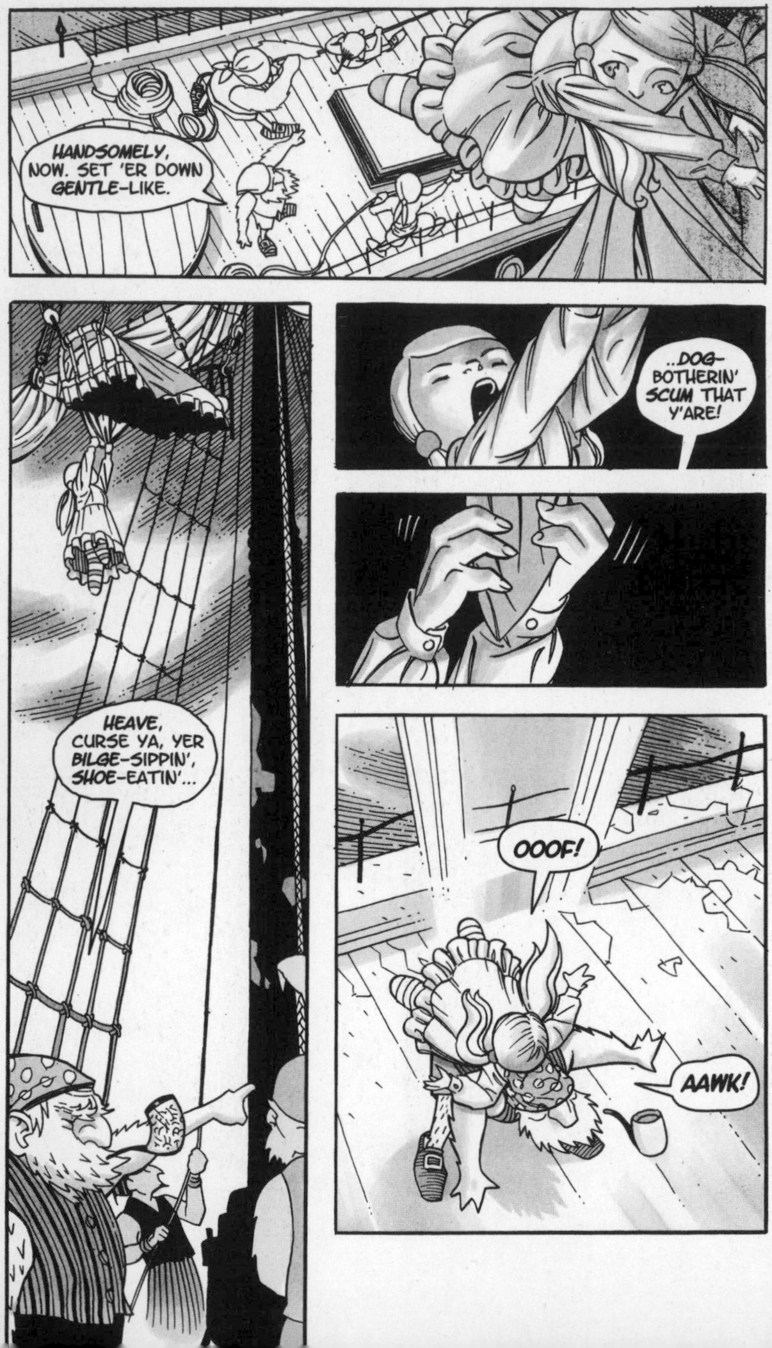
HANDSOMELY, NOW. SET 'ER DOWN GENTLE-LIKE.
HEAVE, CURSE YA, YER BILGE-SIPPIN', SHOE-EATIN'...
...DOG-BOTHERIN' SCUM THAT Y'ARE!
OOOF!
AAWK!

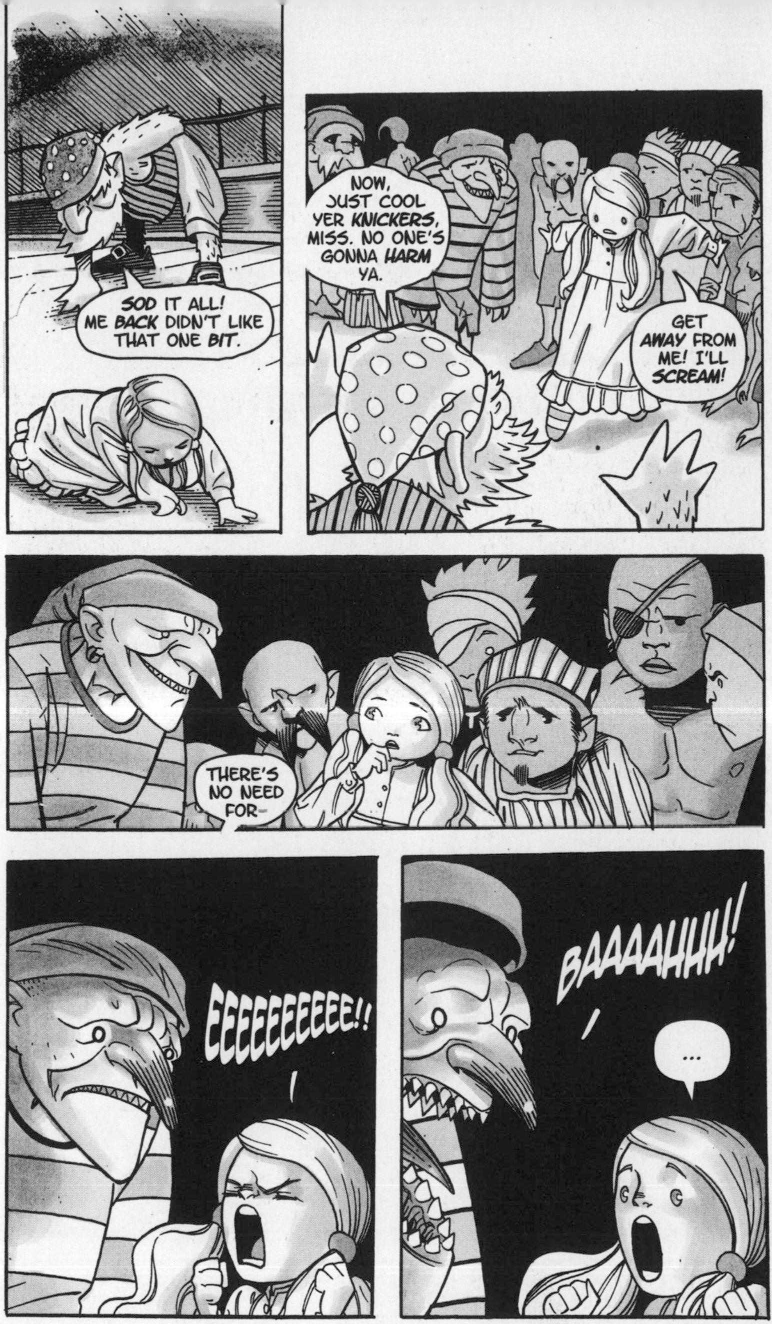
SOD IT ALL! ME BACK DIDN'T LIKE THAT ONE BIT.
NOW, JUST COOL YER KNICKERS, MISS. NO ONE'S GONNA HARM YA.
GET AWAY FROM ME! I'LL SCREAM!
THERE'S NO NEED FOR-
EEEEEEEEEE!!
BAAAAHHH!
...

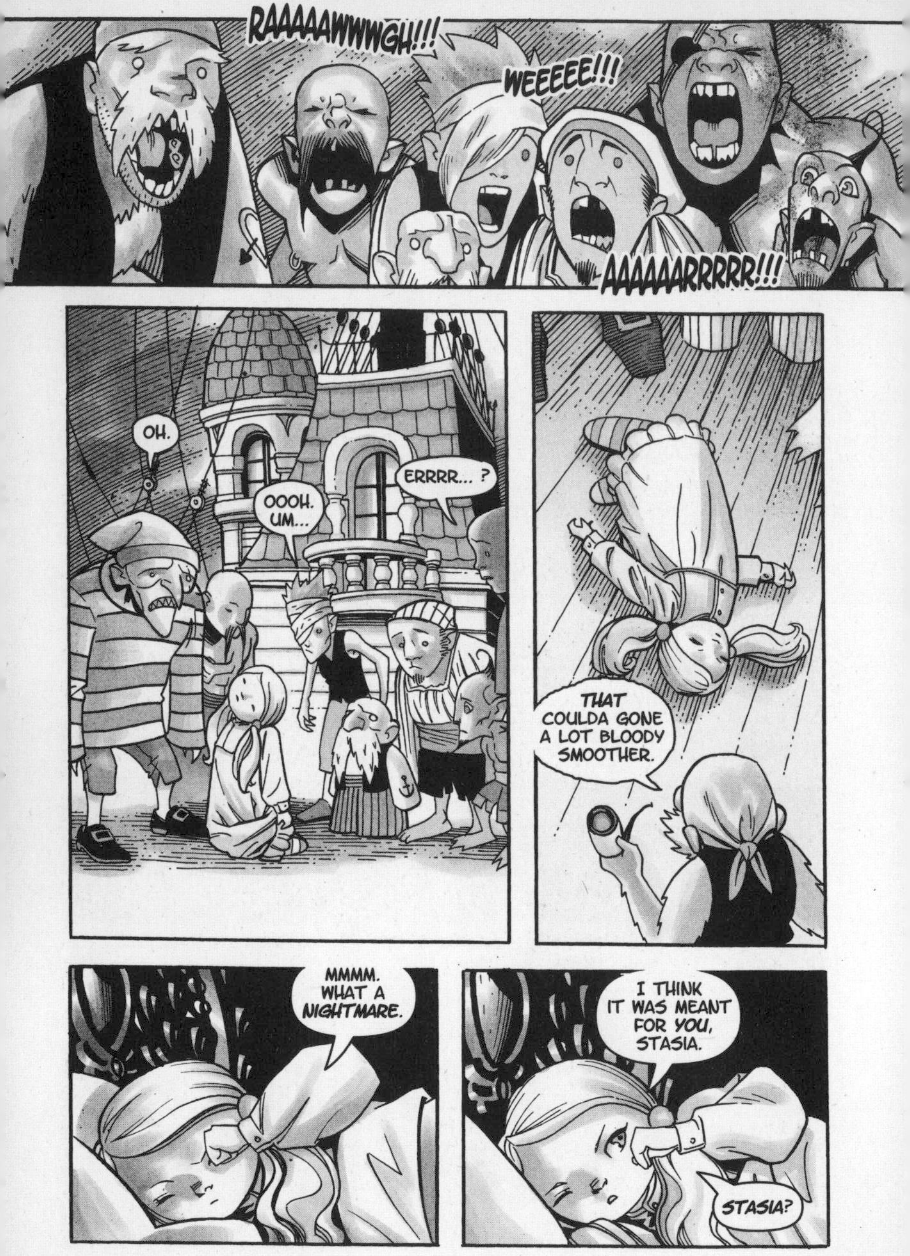
RAAAAAWWWGH!!!
WEEEEE!!!
AAAAAARRRRR!!!
OH.
OOOH. UM...
ERRRR... ?
THAT COULDA GONE A LOT BLOODY SMOOTHER.
MMMM. WHAT A NIGHTMARE.
I THINK IT WAS MEANT FOR YOU, STASIA.
STASIA?

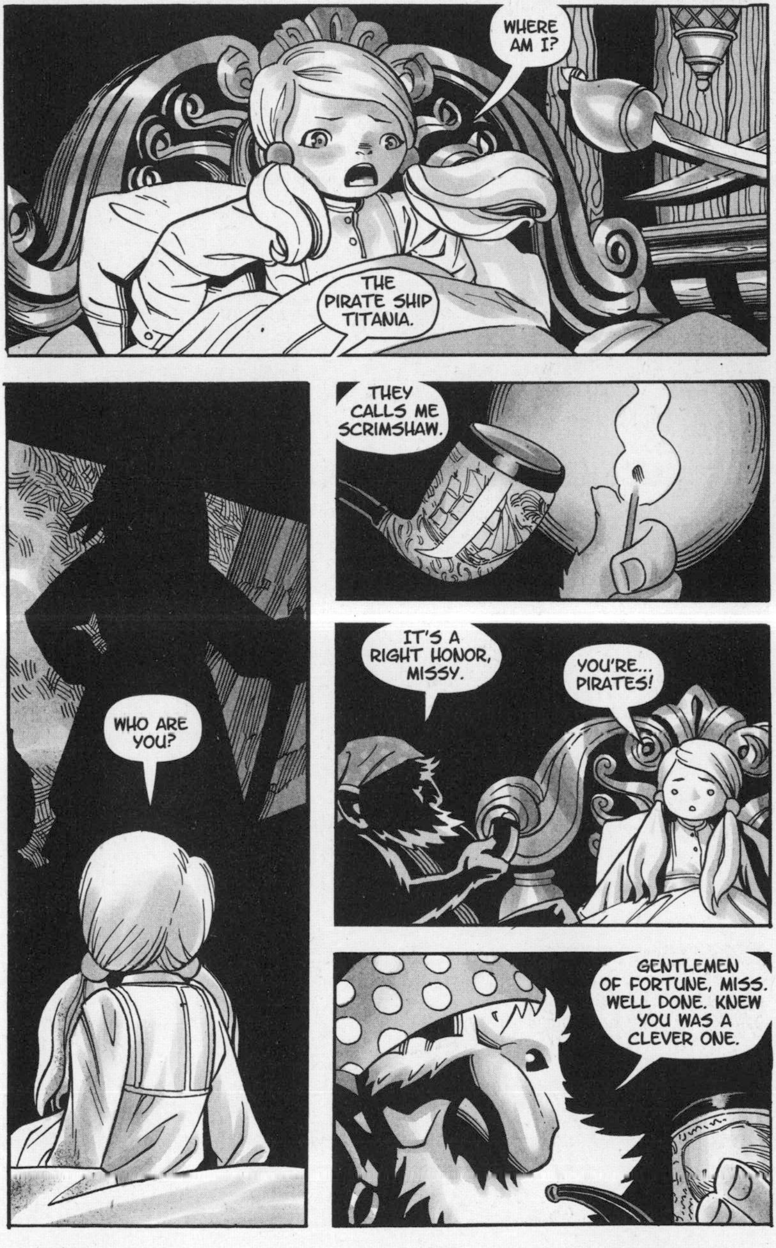
WHERE AM I?
THE PIRATE SHIP TITANIA.
WHO ARE YOU?
THEY CALLS ME SCRIMSHAW.
IT'S A RIGHT HONOR, MISSY.
YOU'RE... PIRATES!
GENTLEMEN OF FORTUNE, MISS. WELL DONE. KNEW YOU WAS A CLEVER ONE.

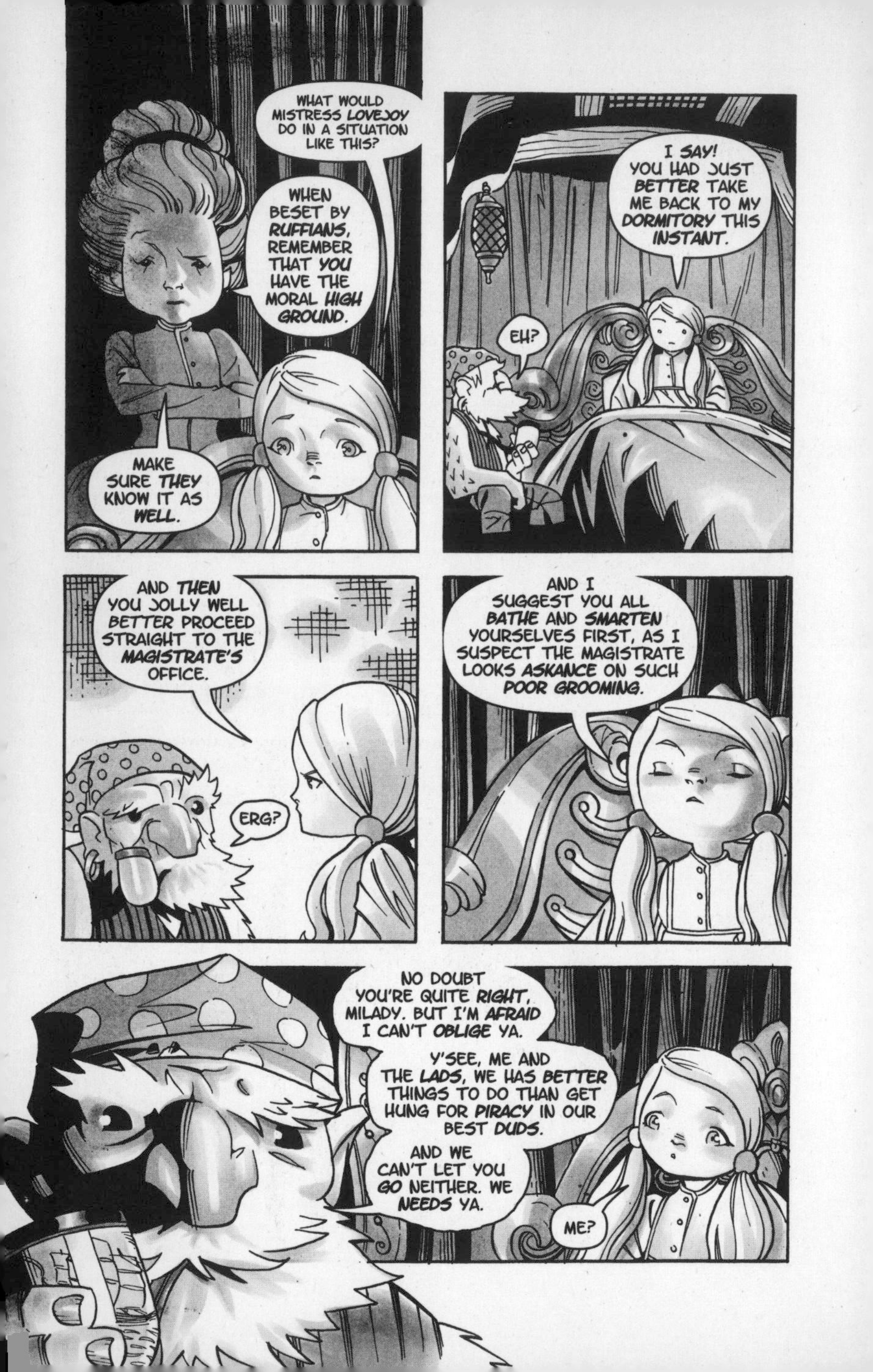
WHAT WOULD MISTRESS LOVEJOY DO IN A SITUATION LIKE THIS?
WHEN BESET BY RUFFIANS, REMEMBER THAT YOU HAVE THE MORAL HIGH GROUND.
MAKE SURE THEY KNOW IT AS WELL.
I SAY! YOU HAD JUST BETTER TAKE ME BACK TO MY DORMITORY THIS INSTANT.
EH?
AND THEN YOU JOLLY WELL BETTER PROCEED STRAIGHT TO THE MAGISTRATE'S OFFICE.
ERG?
AND I SUGGEST YOU ALL BATHE AND SMARTEN YOURSELVES FIRST, AS I SUSPECT THE MAGISTRATE LOOKS ASKANCE ON SUCH POOR GROOMING.
NO DOUBT YOU'RE QUITE RIGHT, MILADY. BUT I'M AFRAID I CAN'T OBLIGE YA.
Y'SEE, ME AND THE LADS, WE HAS BETTER THINGS TO DO THAN GET HUNG FOR PIRACY IN OUR BEST DUDS.
AND WE CAN'T LET YOU GO NEITHER. WE NEEDS YA.
ME?

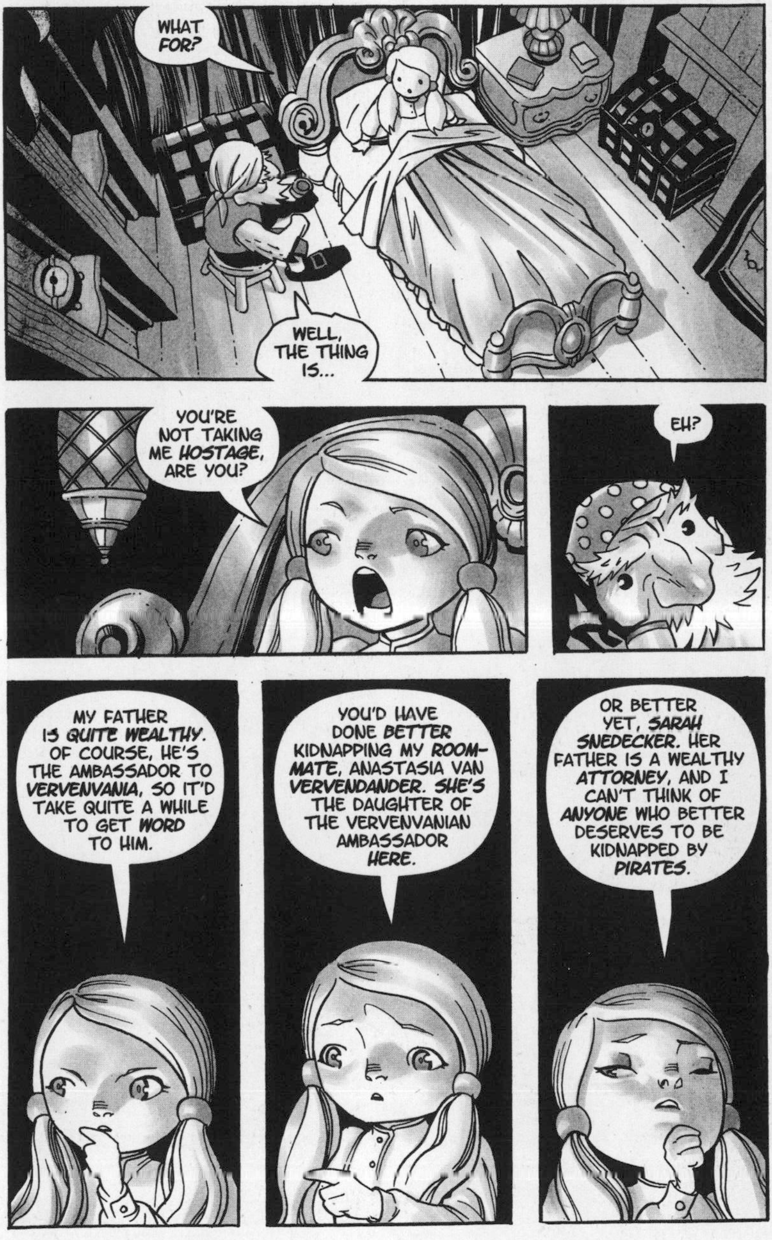
WHAT FOR?
WELL, THE THING IS...
YOU'RE NOT TAKING ME HOSTAGE, ARE YOU?
EH?
MY FATHER IS QUITE WEALTHY. OF COURSE, HE'S THE AMBASSADOR TO VERVENVANIA, SO IT'D TAKE QUITE A WHILE TO GET WORD TO HIM.
YOU'D HAVE DONE BETTER KIDNAPPING MY ROOM-MATE, ANASTASIA VAN VERVENDANDER. SHE'S THE DAUGHTER OF THE VERVENVANIAN AMBASSADOR HERE.
OR BETTER YET, SARAH SNEDECKER. HER FATHER IS A WEALTHY ATTORNEY, AND I CAN'T THINK OF ANYONE WHO BETTER DESERVES TO BE KIDNAPPED BY PIRATES.

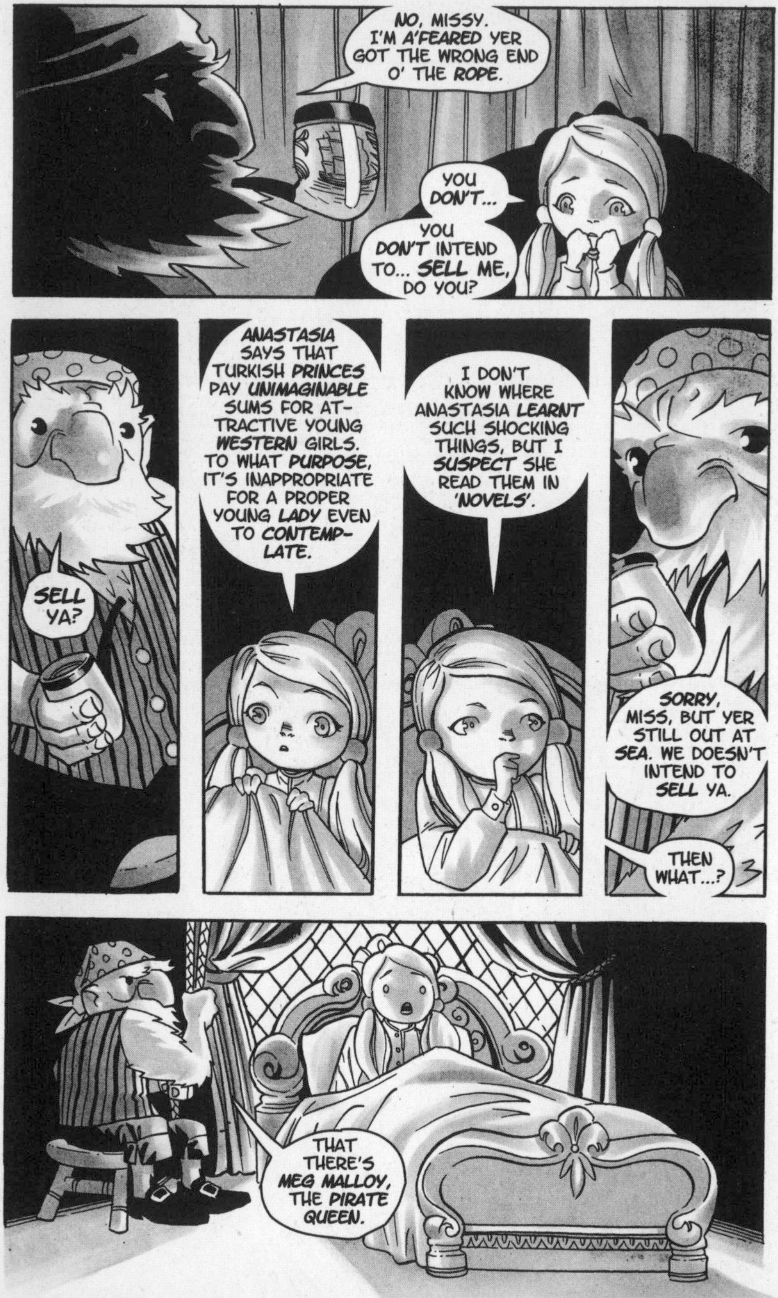
NO, MISSY. I'M A'FEARED YER GOT THE WRONG END O' THE ROPE.
YOU DON'T...
YOU DON'T INTEND TO... SELL ME, DO YOU?
SELL YA?
ANASTASIA SAYS THAT TURKISH PRINCES PAY UNIMAGINABLE SUMS FOR AT-TRACTIVE YOUNG WESTERN GIRLS. TO WHAT PURPOSE, IT'S INAPPROPRIATE FOR A PROPER YOUNG LADY EVEN TO CONTEMP-LATE.
I DON'T KNOW WHERE ANASTASIA LEARNT SUCH SHOCKING THINGS, BUT I SUSPECT SHE READ THEM IN 'NOVELS'.
SORRY, MISS, BUT YER STILL OUT AT SEA. WE DOESN'T INTEND TO SELL YA.
THEN WHAT...?
THAT THERE'S MEG MALLOY, THE PIRATE QUEEN.

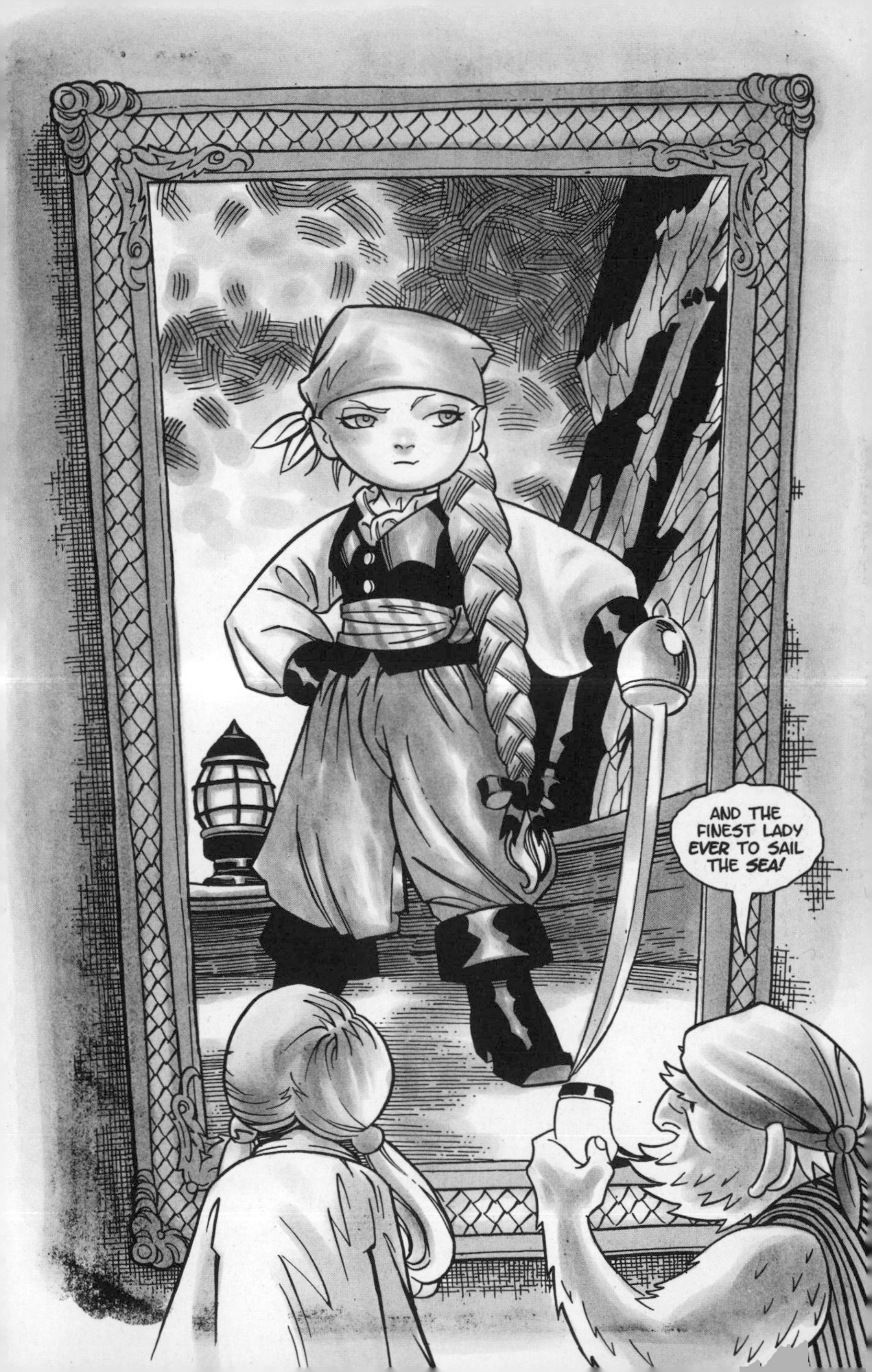
AND THE FINEST LADY EVER TO SAIL THE SEA!

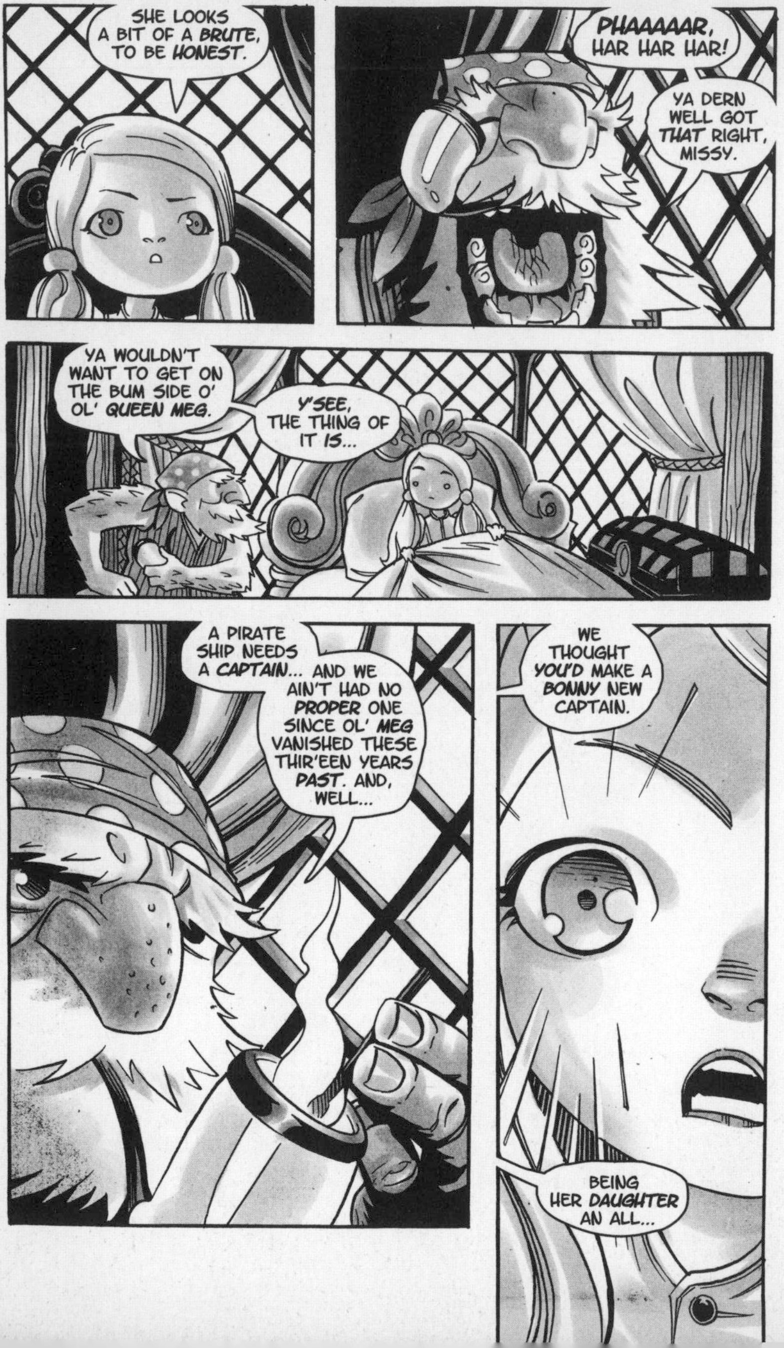
SHE LOOKS A BIT OF A BRUTE, TO BE HONEST.
PHAAAAAR, HAR HAR HAR!
YA DERN WELL GOT THAT RIGHT, MISSY.
YA WOULDN'T WANT TO GET ON THE BUM SIDE O' OL' QUEEN MEG.
Y'SEE, THE THING OF IT IS...
A PIRATE SHIP NEEDS A CAPTAIN... AND WE AIN'T HAD NO PROPER ONE SINCE OL' MEG VANISHED THESE THIR'EEN YEARS PAST. AND, WELL...
WE THOUGHT YOU'D MAKE A BONNY NEW CAPTAIN.
BEING HER DAUGHTER AN ALL...

Chapter 2

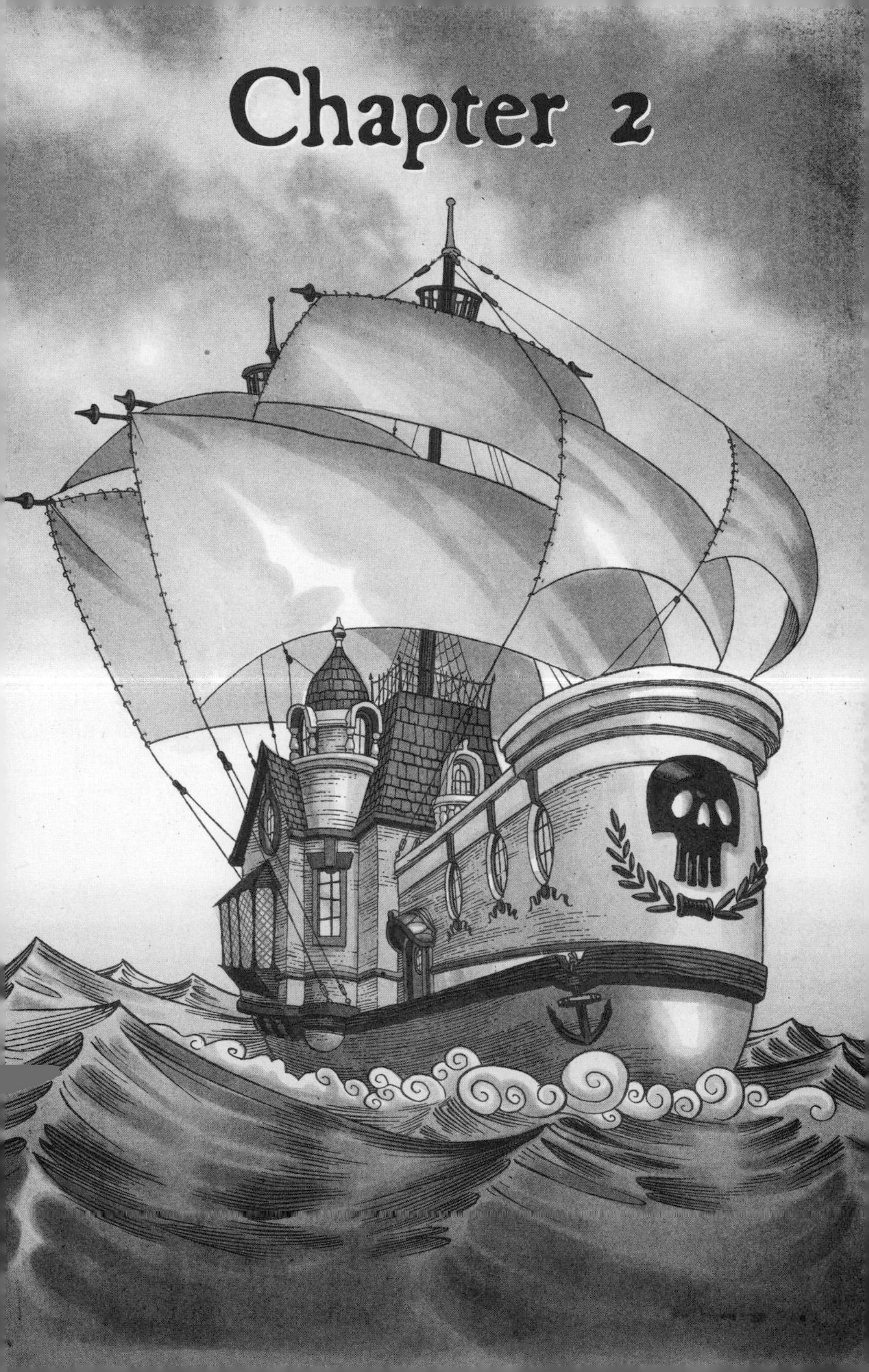

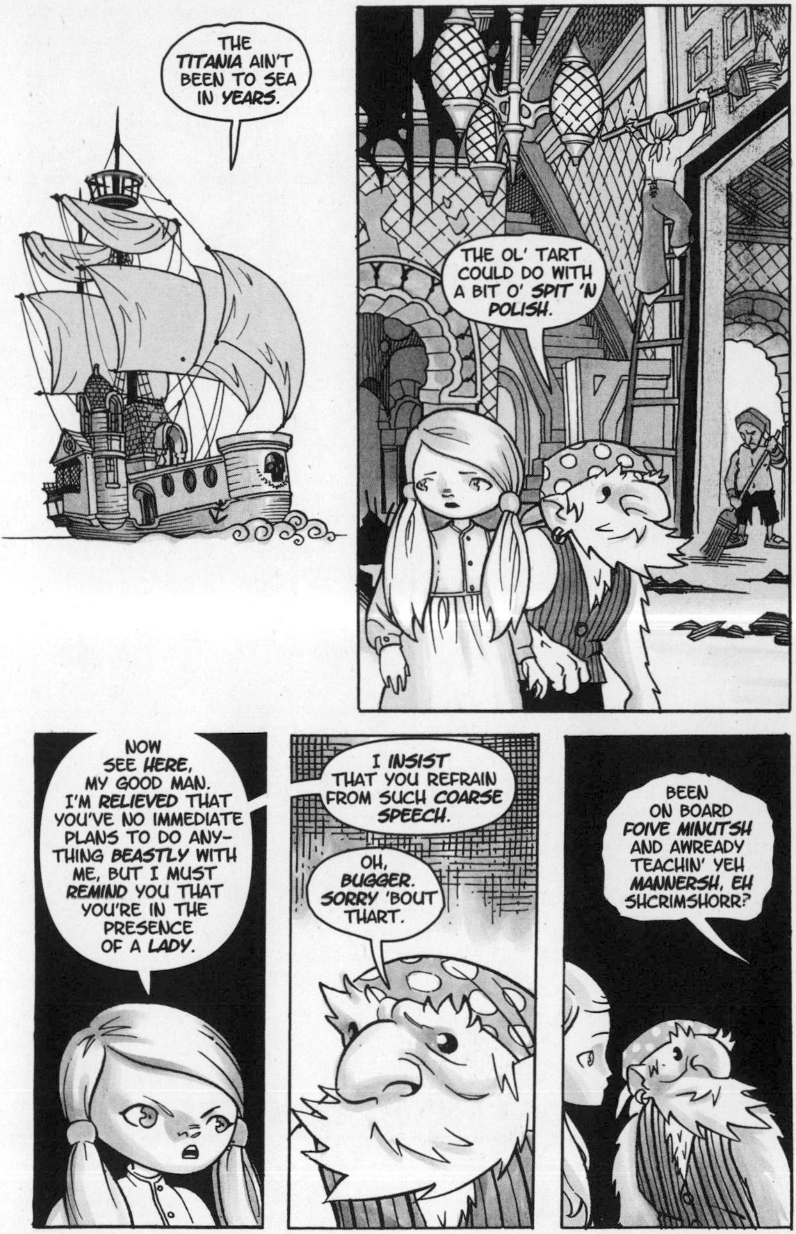
THE TITANIA AIN'T BEEN TO SEA IN YEARS.
THE OL' TART COULD DO WITH A BIT O' SPIT 'N POLISH.
NOW SEE HERE, MY GOOD MAN. I'M RELIEVED THAT YOU'VE NO IMMEDIATE PLANS TO DO ANY-THING BEASTLY WITH ME, BUT I MUST REMIND YOU THAT YOU'RE IN THE PRESENCE OF A LADY.
I INSIST THAT YOU REFRAIN FROM SUCH COARSE SPEECH.
OH, BUGGER. SORRY 'BOUT THART.
BEEN ON BOARD FOIVE MINUTSH AND AWREADY TEACHIN' YEH MANNERSH, EH SHCRIMSHORR?

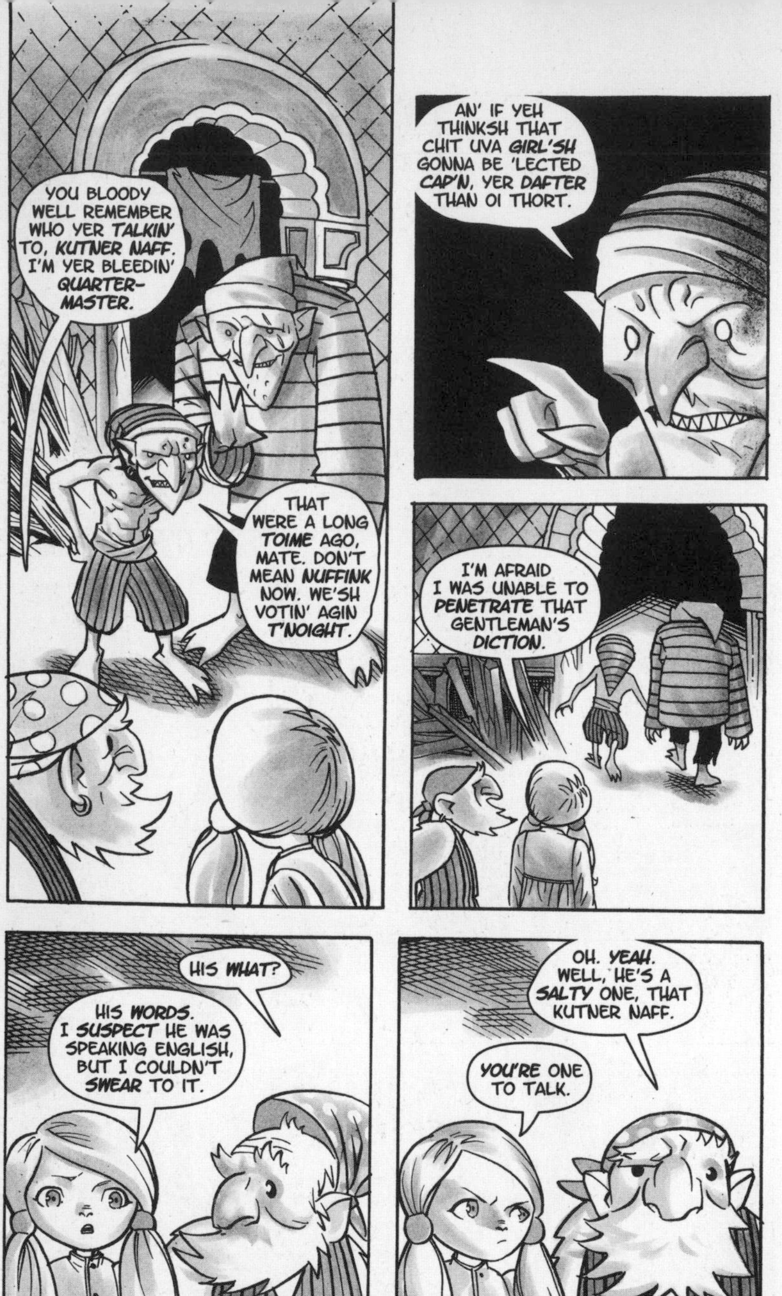
YOU BLOODY WELL REMEMBER WHO YER TALKIN' TO, KUTNER NAFF. I'M YER BLEEDIN' QUARTER-MASTER.
THAT WERE A LONG TOIME AGO, MATE. DON'T MEAN NUFFINK NOW. WE'SH VOTIN' AGIN T'NOIGHT.
AN' IF YEH THINKSH THAT CHIT UVA GIRL'SH GONNA BE 'LECTED CAP'N, YER DAFTER THAN OI THORT.
I'M AFRAID I WAS UNABLE TO PENETRATE THAT GENTLEMAN'S DICTION.
HIS WHAT?
HIS WORDS. I SUSPECT HE WAS SPEAKING ENGLISH, BUT I COULDN'T SWEAR TO IT.
OH. YEAH. WELL, HE'S A SALTY ONE, THAT KUTNER NAFF.
YOU'RE ONE TO TALK.

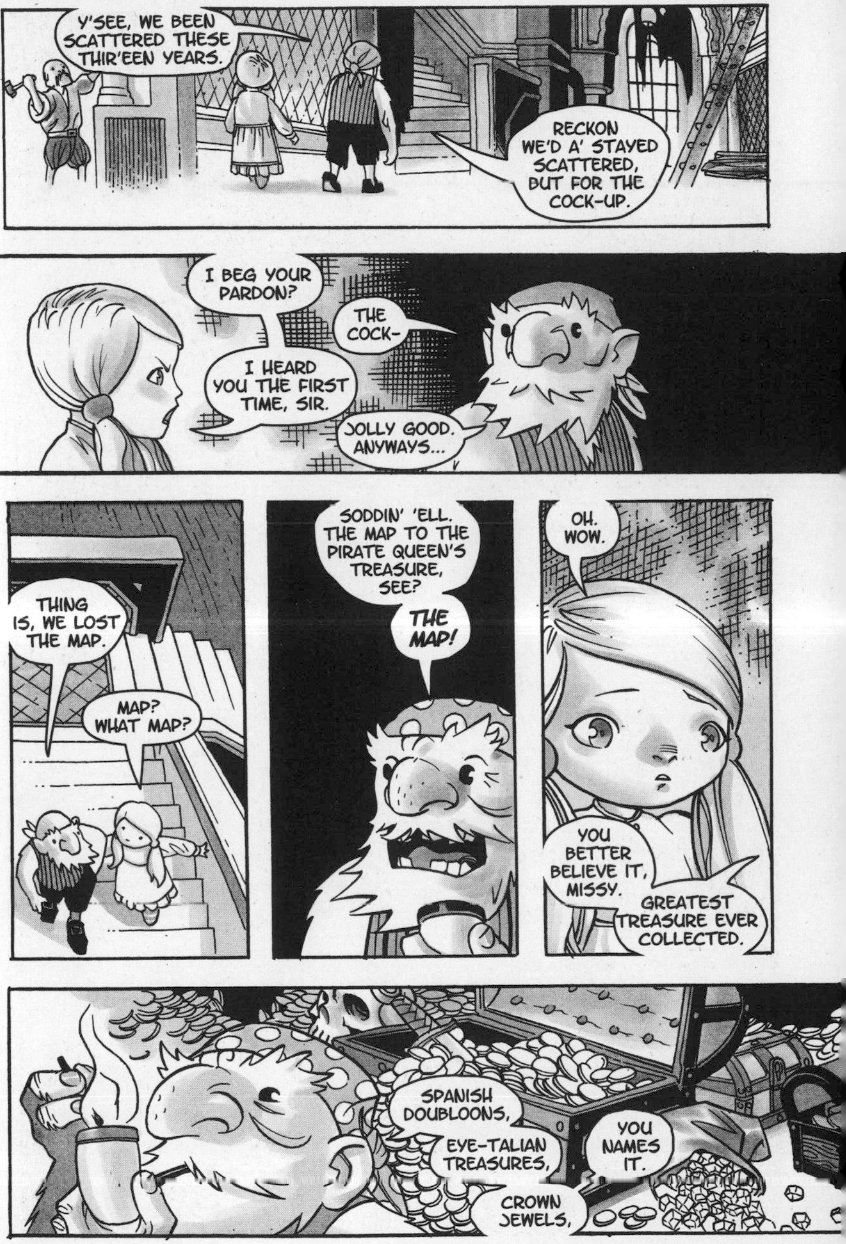
Y'SEE, WE BEEN SCATTERED THESE THIR'EEN YEARS.
RECKON WE'D A' STAYED SCATTERED, BUT FOR THE COCK-UP.
I BEG YOUR PARDON?
THE COCK-
I HEARD YOU THE FIRST TIME, SIR.
JOLLY GOOD. ANYWAYS...
THING IS, WE LOST THE MAP.
MAP? WHAT MAP?
SODDIN' 'ELL. THE MAP TO THE PIRATE QUEEN'S TREASURE, SEE?
THE MAP!
OH. WOW.
YOU BETTER BELIEVE IT, MISSY.
GREATEST TREASURE EVER COLLECTED.
SPANISH DOUBLOONS,
EYE-TALIAN TREASURES,
CROWN JEWELS,
YOU NAMES IT.

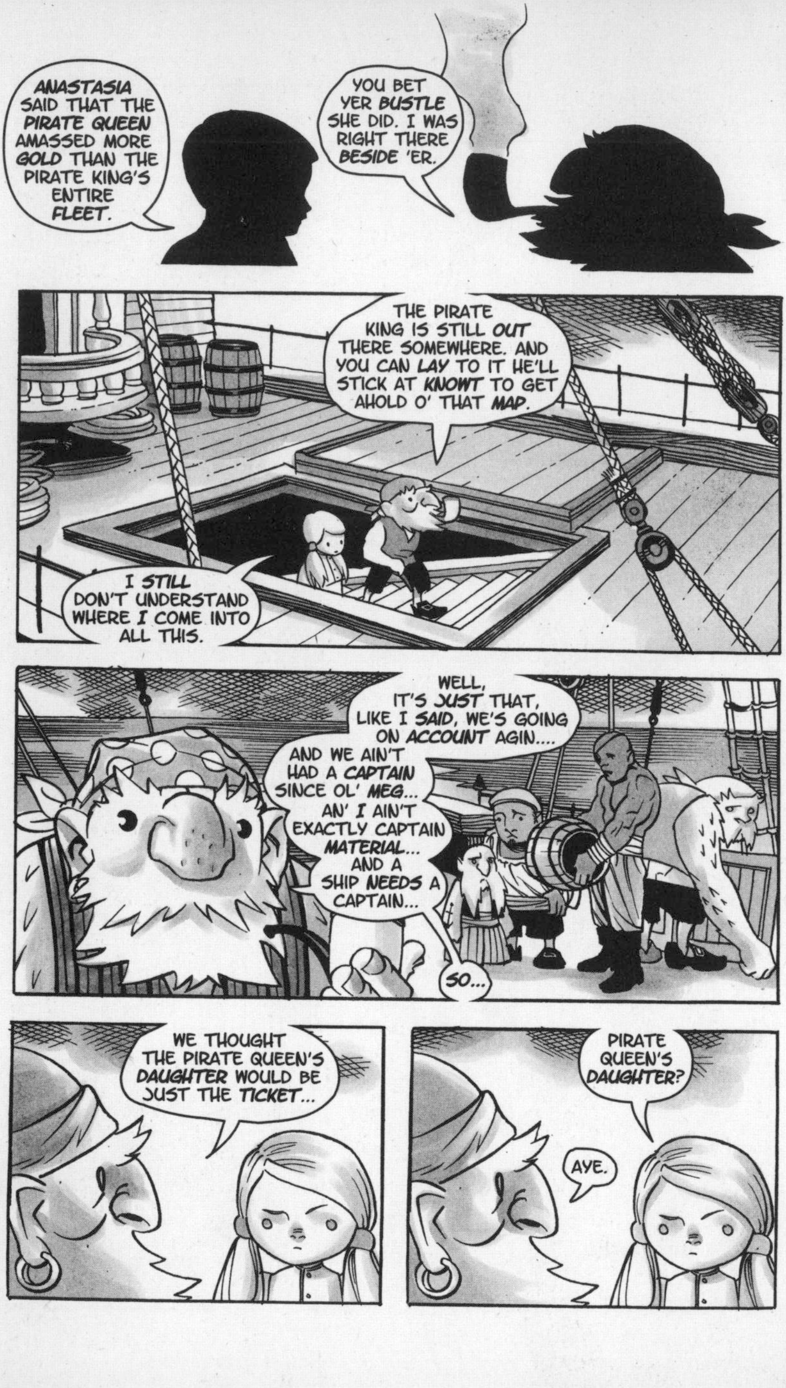
ANASTASIA SAID THAT THE PIRATE QUEEN AMASSED MORE GOLD THAN THE PIRATE KING'S ENTIRE FLEET.
YOU BET YER BUSTLE SHE DID. I WAS RIGHT THERE BESIDE 'ER.
THE PIRATE KING IS STILL OUT THERE SOMEWHERE. AND YOU CAN LAY TO IT HE'LL STICK AT KNOWT TO GET AHOLD O' THAT MAP.
I STILL DON'T UNDERSTAND WHERE I COME INTO ALL THIS.
WELL, IT'S JUST THAT, LIKE I SAID, WE'S GOING ON ACCOUNT AGIN....
AND WE AIN'T HAD A CAPTAIN SINCE OL' MEG... AN' I AIN'T EXACTLY CAPTAIN MATERIAL... AND A SHIP NEEDS A CAPTAIN...
SO...
WE THOUGHT THE PIRATE QUEEN'S DAUGHTER WOULD BE JUST THE TICKET...
PIRATE QUEEN'S DAUGHTER?
AYE.

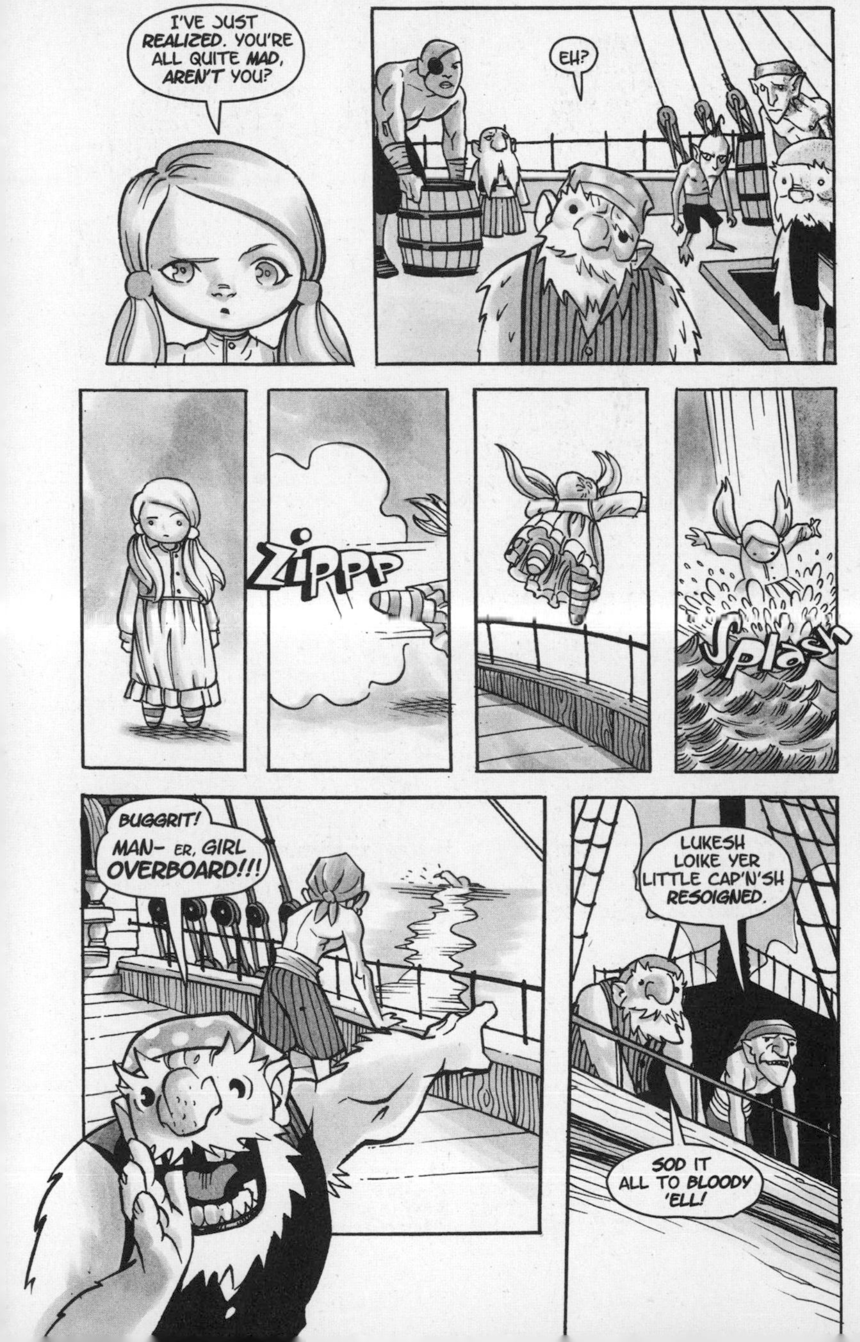
I'VE JUST REALIZED. YOU'RE ALL QUITE MAD, AREN'T YOU?
EH?
ZIPPP
SPLASH
BUGGRIT! MAN- ER, GIRL OVERBOARD!!!
LUKESH LOIKE YER LITTLE CAP'N'SH RESOIGNED.
SOD IT ALL TO BLOODY 'ELL!

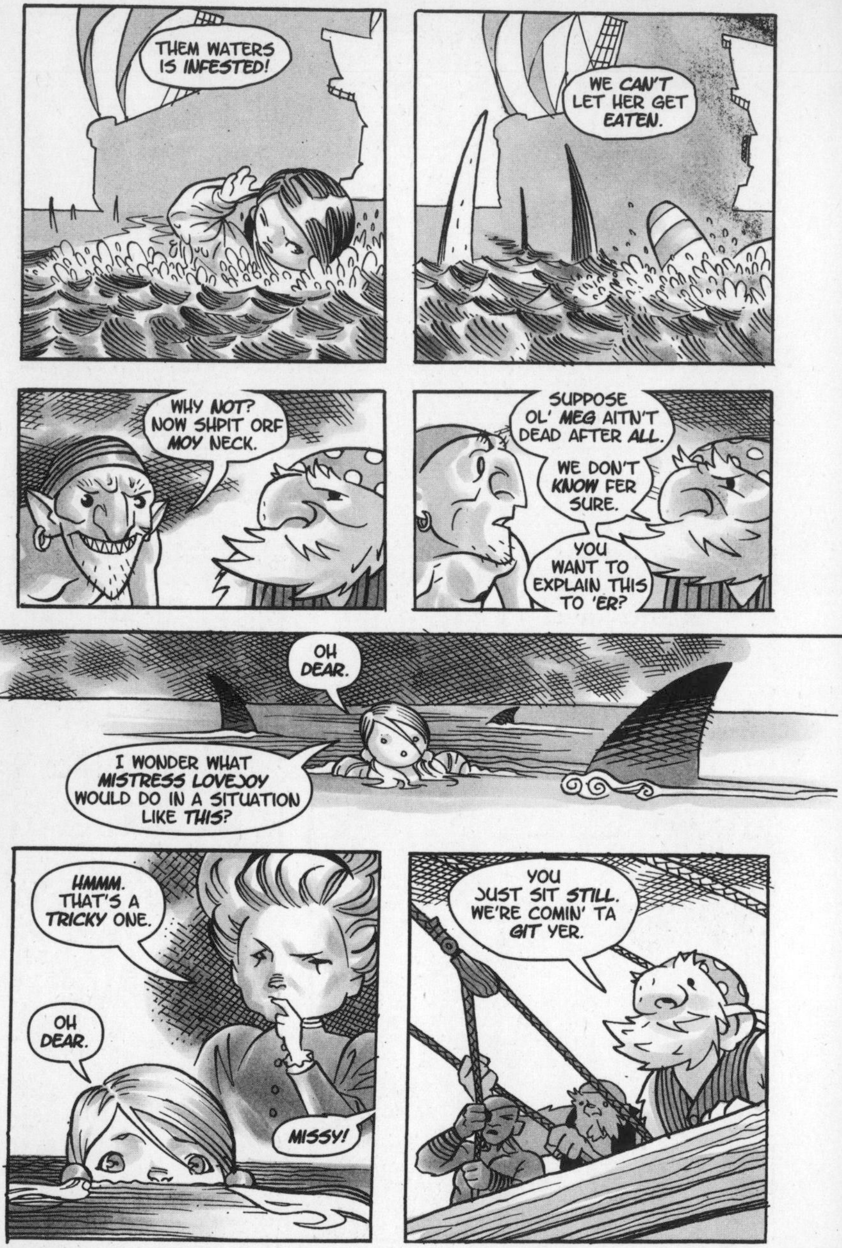
THEM WATERS IS INFESTED!
WE CAN'T LET HER GET EATEN.
WHY NOT? NOW SHPIT ORF MOY NECK.
SUPPOSE OL' MEG AITN'T DEAD AFTER ALL.
WE DON'T KNOW FER SURE.
YOU WANT TO EXPLAIN THIS TO 'ER?
OH DEAR.
I WONDER WHAT MISTRESS LOVEJOY WOULD DO IN A SITUATION LIKE THIS?
HMMM. THAT'S A TRICKY ONE.
OH DEAR.
MISSY!
YOU JUST SIT STILL. WE'RE COMIN' TA GIT YER.

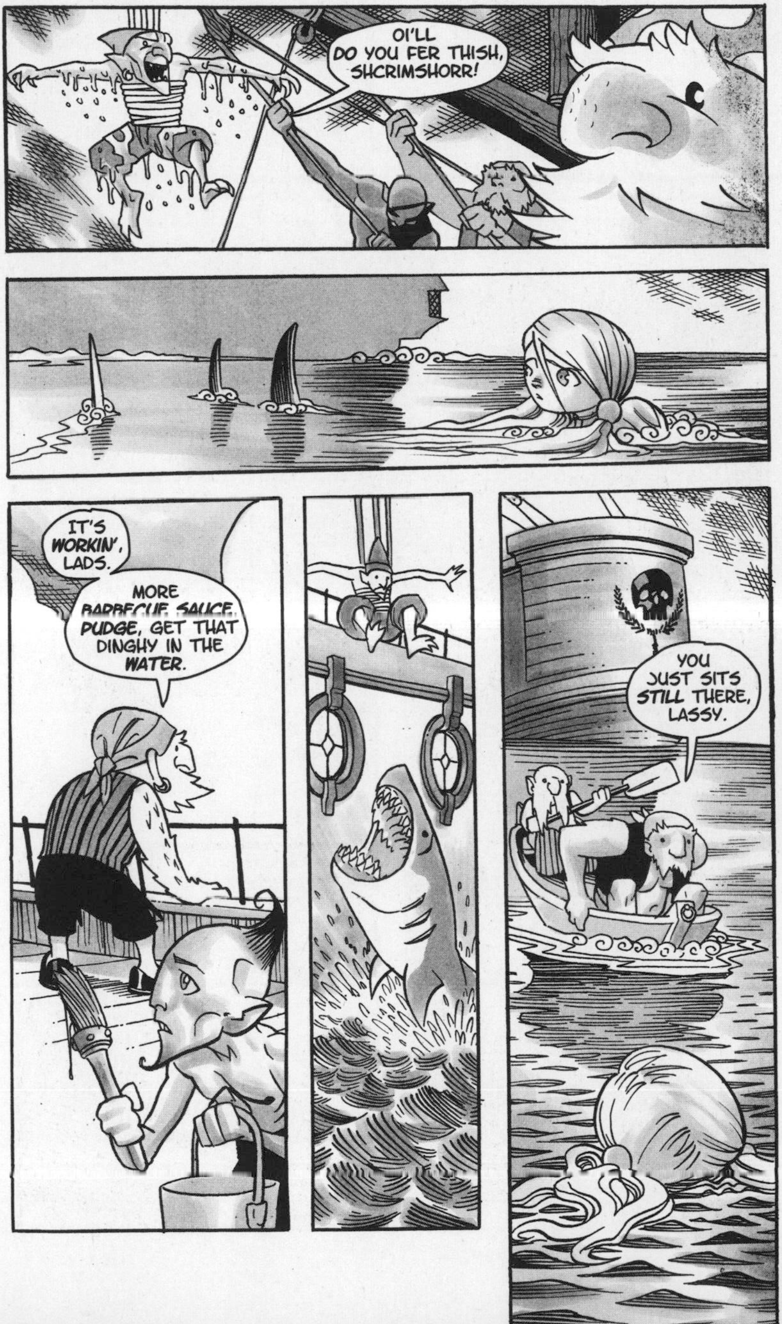
OI'LL DO YOU FER THISH, SHCRIMSHORR!
IT'S WORKIN', LADS.
MORE BARBECUE SAUCE. PUDGE, GET THAT DINGHY IN THE WATER.
YOU JUST SITS STILL THERE, LASSY.

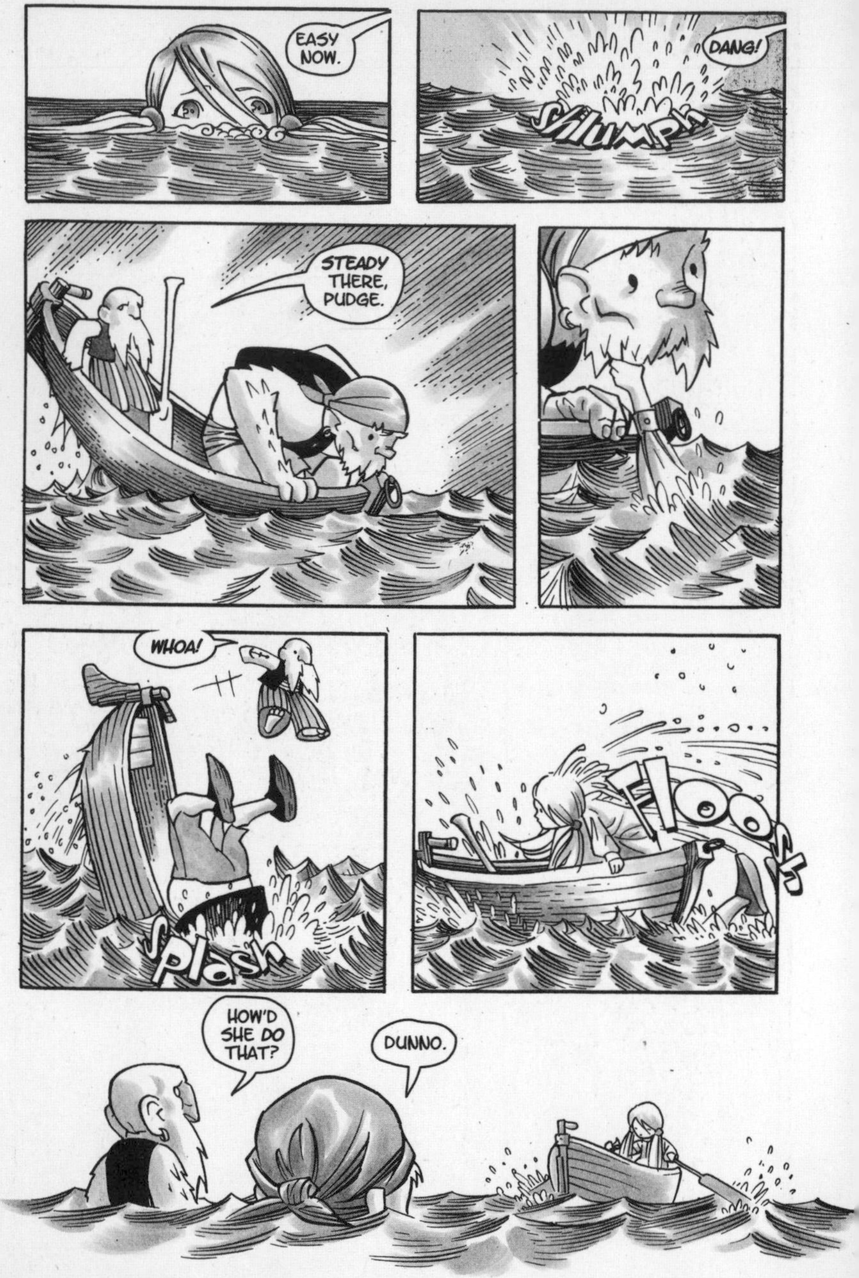
EASY NOW.
DANG!
SHLUMPH
STEADY THERE, PUDGE.
WHOA!
SPLASH
FLOOOSH
HOW'D SHE DO THAT?
DUNNO.

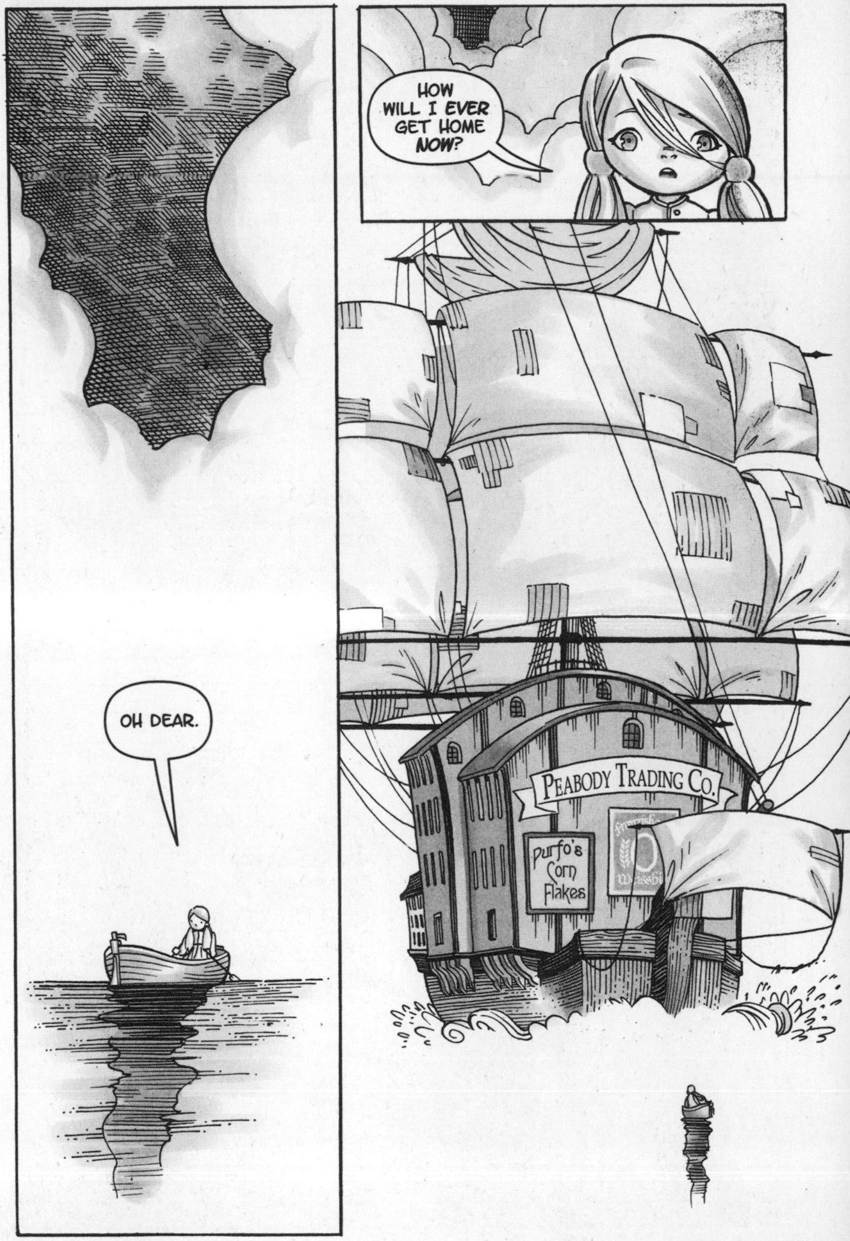
OH DEAR.
HOW WILL I EVER GET HOME NOW?
PEABODY TRADING CO.
Purfo's Corn Flakes

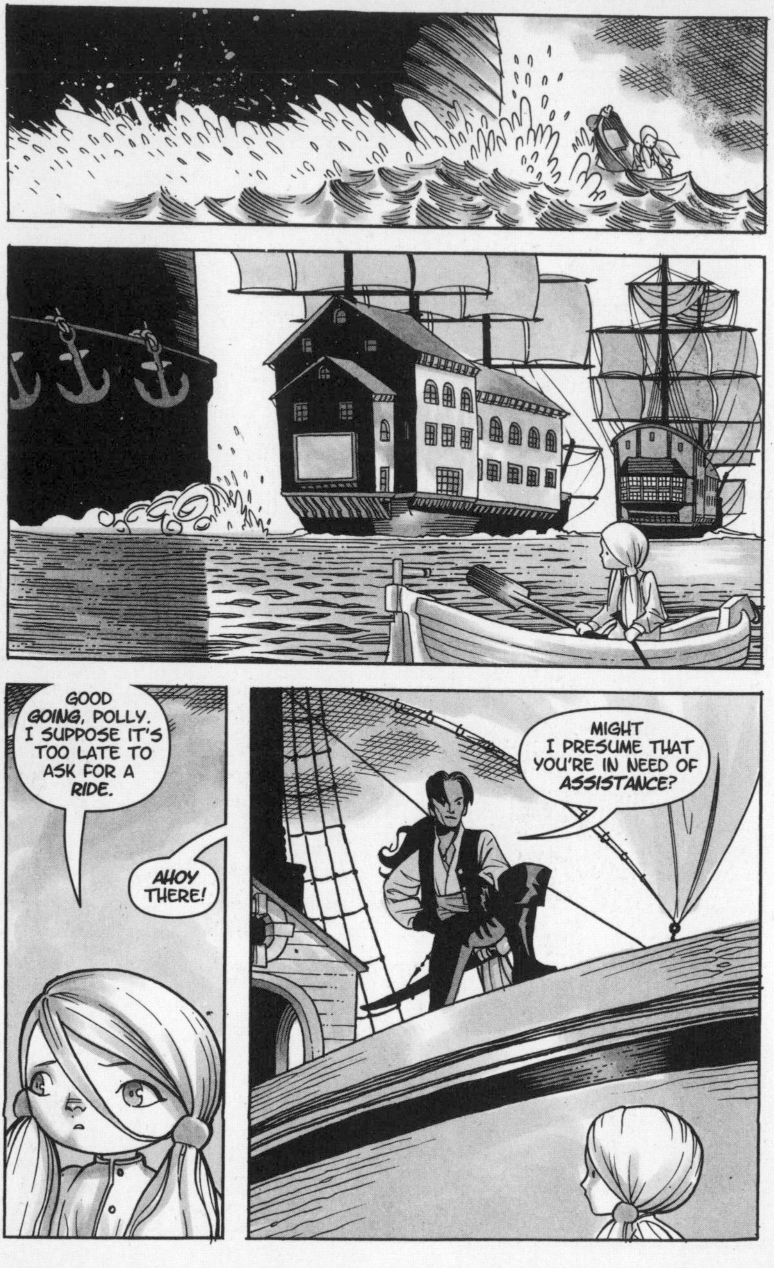
GOOD GOING, POLLY. I SUPPOSE IT'S TOO LATE TO ASK FOR A RIDE.
AHOY THERE!
MIGHT I PRESUME THAT YOU'RE IN NEED OF ASSISTANCE?

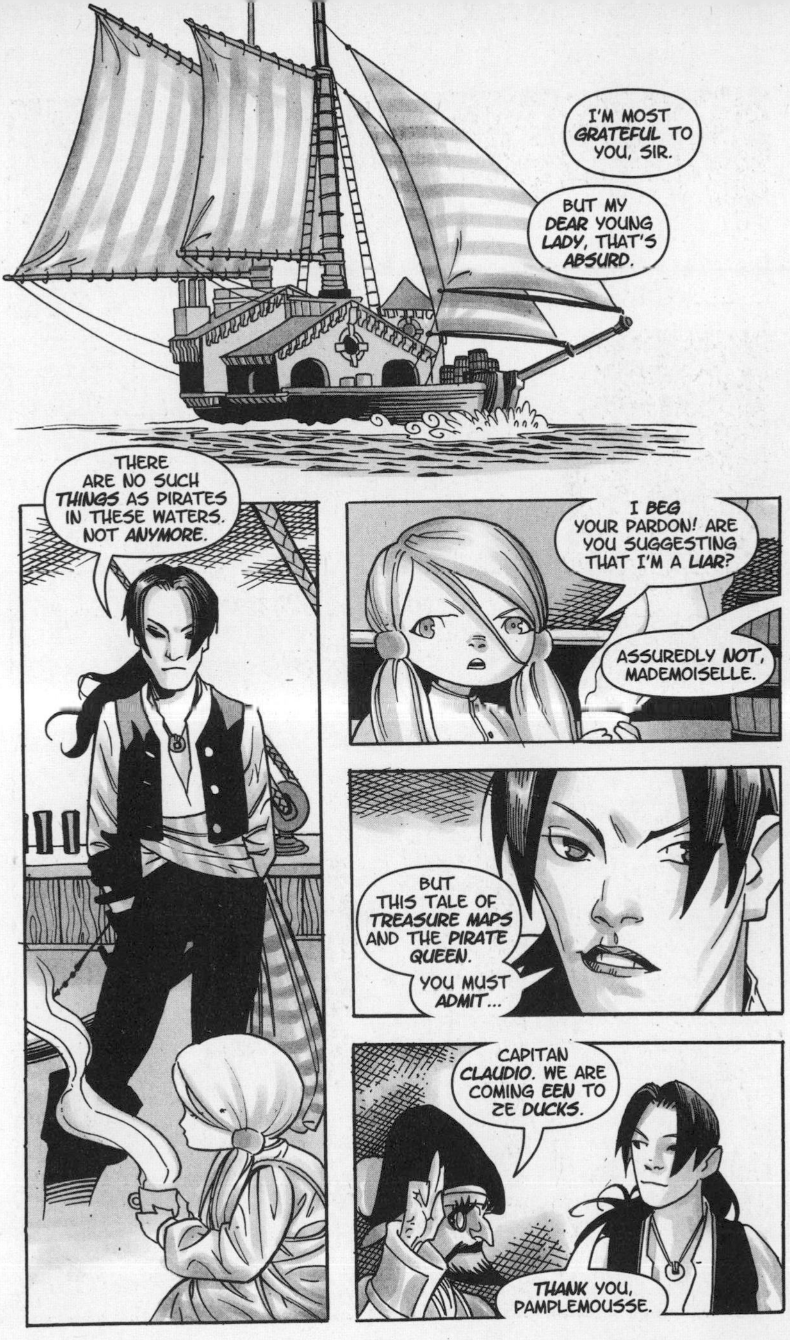
I'M MOST GRATEFUL TO YOU, SIR.
BUT MY DEAR YOUNG LADY, THAT'S ABSURD.
THERE ARE NO SUCH THINGS AS PIRATES IN THESE WATERS. NOT ANYMORE.
I BEG YOUR PARDON! ARE YOU SUGGESTING THAT I'M A LIAR?
ASSUREDLY NOT, MADEMOISELLE.
BUT THIS TALE OF TREASURE MAPS AND THE PIRATE QUEEN.
YOU MUST ADMIT...
CAPITAN CLAUDIO. WE ARE COMING EEN TO ZE DUCKS.
THANK YOU, PAMPLEMOUSSE.

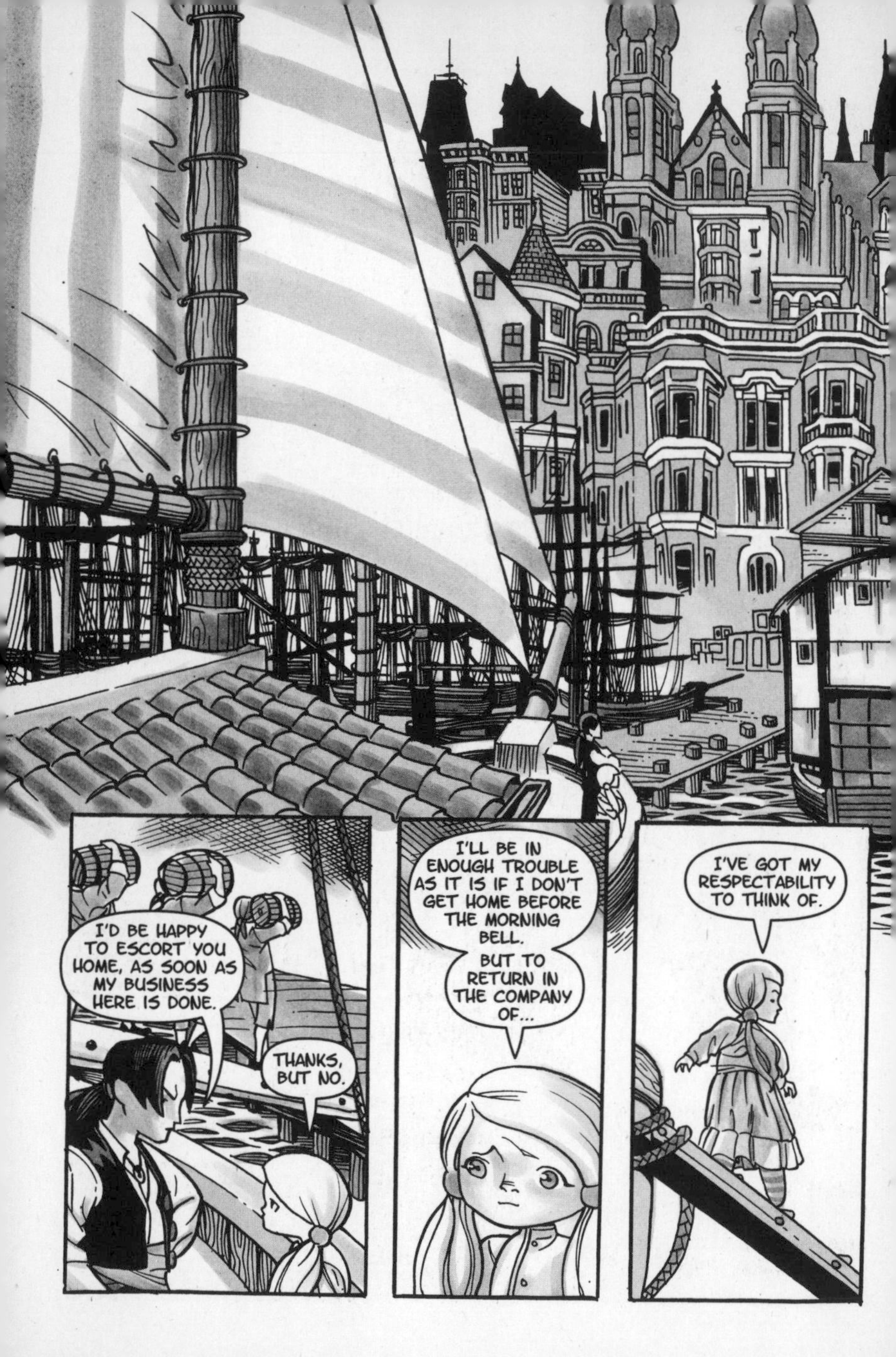
I'D BE HAPPY TO ESCORT YOU HOME, AS SOON AS MY BUSINESS HERE IS DONE.
THANKS, BUT NO.
I'LL BE IN ENOUGH TROUBLE AS IT IS IF I DON'T GET HOME BEFORE THE MORNING BELL.
BUT TO RETURN IN THE COMPANY OF...
I'VE GOT MY RESPECTABILITY TO THINK OF.

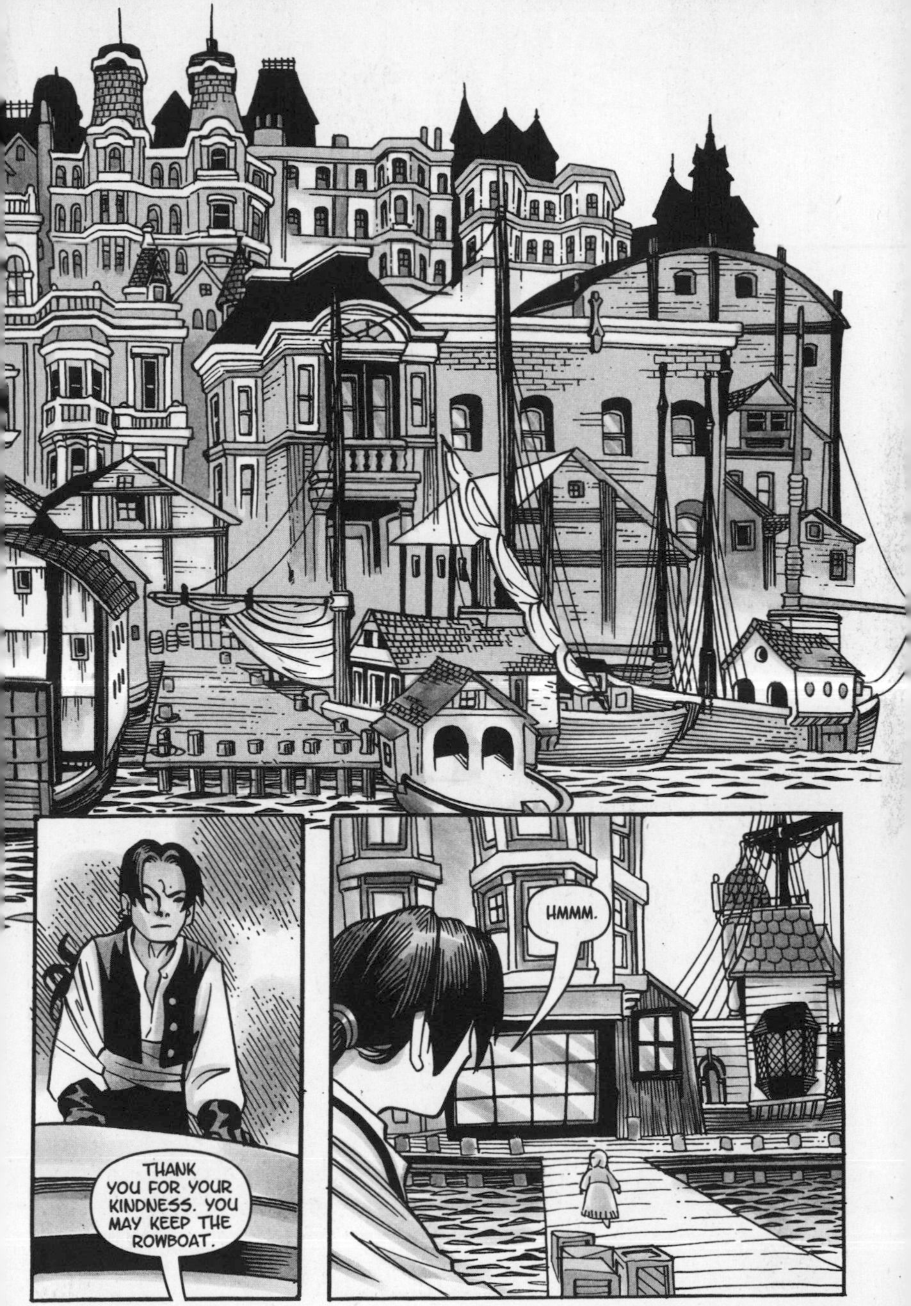
THANK YOU FOR YOUR KINDNESS. YOU MAY KEEP THE ROWBOAT.
HMMM.

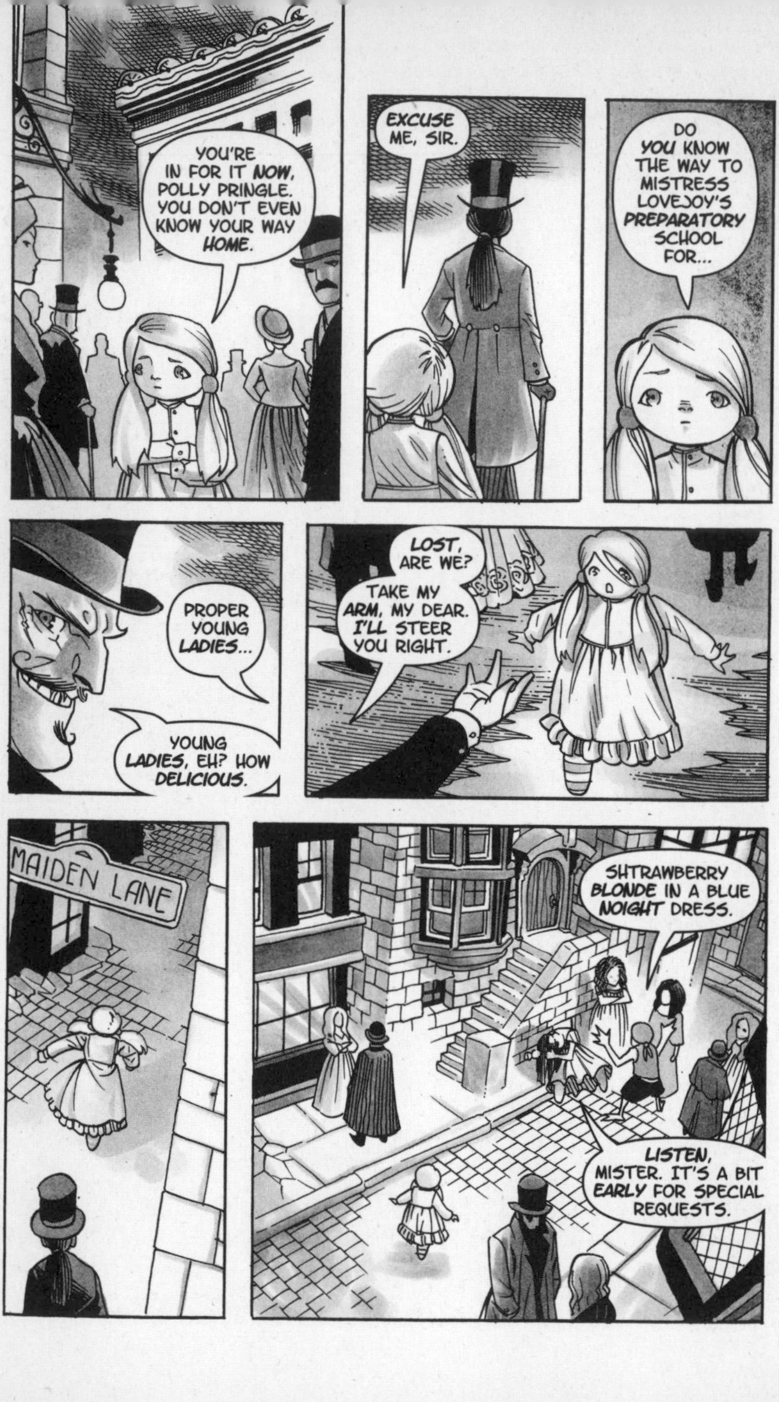
YOU'RE IN FOR IT NOW, POLLY PRINGLE. YOU DON'T EVEN KNOW YOUR WAY HOME.
EXCUSE ME, SIR.
DO YOU KNOW THE WAY TO MISTRESS LOVEJOY'S PREPARATORY SCHOOL FOR...
PROPER YOUNG LADIES...
YOUNG LADIES, EH? HOW DELICIOUS.
LOST, ARE WE?
TAKE MY ARM, MY DEAR. I'LL STEER YOU RIGHT.
MAIDEN LANE
SHTRAWBERRY BLONDE IN A BLUE NOIGHT DRESS.
LISTEN, MISTER. IT'S A BIT EARLY FOR SPECIAL REQUESTS.

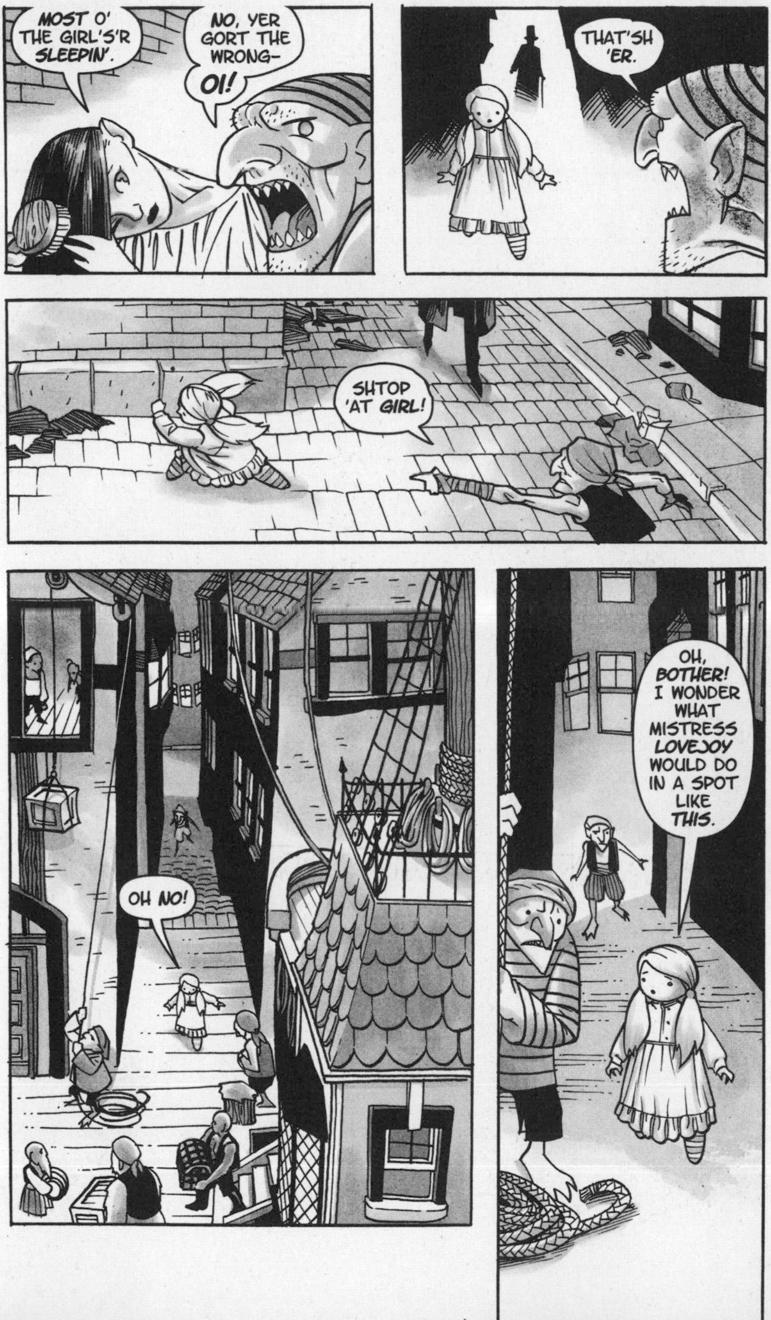
MOST O' THE GIRL'S'R SLEEPIN'.
NO, YER GORT THE WRONG-
OI!
THAT'SH 'ER.
SHTOP 'AT GIRL!
OH NO!
OH, BOTHER! I WONDER WHAT MISTRESS LOVEJOY WOULD DO IN A SPOT LIKE THIS.

I'D USE MY HEAD, YOU SILLY GIRL!

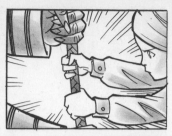

BONK

GREAT WALLABIES!

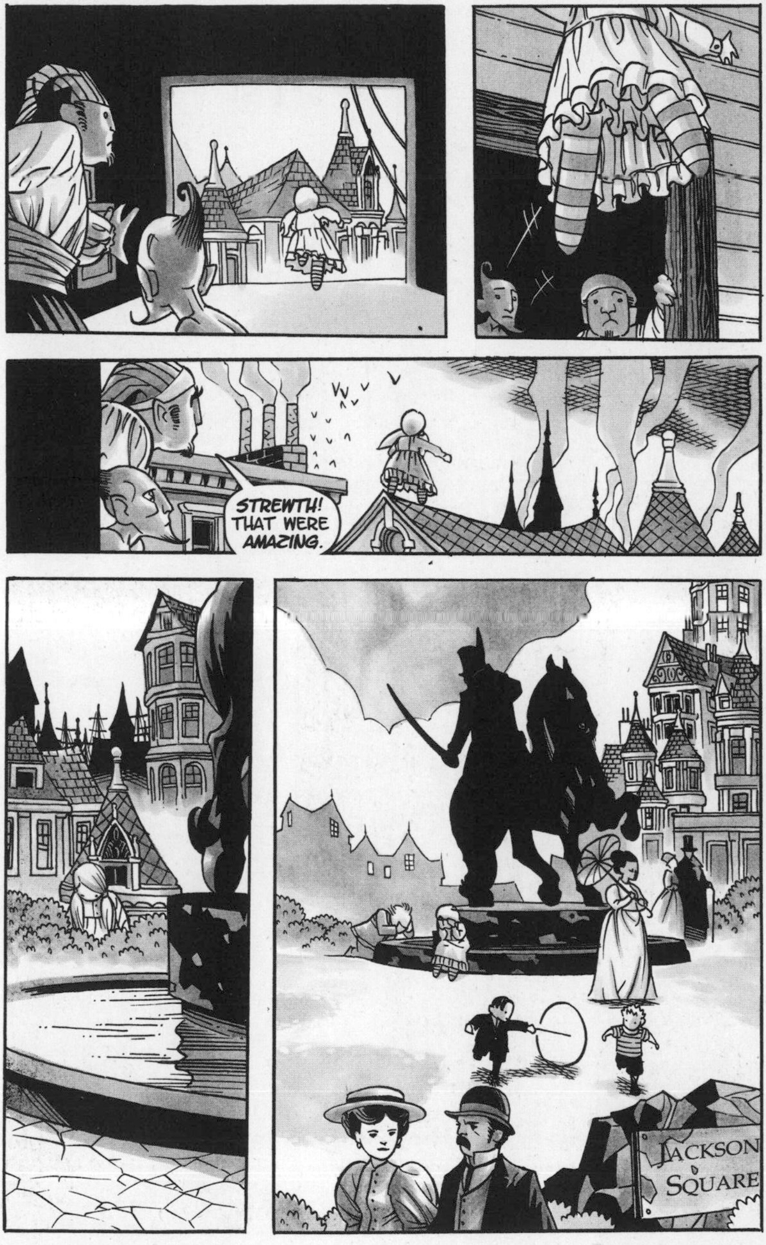
STREWTH! THAT WERE AMAZING.
JACKSON SQUARE

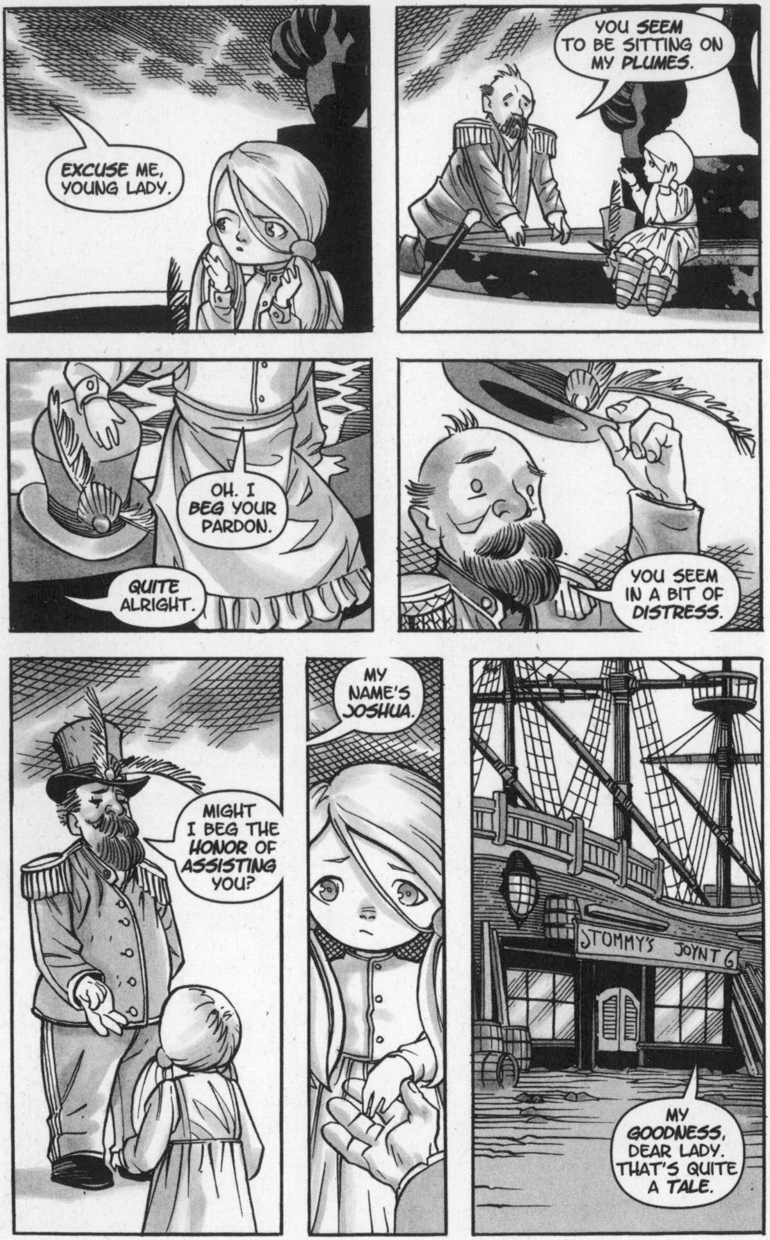
EXCUSE ME, YOUNG LADY.
YOU SEEM TO BE SITTING ON MY PLUMES.
OH. I BEG YOUR PARDON.
QUITE ALRIGHT.
YOU SEEM IN A BIT OF DISTRESS.
MIGHT I BEG THE HONOR OF ASSISTING YOU?
MY NAME'S JOSHUA.
STOMMY'S JOYNT
MY GOODNESS, DEAR LADY. THAT'S QUITE A TALE.

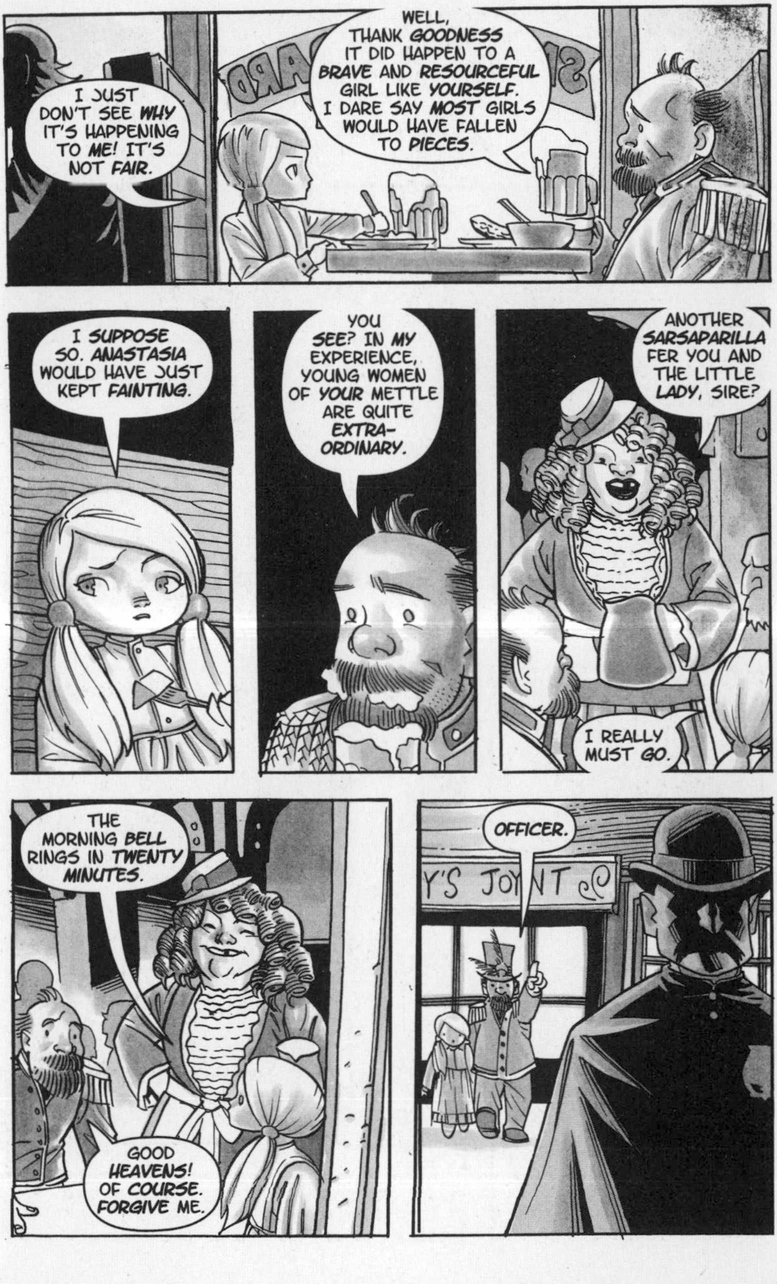
I JUST DON'T SEE WHY IT'S HAPPENING TO ME! IT'S NOT FAIR.
WELL, THANK GOODNESS IT DID HAPPEN TO A BRAVE AND RESOURCEFUL GIRL LIKE YOURSELF. I DARE SAY MOST GIRLS WOULD HAVE FALLEN TO PIECES.
I SUPPOSE SO. ANASTASIA WOULD HAVE JUST KEPT FAINTING.
YOU SEE? IN MY EXPERIENCE, YOUNG WOMEN OF YOUR METTLE ARE QUITE EXTRA-ORDINARY.
ANOTHER SARSAPARILLA FER YOU AND THE LITTLE LADY, SIRE?
I REALLY MUST GO.
THE MORNING BELL RINGS IN TWENTY MINUTES.
GOOD HEAVENS! OF COURSE. FORGIVE ME.
Y'S JOYNT
OFFICER.

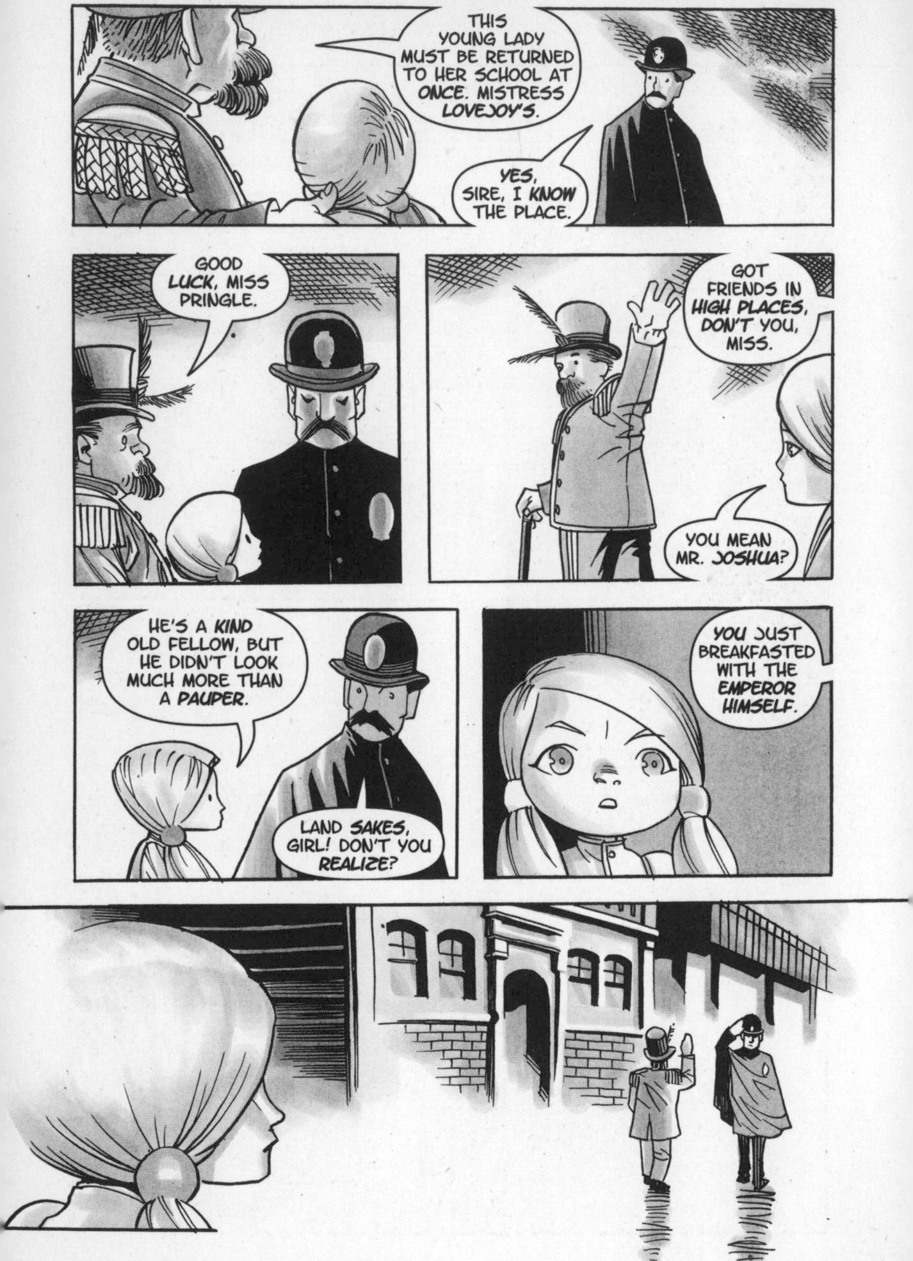
THIS YOUNG LADY MUST BE RETURNED TO HER SCHOOL AT ONCE. MISTRESS LOVEJOY'S.
YES, SIRE, I KNOW THE PLACE.
GOOD LUCK, MISS PRINGLE.
GOT FRIENDS IN HIGH PLACES, DON'T YOU, MISS.
YOU MEAN MR. JOSHUA?
HE'S A KIND OLD FELLOW, BUT HE DIDN'T LOOK MUCH MORE THAN A PAUPER.
LAND SAKES, GIRL! DON'T YOU REALIZE?
YOU JUST BREAKFASTED WITH THE EMPEROR HIMSELF.

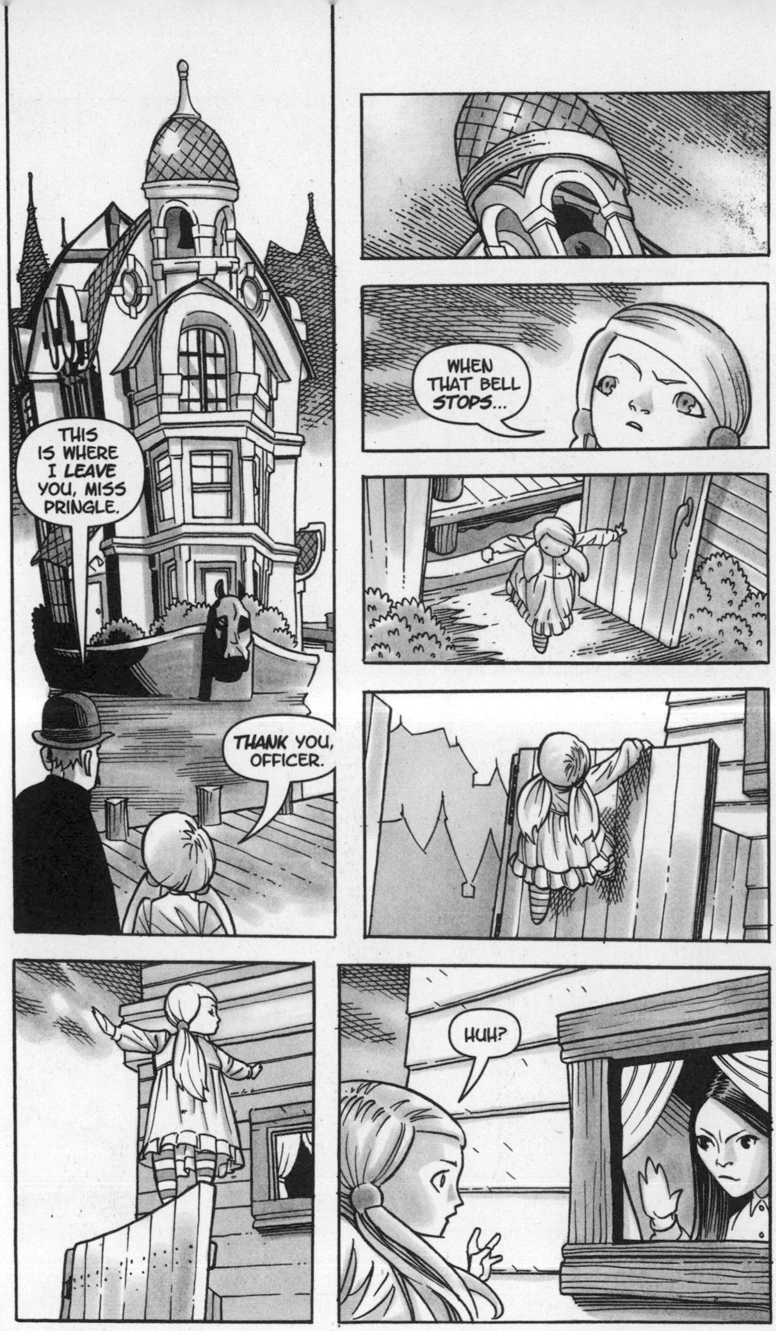
THIS IS WHERE I LEAVE YOU, MISS PRINGLE.
THANK YOU, OFFICER.
WHEN THAT BELL STOPS...
HUH?

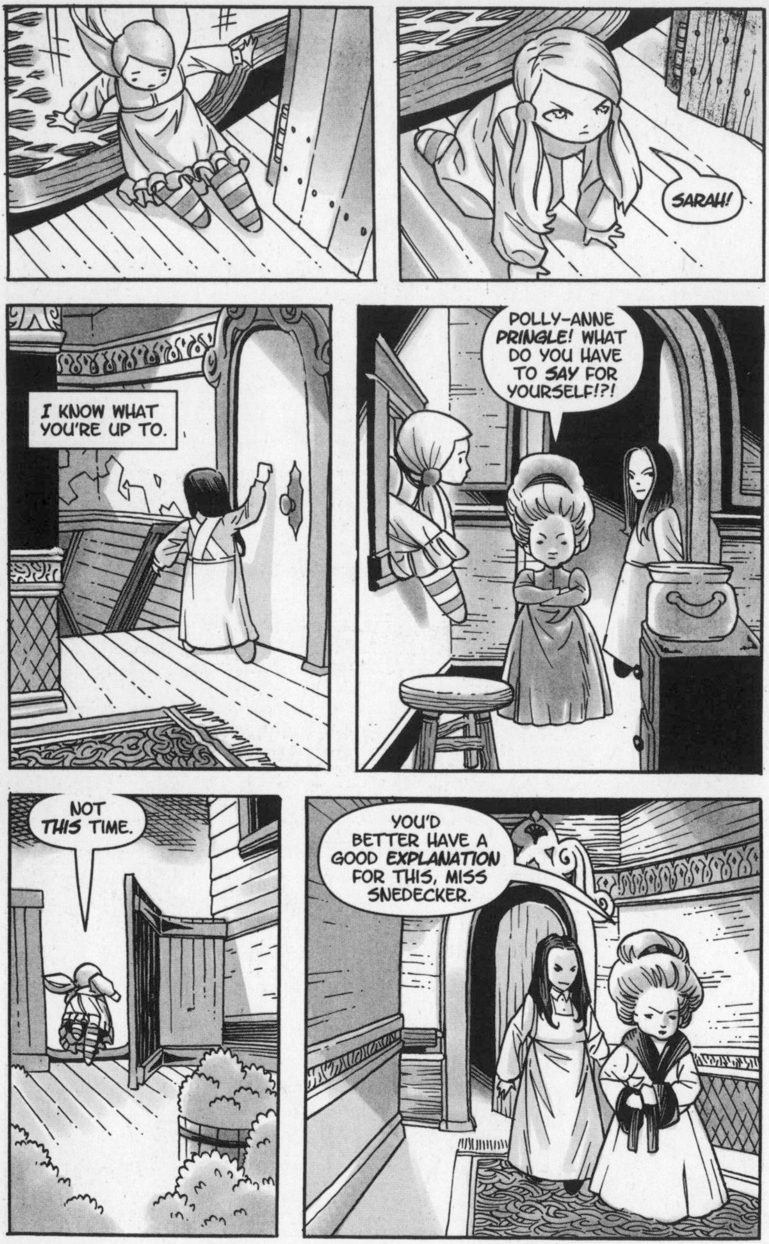
SARAH!
I KNOW WHAT YOU'RE UP TO.
POLLY-ANNE PRINGLE! WHAT DO YOU HAVE TO SAY FOR YOURSELF!?!
NOT THIS TIME.
YOU'D BETTER HAVE A GOOD EXPLANATION FOR THIS, MISS SNEDECKER.

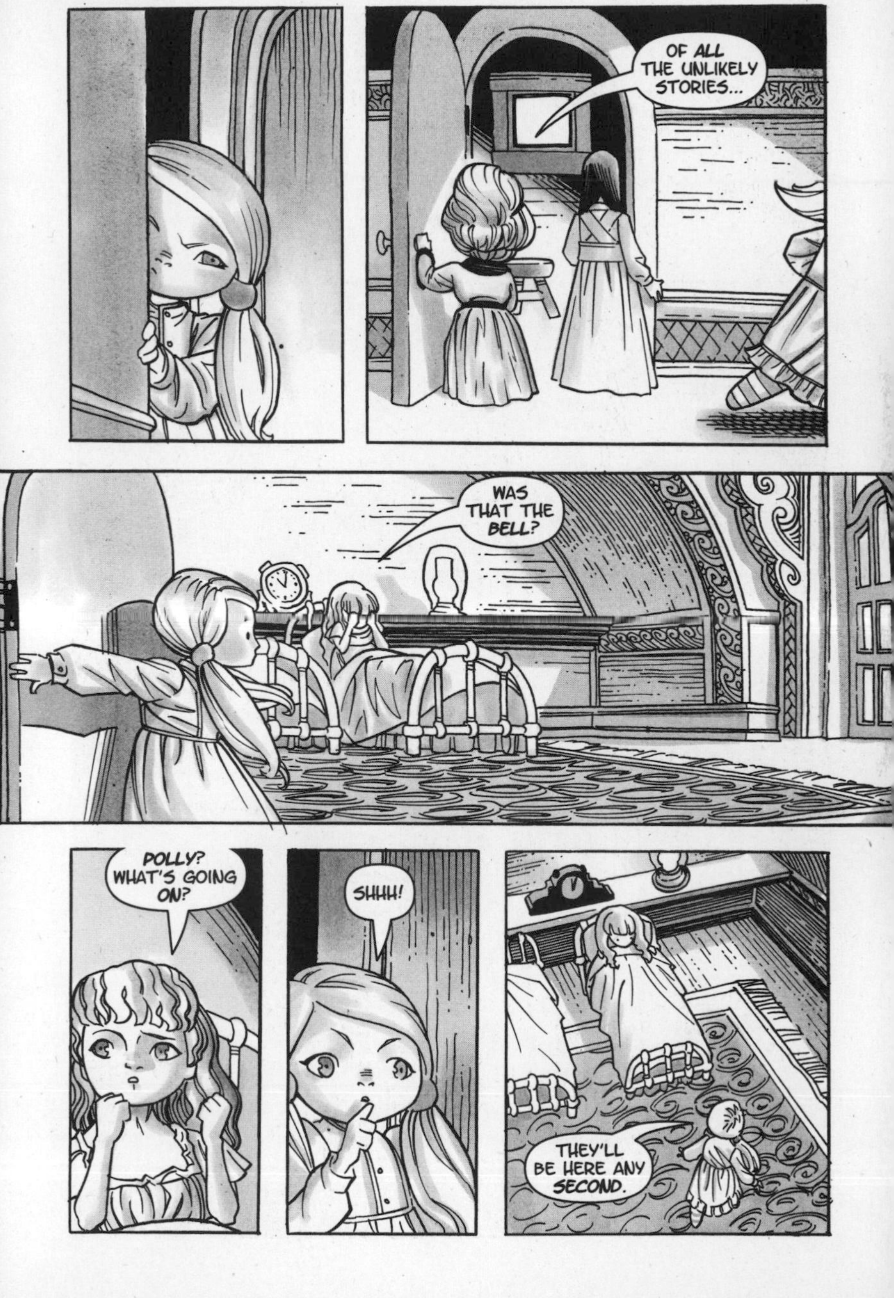
OF ALL THE UNLIKELY STORIES...
WAS THAT THE BELL?
POLLY? WHAT'S GOING ON?
SHHH!
THEY'LL BE HERE ANY SECOND.

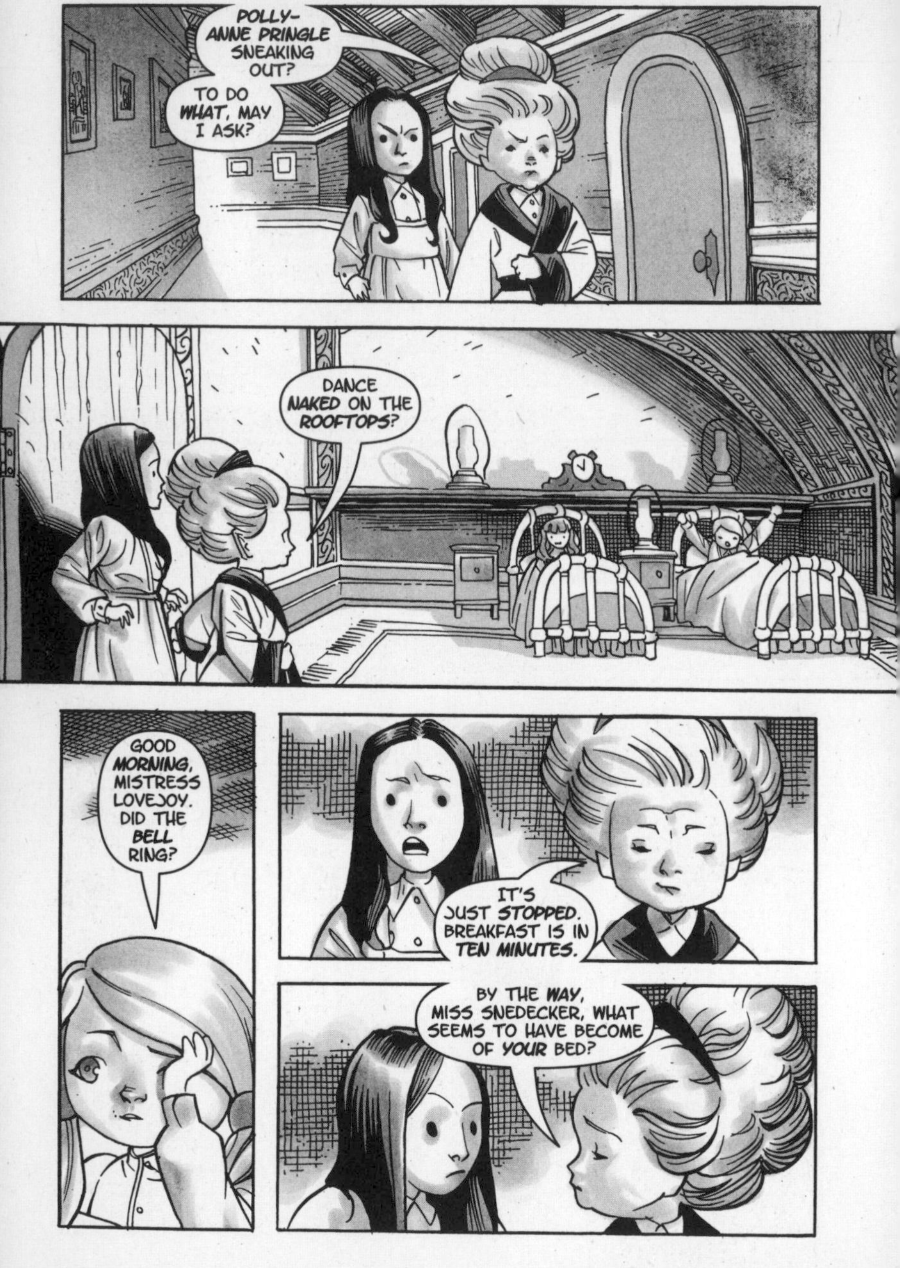
POLLY-ANNE PRINGLE SNEAKING OUT?
TO DO WHAT, MAY I ASK?
DANCE NAKED ON THE ROOFTOPS?
GOOD MORNING, MISTRESS LOVEJOY. DID THE BELL RING?
IT'S JUST STOPPED. BREAKFAST IS IN TEN MINUTES.
BY THE WAY, MISS SNEDECKER, WHAT SEEMS TO HAVE BECOME OF YOUR BED?

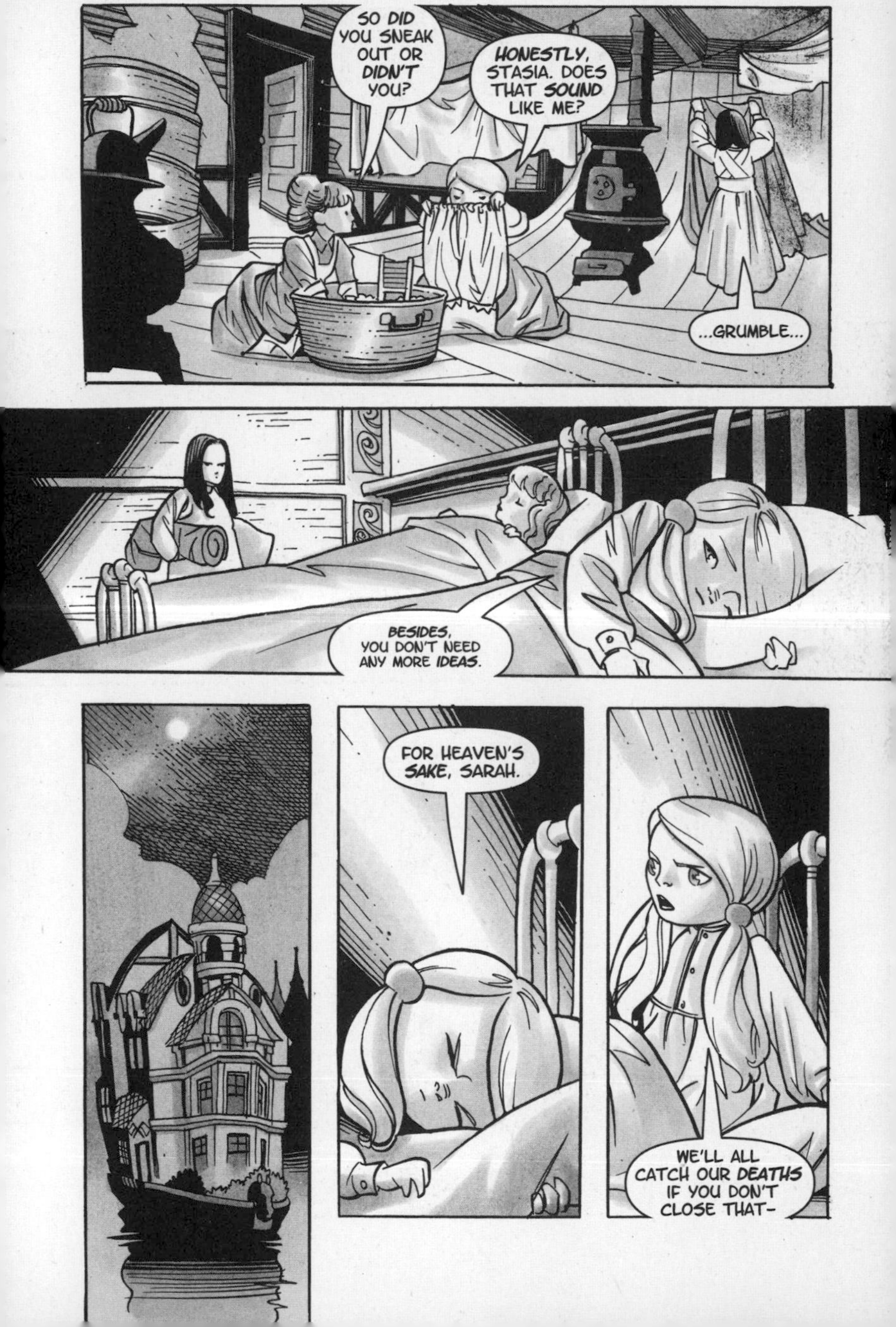
SO DID YOU SNEAK OUT OR DIDN'T YOU?
HONESTLY, STASIA. DOES THAT SOUND LIKE ME?
...GRUMBLE...
BESIDES, YOU DON'T NEED ANY MORE IDEAS.
FOR HEAVEN'S SAKE, SARAH.
WE'LL ALL CATCH OUR DEATHS IF YOU DON'T CLOSE THAT-

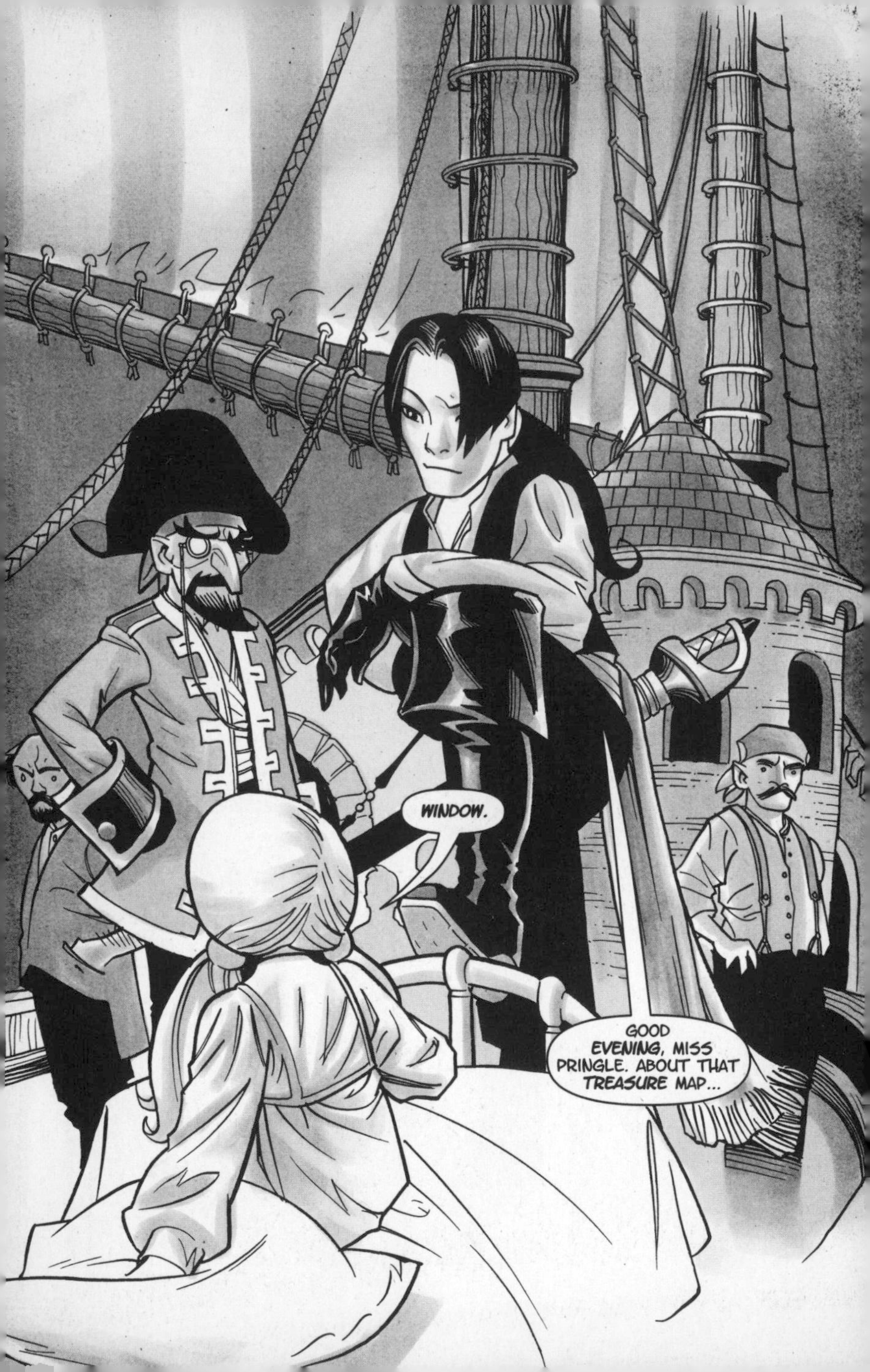
WINDOW.
GOOD EVENING, MISS PRINGLE. ABOUT THAT TREASURE MAP...

Chapter 3

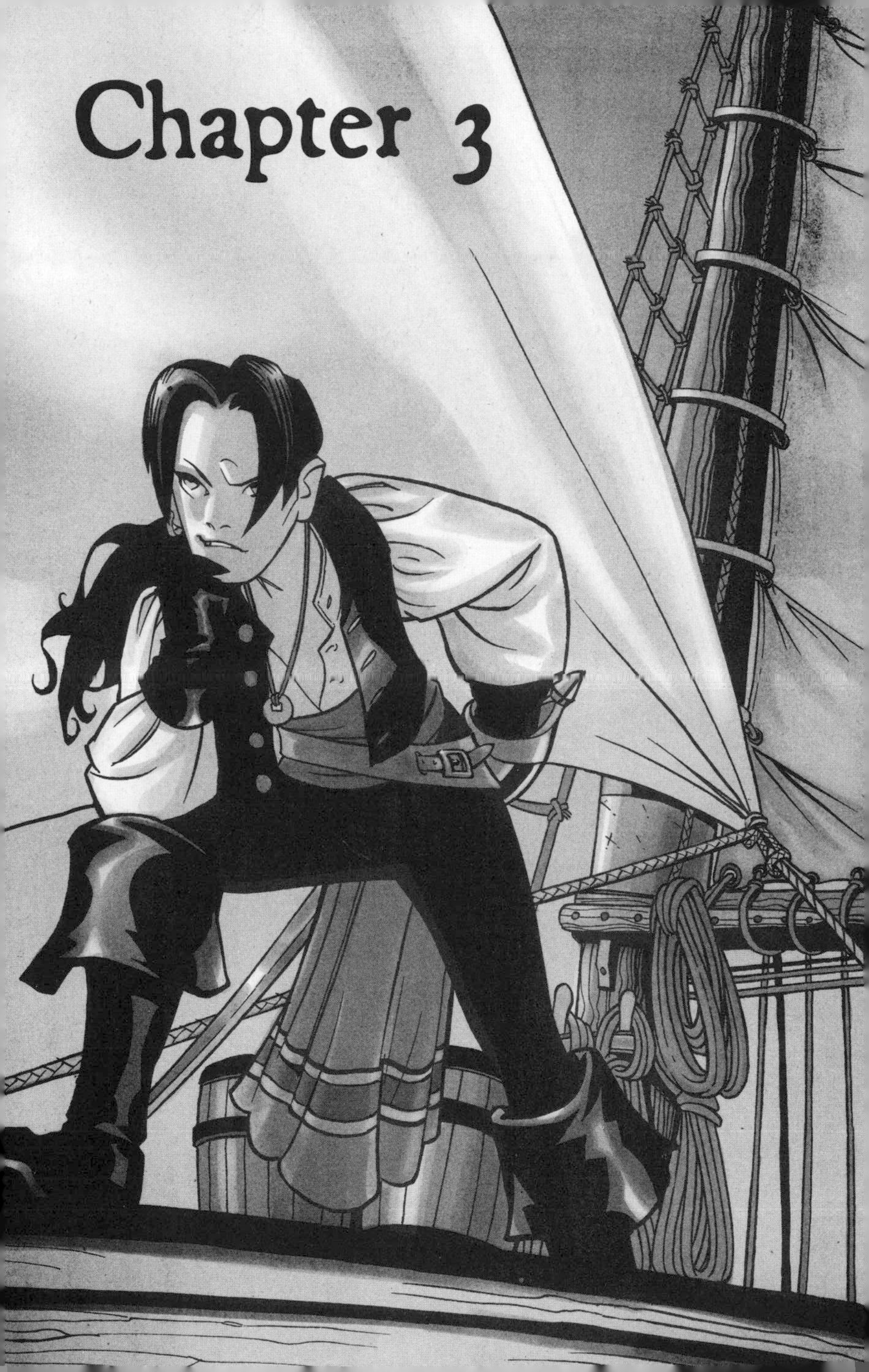

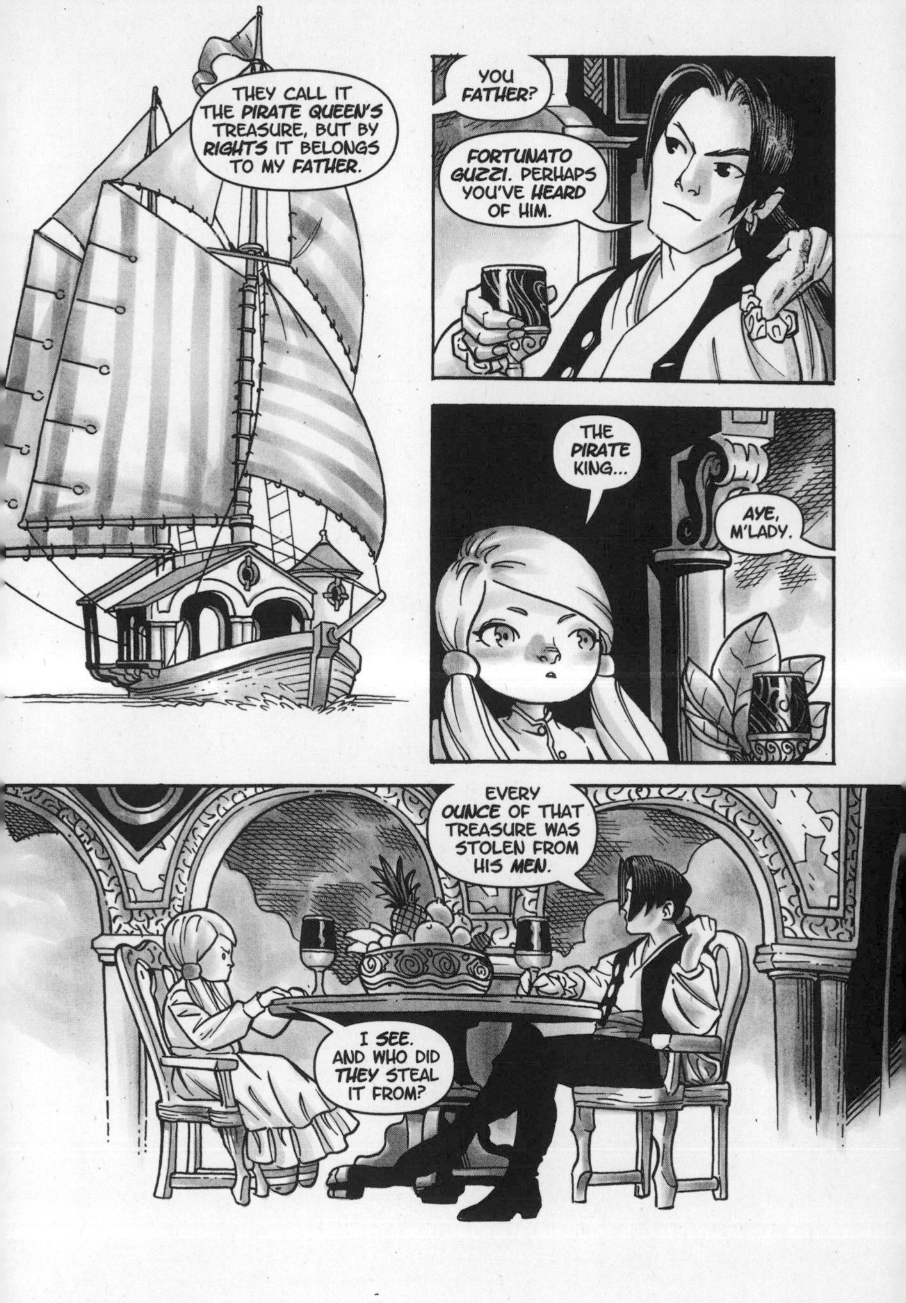
THEY CALL IT THE PIRATE QUEEN'S TREASURE, BUT BY RIGHTS IT BELONGS TO MY FATHER.
YOU FATHER?
FORTUNATO GUZZI. PERHAPS YOU'VE HEARD OF HIM.
THE PIRATE KING...
AYE, M'LADY.
EVERY OUNCE OF THAT TREASURE WAS STOLEN FROM HIS MEN.
I SEE. AND WHO DID THEY STEAL IT FROM?

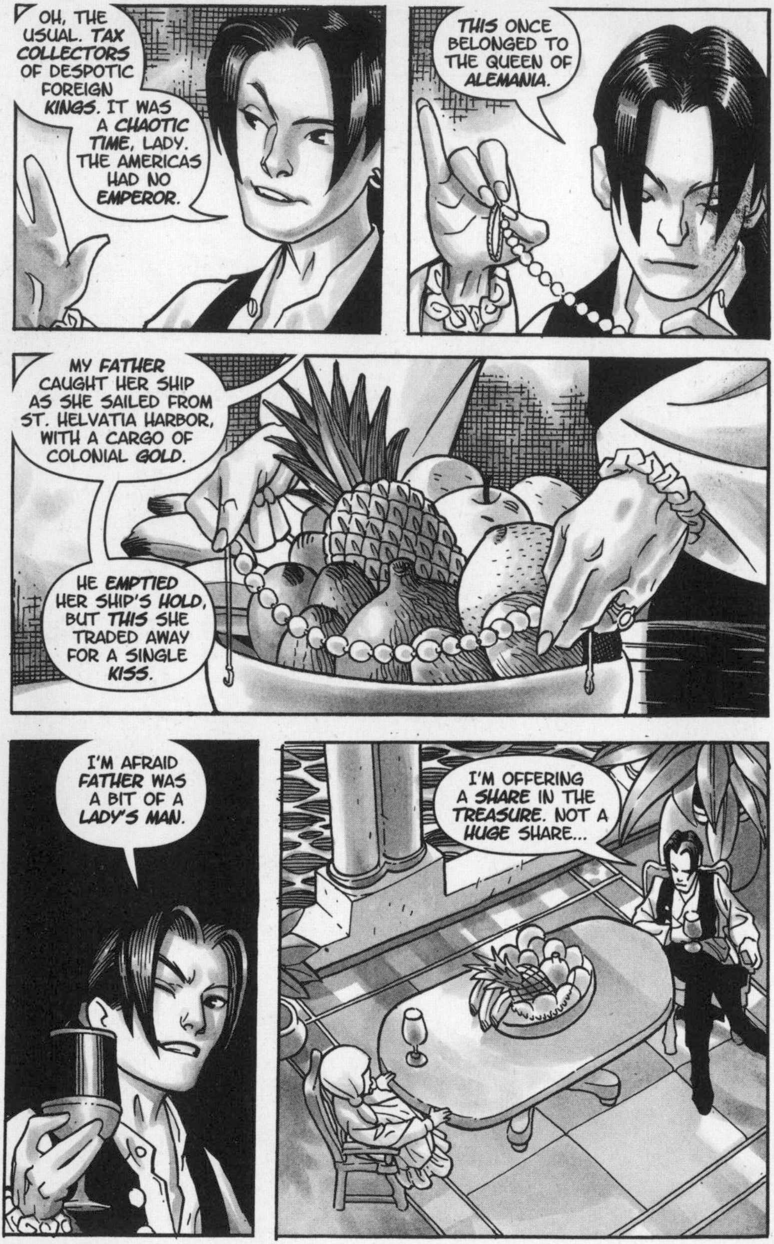
OH, THE USUAL. TAX COLLECTORS OF DESPOTIC FOREIGN KINGS. IT WAS A CHAOTIC TIME, LADY. THE AMERICAS HAD NO EMPEROR.
THIS ONCE BELONGED TO THE QUEEN OF ALEMANIA.
MY FATHER CAUGHT HER SHIP AS SHE SAILED FROM ST. HELVATIA HARBOR, WITH A CARGO OF COLONIAL GOLD.
HE EMPTIED HER SHIP'S HOLD, BUT THIS SHE TRADED AWAY FOR A SINGLE KISS.
I'M AFRAID FATHER WAS A BIT OF A LADY'S MAN.
I'M OFFERING A SHARE IN THE TREASURE. NOT A HUGE SHARE...

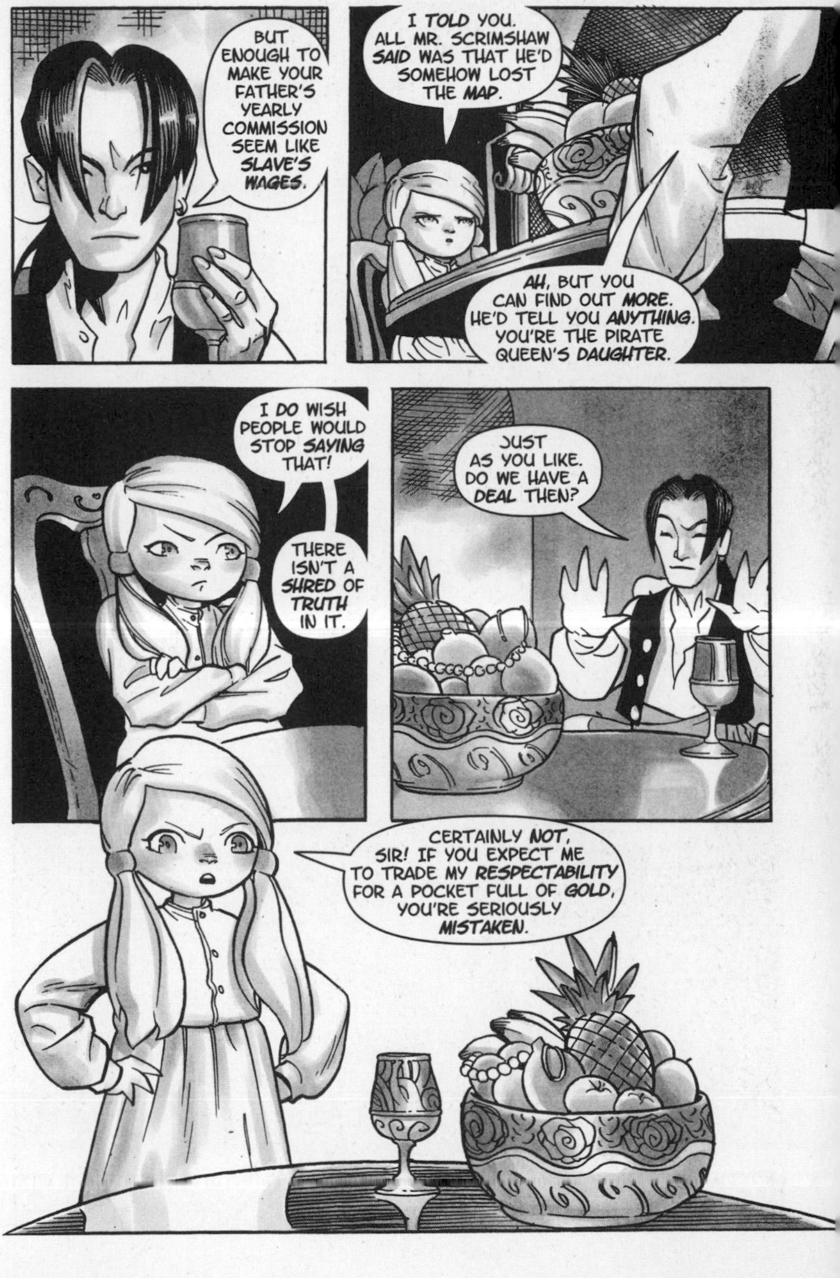
BUT ENOUGH TO MAKE YOUR FATHER'S YEARLY COMMISSION SEEM LIKE SLAVE'S WAGES.
I TOLD YOU. ALL MR. SCRIMSHAW SAID WAS THAT HE'D SOMEHOW LOST THE MAP.
AH, BUT YOU CAN FIND OUT MORE. HE'D TELL YOU ANYTHING. YOU'RE THE PIRATE QUEEN'S DAUGHTER.
I DO WISH PEOPLE WOULD STOP SAYING THAT!
THERE ISN'T A SHRED OF TRUTH IN IT.
JUST AS YOU LIKE. DO WE HAVE A DEAL THEN?
CERTAINLY NOT, SIR! IF YOU EXPECT ME TO TRADE MY RESPECTABILITY FOR A POCKET FULL OF GOLD, YOU'RE SERIOUSLY MISTAKEN.

YOU MAY CONSIDER YOUR OFFER DECLINED.

GOOD *GIRL*, POLLY.

YOUR *RESPECTABILITY* IS MORE VALUABLE THAN *GOLD*, IS IT?

THEN YOU WOULDN'T WANT ME TO TELL YOUR CHARMING HEAD-MISTRESS ALL ABOUT...

...US.

WHAT ON *EARTH* ARE YOU *TALKING* ABOUT?

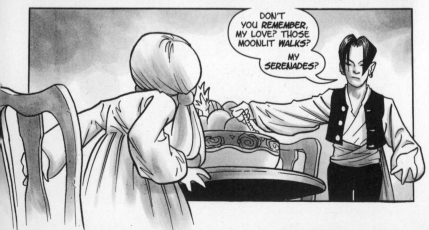

DON'T YOU *REMEMBER*, MY LOVE? THOSE *MOONLIT WALKS*?

MY *SERENADES*?

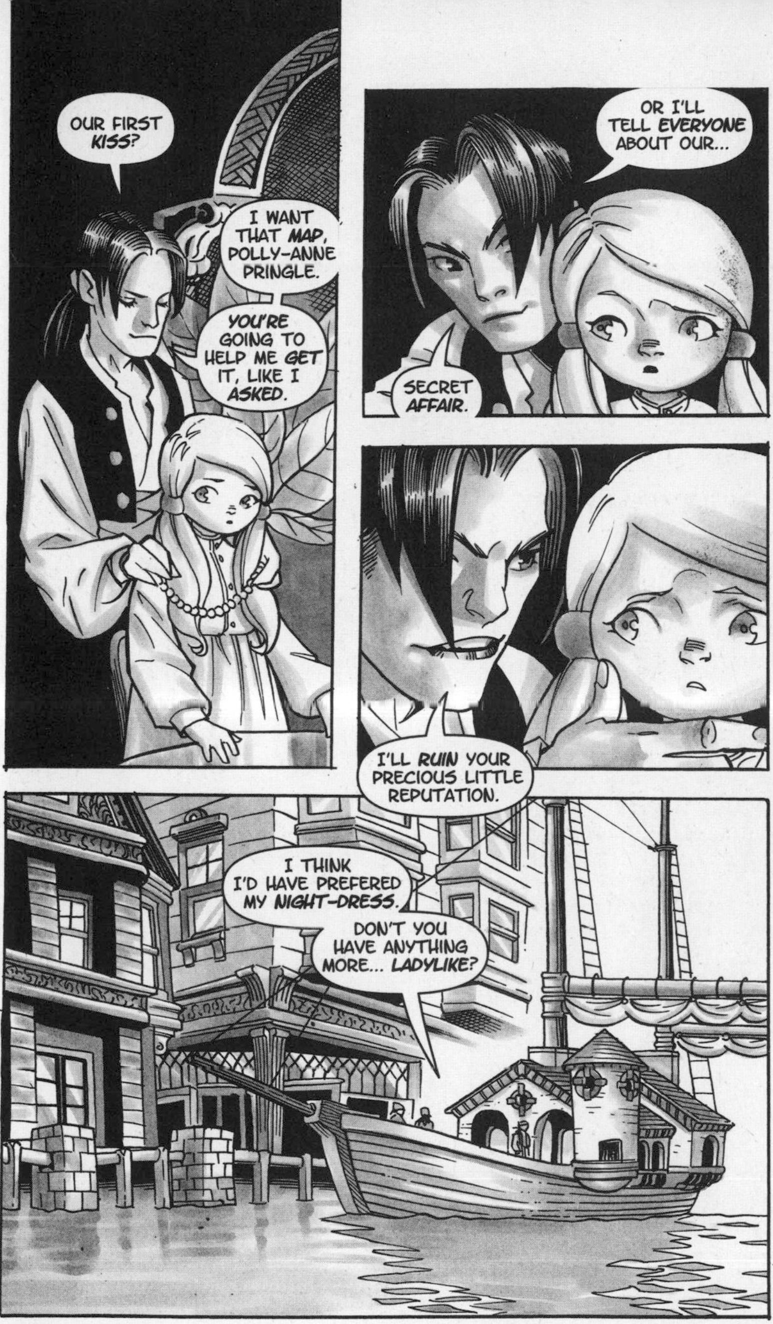
OUR FIRST KISS?
I WANT THAT MAP, POLLY-ANNE PRINGLE.
YOU'RE GOING TO HELP ME GET IT, LIKE I ASKED.
OR I'LL TELL EVERYONE ABOUT OUR...
SECRET AFFAIR.
I'LL RUIN YOUR PRECIOUS LITTLE REPUTATION.
I THINK I'D HAVE PREFERED MY NIGHT-DRESS.
DON'T YOU HAVE ANYTHING MORE... LADYLIKE?

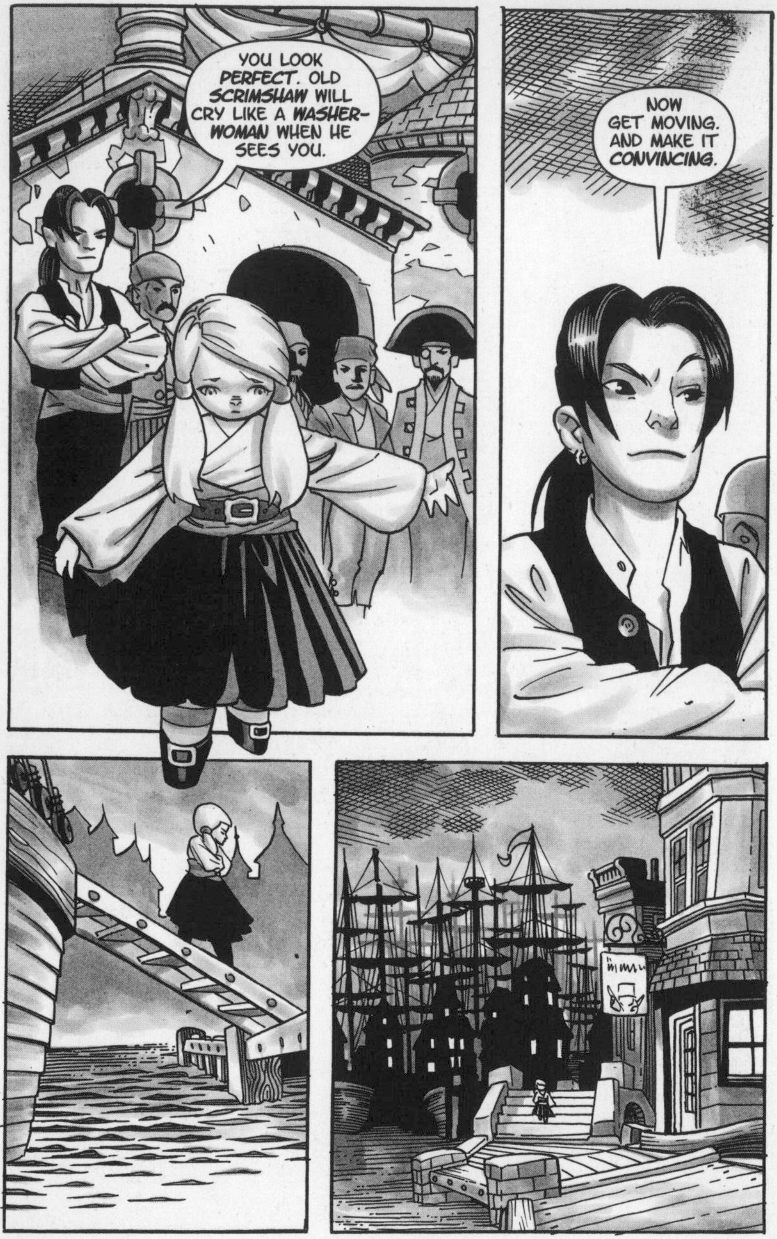
YOU LOOK PERFECT. OLD SCRIMSHAW WILL CRY LIKE A WASHER-WOMAN WHEN HE SEES YOU.
NOW GET MOVING. AND MAKE IT CONVINCING.

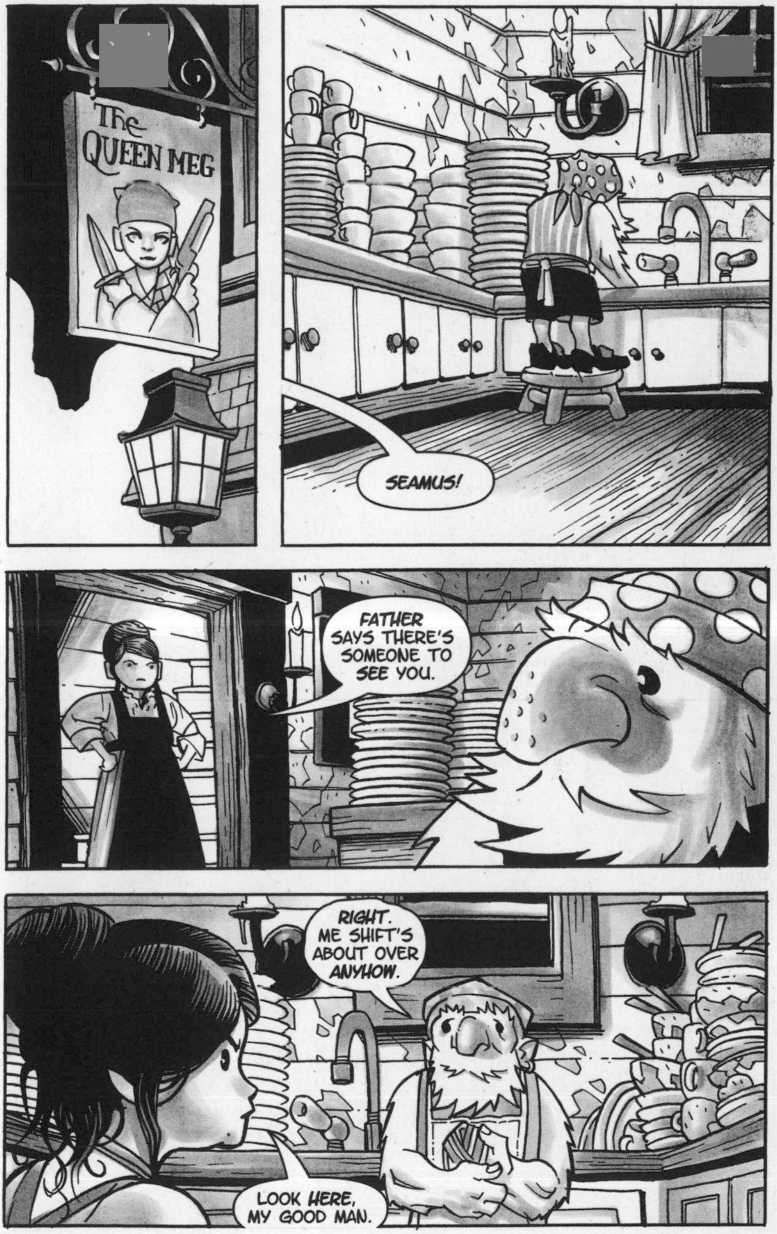
The QUEEN MEG
SEAMUS!
FATHER SAYS THERE'S SOMEONE TO SEE YOU.
RIGHT. ME SHIFT'S ABOUT OVER ANYHOW.
LOOK HERE, MY GOOD MAN.

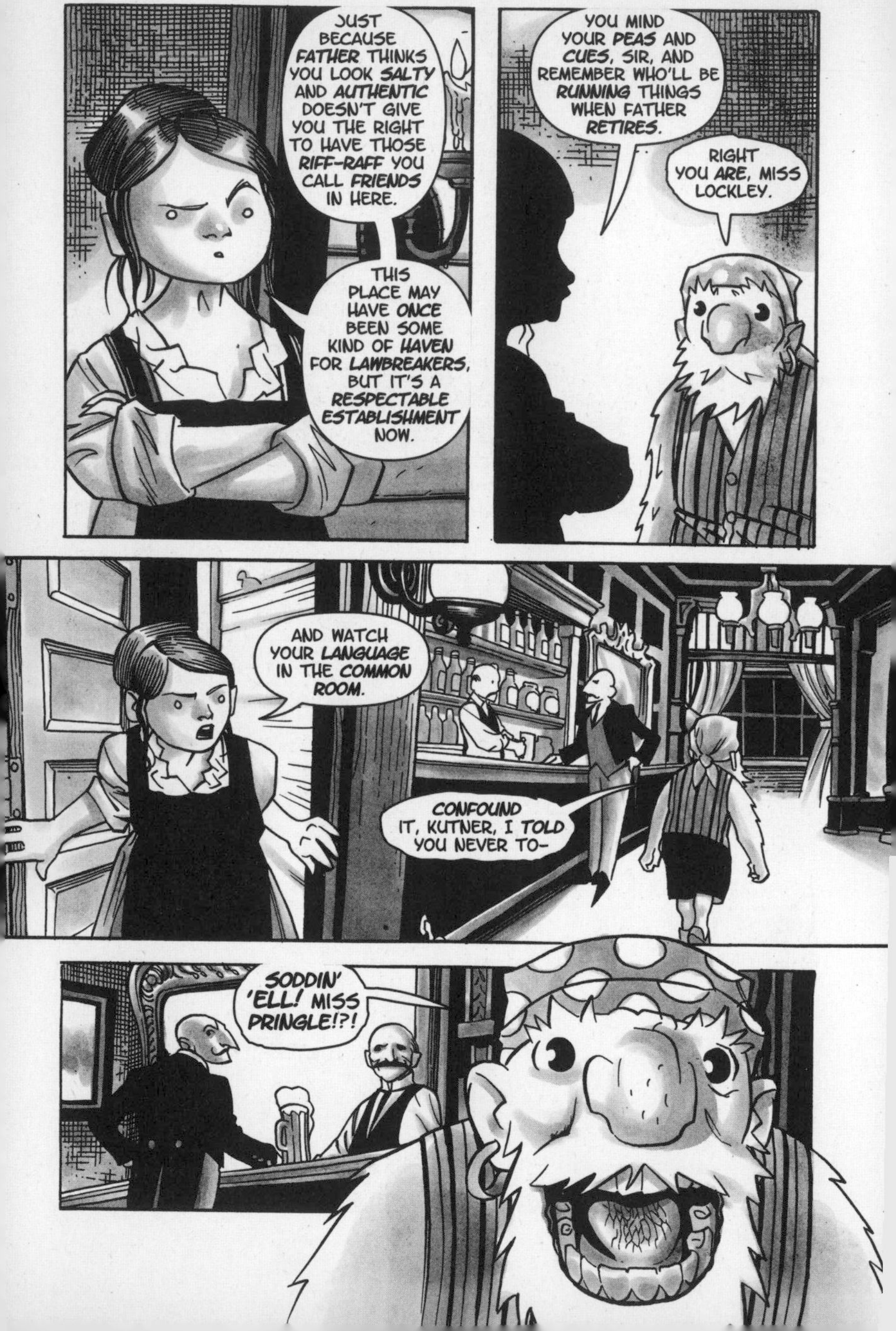
JUST BECAUSE FATHER THINKS YOU LOOK SALTY AND AUTHENTIC DOESN'T GIVE YOU THE RIGHT TO HAVE THOSE RIFF-RAFF YOU CALL FRIENDS IN HERE.
THIS PLACE MAY HAVE ONCE BEEN SOME KIND OF HAVEN FOR LAWBREAKERS, BUT IT'S A RESPECTABLE ESTABLISHMENT NOW.
YOU MIND YOUR PEAS AND CUES, SIR, AND REMEMBER WHO'LL BE RUNNING THINGS WHEN FATHER RETIRES.
RIGHT YOU ARE, MISS LOCKLEY.
AND WATCH YOUR LANGUAGE IN THE COMMON ROOM.
CONFOUND IT, KUTNER, I TOLD YOU NEVER TO-
SODDIN' 'ELL! MISS PRINGLE!?!

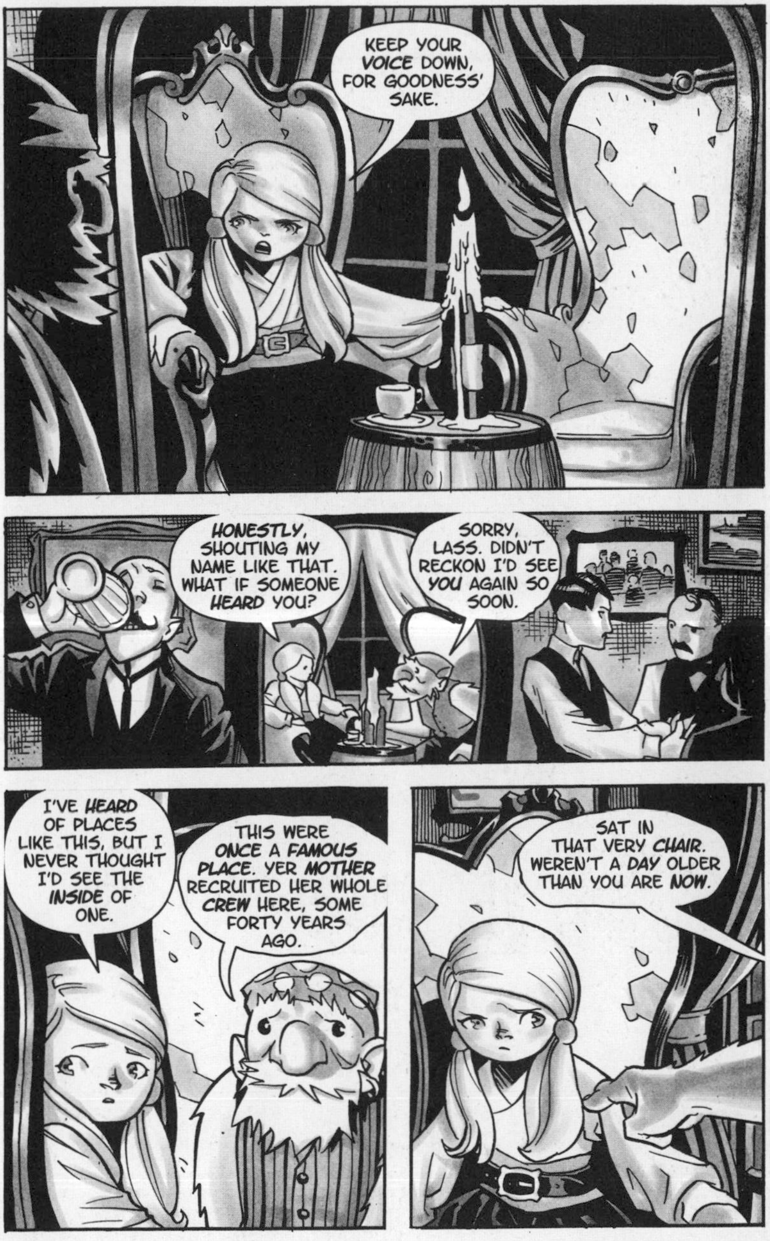
KEEP YOUR VOICE DOWN, FOR GOODNESS' SAKE.
HONESTLY, SHOUTING MY NAME LIKE THAT. WHAT IF SOMEONE HEARD YOU?
SORRY, LASS. DIDN'T RECKON I'D SEE YOU AGAIN SO SOON.
I'VE HEARD OF PLACES LIKE THIS, BUT I NEVER THOUGHT I'D SEE THE INSIDE OF ONE.
THIS WERE ONCE A FAMOUS PLACE. YER MOTHER RECRUITED HER WHOLE CREW HERE, SOME FORTY YEARS AGO.
SAT IN THAT VERY CHAIR. WEREN'T A DAY OLDER THAN YOU ARE NOW.

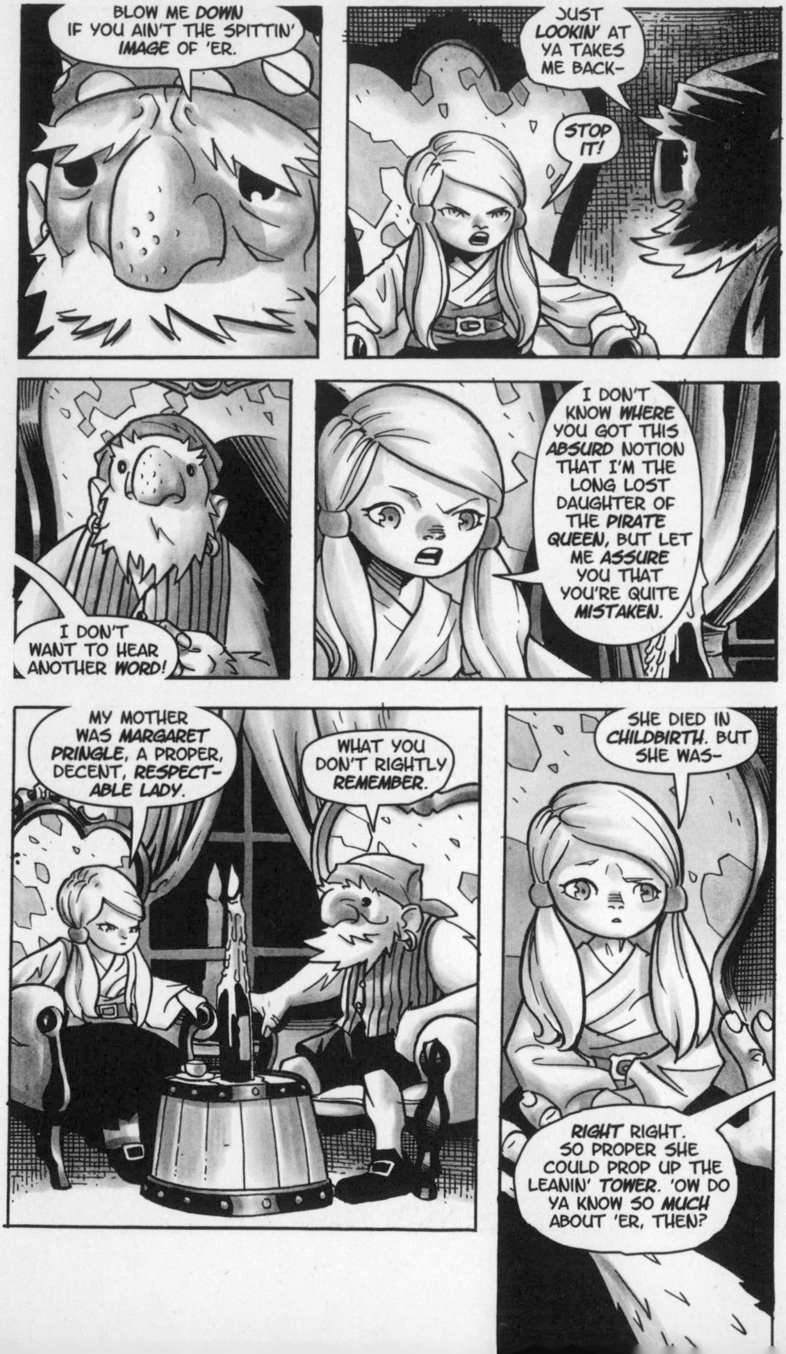
BLOW ME DOWN IF YOU AIN'T THE SPITTIN' IMAGE OF 'ER.
JUST LOOKIN' AT YA TAKES ME BACK-
STOP IT!
I DON'T WANT TO HEAR ANOTHER WORD!
I DON'T KNOW WHERE YOU GOT THIS ABSURD NOTION THAT I'M THE LONG LOST DAUGHTER OF THE PIRATE QUEEN, BUT LET ME ASSURE YOU THAT YOU'RE QUITE MISTAKEN.
MY MOTHER WAS MARGARET PRINGLE, A PROPER, DECENT, RESPECT-ABLE LADY.
WHAT YOU DON'T RIGHTLY REMEMBER.
SHE DIED IN CHILDBIRTH. BUT SHE WAS-
RIGHT RIGHT. SO PROPER SHE COULD PROP UP THE LEANIN' TOWER. 'OW DO YA KNOW SO MUCH ABOUT 'ER, THEN?

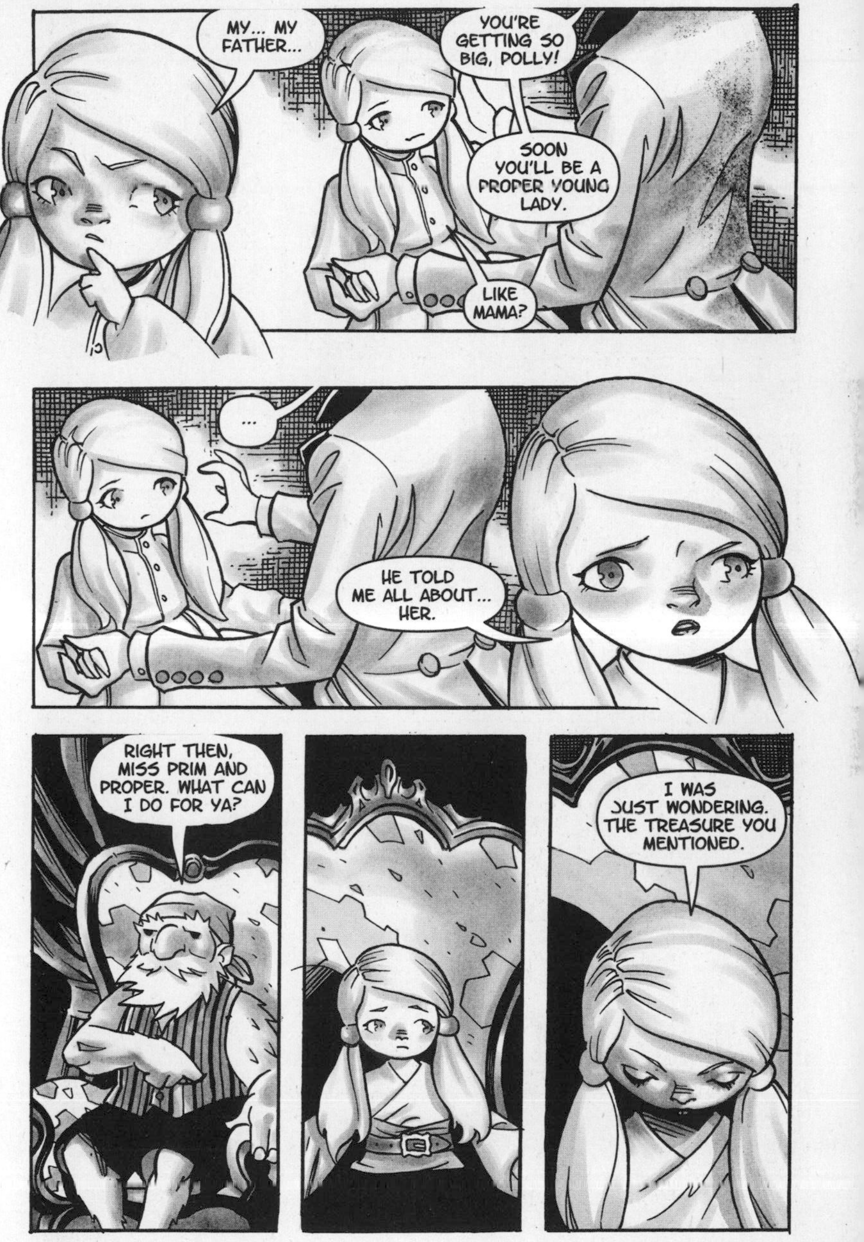
MY... MY FATHER...
YOU'RE GETTING SO BIG, POLLY!
SOON YOU'LL BE A PROPER YOUNG LADY.
LIKE MAMA?
...
HE TOLD ME ALL ABOUT... HER.
RIGHT THEN, MISS PRIM AND PROPER. WHAT CAN I DO FOR YA?
I WAS JUST WONDERING. THE TREASURE YOU MENTIONED.

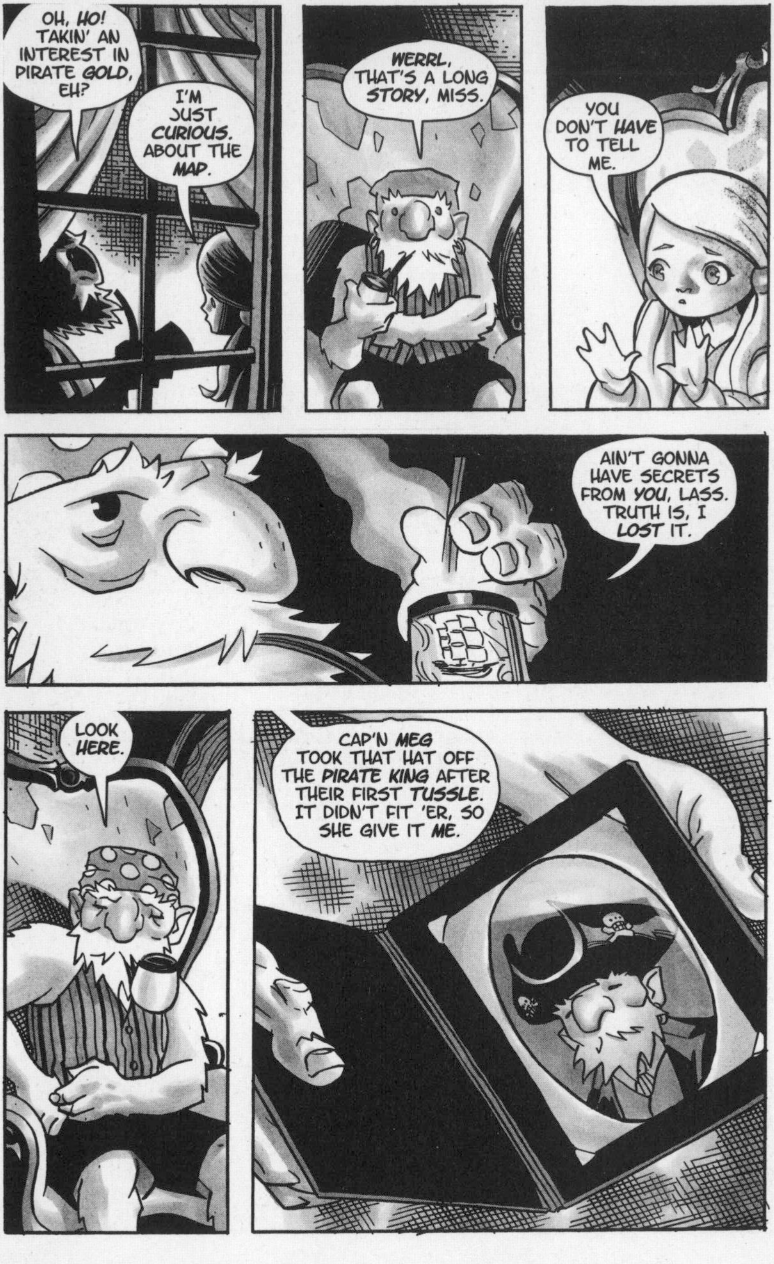
OH, HO! TAKIN' AN INTEREST IN PIRATE GOLD, EH?
I'M JUST CURIOUS. ABOUT THE MAP.
WERRL, THAT'S A LONG STORY, MISS.
YOU DON'T HAVE TO TELL ME.
AIN'T GONNA HAVE SECRETS FROM YOU, LASS. TRUTH IS, I LOST IT.
LOOK HERE.
CAP'N MEG TOOK THAT HAT OFF THE PIRATE KING AFTER THEIR FIRST TUSSLE. IT DIDN'T FIT 'ER, SO SHE GIVE IT ME.

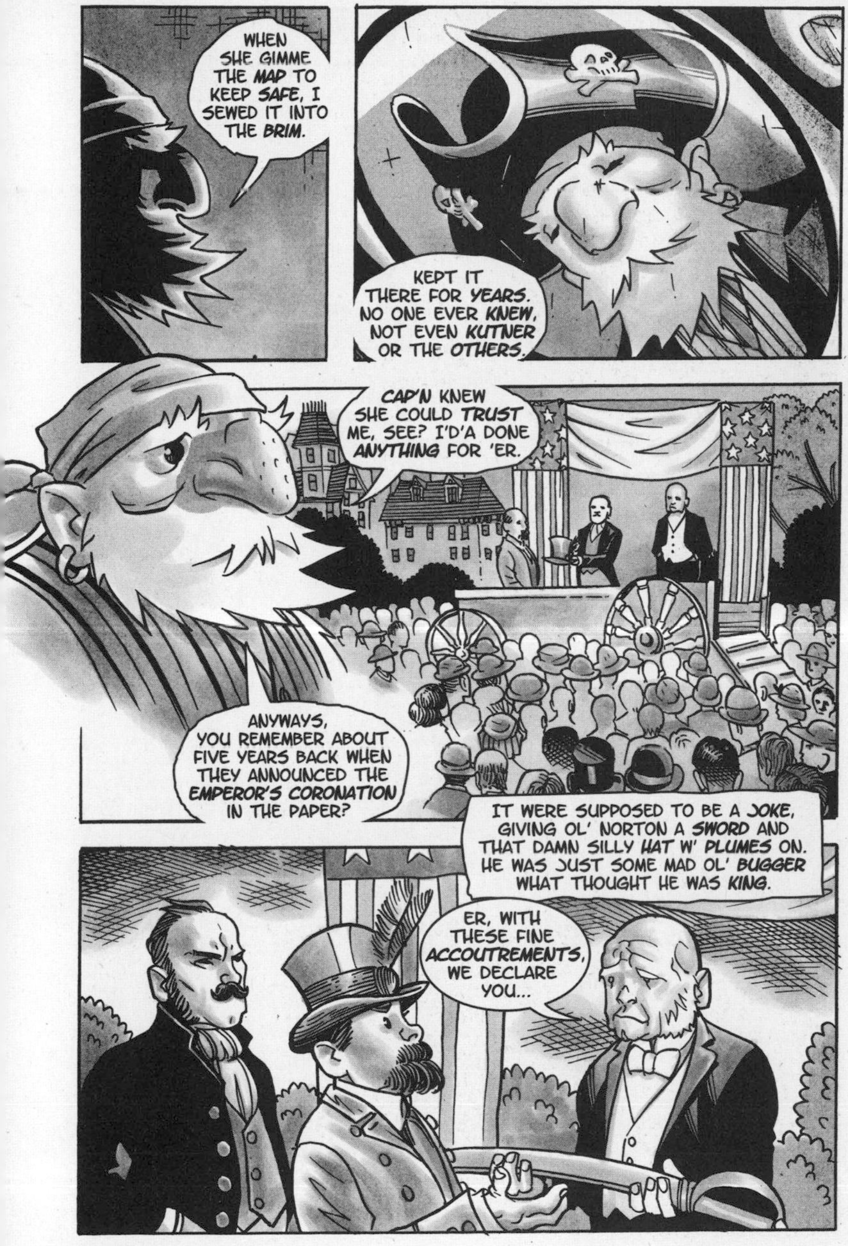
WHEN SHE GIMME THE MAP TO KEEP SAFE, I SEWED IT INTO THE BRIM.
KEPT IT THERE FOR YEARS. NO ONE EVER KNEW, NOT EVEN KUTNER OR THE OTHERS.
CAP'N KNEW SHE COULD TRUST ME, SEE? I'D'A DONE ANYTHING FOR 'ER.
ANYWAYS, YOU REMEMBER ABOUT FIVE YEARS BACK WHEN THEY ANNOUNCED THE EMPEROR'S CORONATION IN THE PAPER?
IT WERE SUPPOSED TO BE A JOKE, GIVING OL' NORTON A SWORD AND THAT DAMN SILLY HAT W' PLUMES ON. HE WAS JUST SOME MAD OL' BUGGER WHAT THOUGHT HE WAS KING.
ER, WITH THESE FINE ACCOUTREMENTS, WE DECLARE YOU...

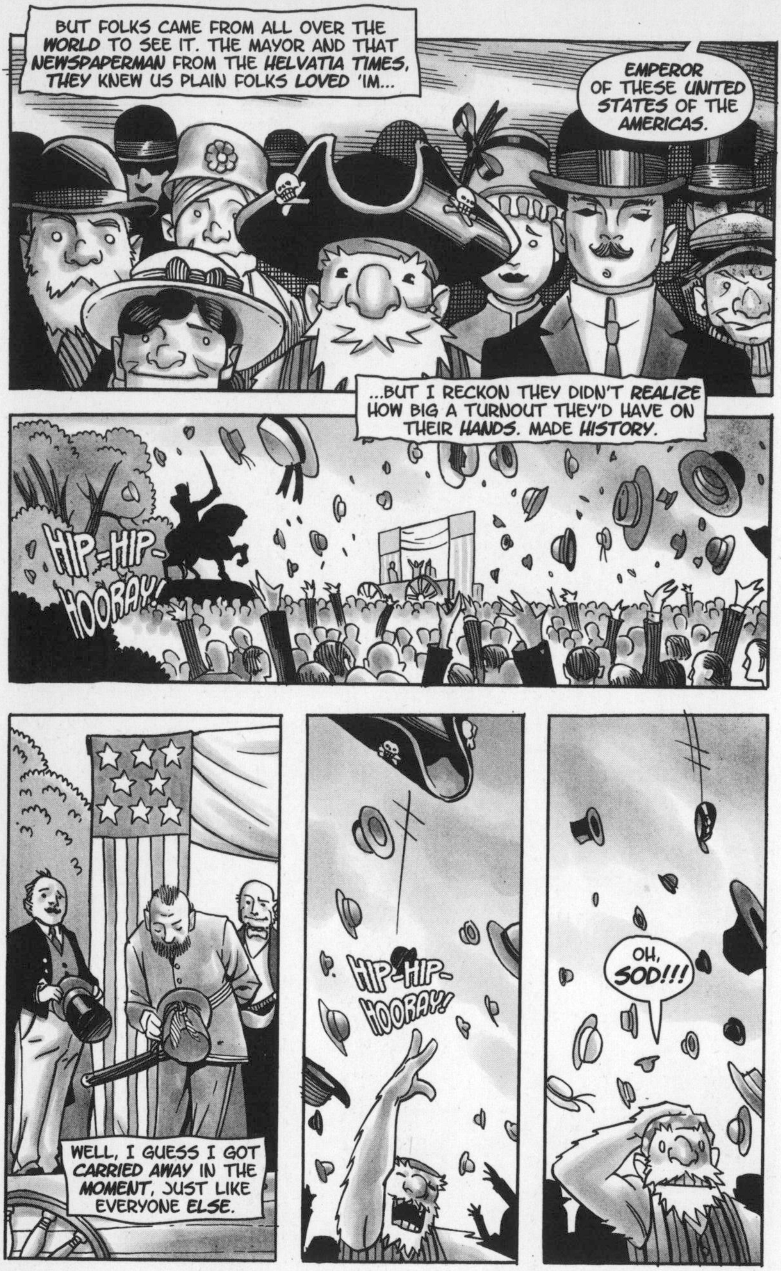
BUT FOLKS CAME FROM ALL OVER THE WORLD TO SEE IT. THE MAYOR AND THAT NEWSPAPERMAN FROM THE HELVATIA TIMES, THEY KNEW US PLAIN FOLKS LOVED 'IM...
EMPEROR OF THESE UNITED STATES OF THE AMERICAS.
...BUT I RECKON THEY DIDN'T REALIZE HOW BIG A TURNOUT THEY'D HAVE ON THEIR HANDS. MADE HISTORY.
HIP-HIP-HOORAY!
WELL, I GUESS I GOT CARRIED AWAY IN THE MOMENT, JUST LIKE EVERYONE ELSE.
HIP-HIP-HOORAY!
OH, SOD!!!

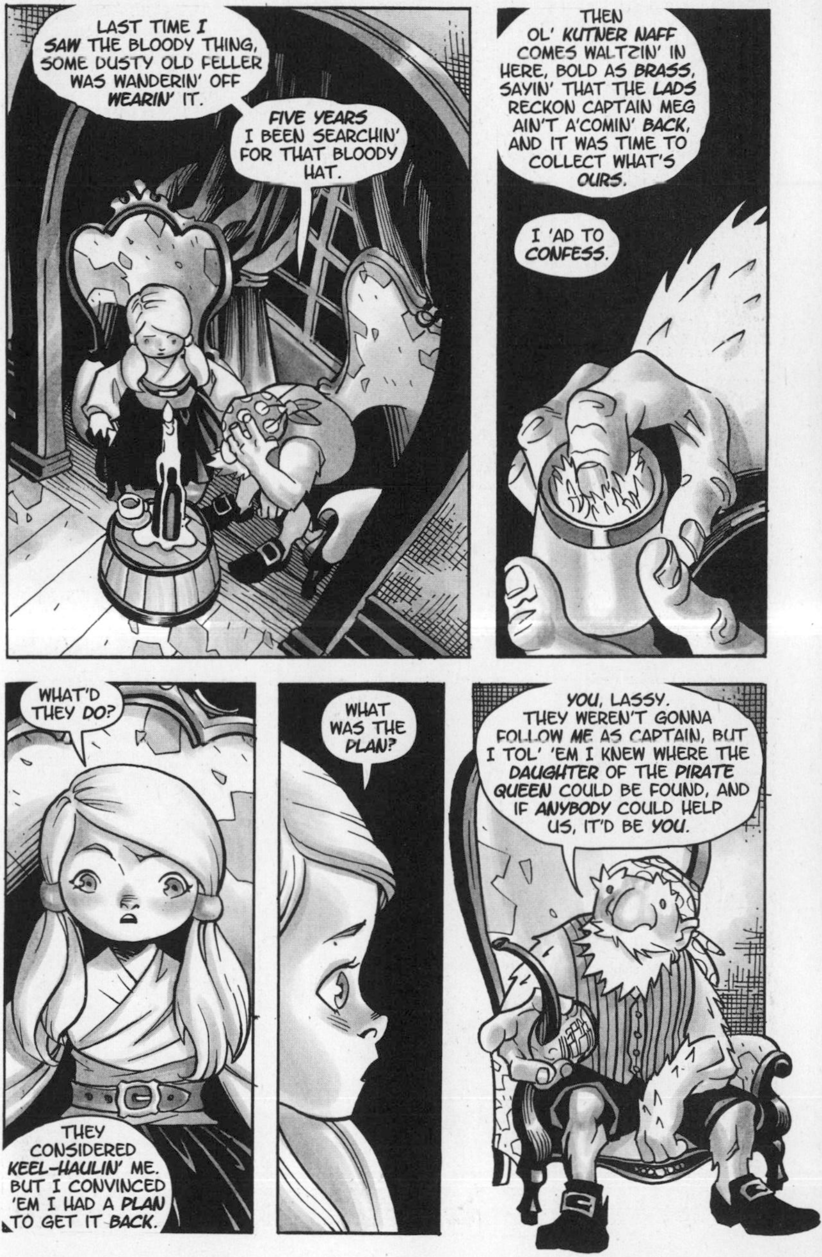
LAST TIME I SAW THE BLOODY THING, SOME DUSTY OLD FELLER WAS WANDERIN' OFF WEARIN' IT.
FIVE YEARS I BEEN SEARCHIN' FOR THAT BLOODY HAT.
THEN OL' KUTNER NAFF COMES WALTZIN' IN HERE, BOLD AS BRASS, SAYIN' THAT THE LADS RECKON CAPTAIN MEG AIN'T A'COMIN' BACK, AND IT WAS TIME TO COLLECT WHAT'S OURS.
I 'AD TO CONFESS.
WHAT'D THEY DO?
THEY CONSIDERED KEEL-HAULIN' ME. BUT I CONVINCED 'EM I HAD A PLAN TO GET IT BACK.
WHAT WAS THE PLAN?
YOU, LASSY. THEY WEREN'T GONNA FOLLOW ME AS CAPTAIN, BUT I TOL' 'EM I KNEW WHERE THE DAUGHTER OF THE PIRATE QUEEN COULD BE FOUND, AND IF ANYBODY COULD HELP US, IT'D BE YOU.

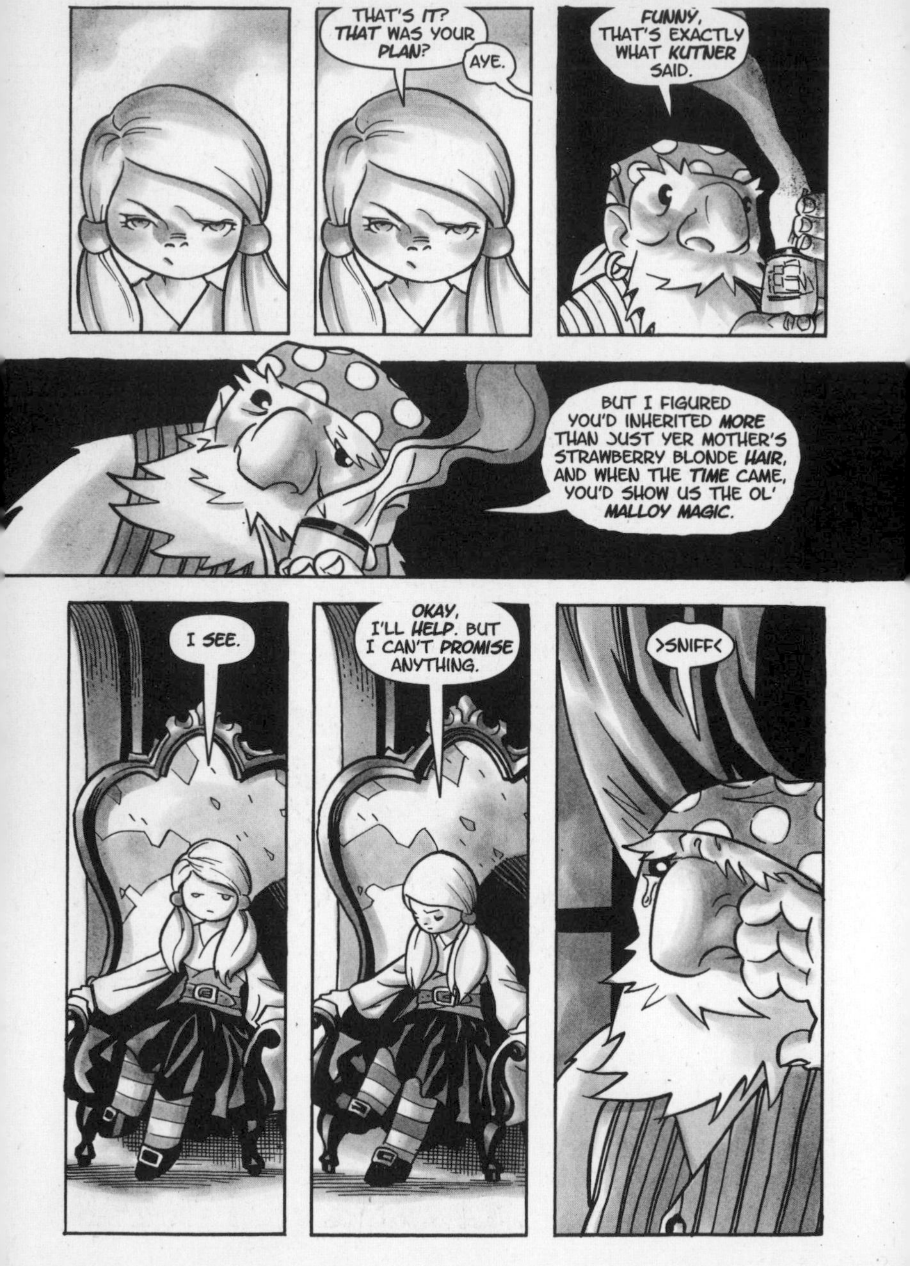

THAT'S IT? THAT WAS YOUR PLAN?
AYE.
FUNNY, THAT'S EXACTLY WHAT KUTNER SAID.
BUT I FIGURED YOU'D INHERITED MORE THAN JUST YER MOTHER'S STRAWBERRY BLONDE HAIR, AND WHEN THE TIME CAME, YOU'D SHOW US THE OL' MALLOY MAGIC.
I SEE.
OKAY, I'LL HELP. BUT I CAN'T PROMISE ANYTHING.
>SNIFF<

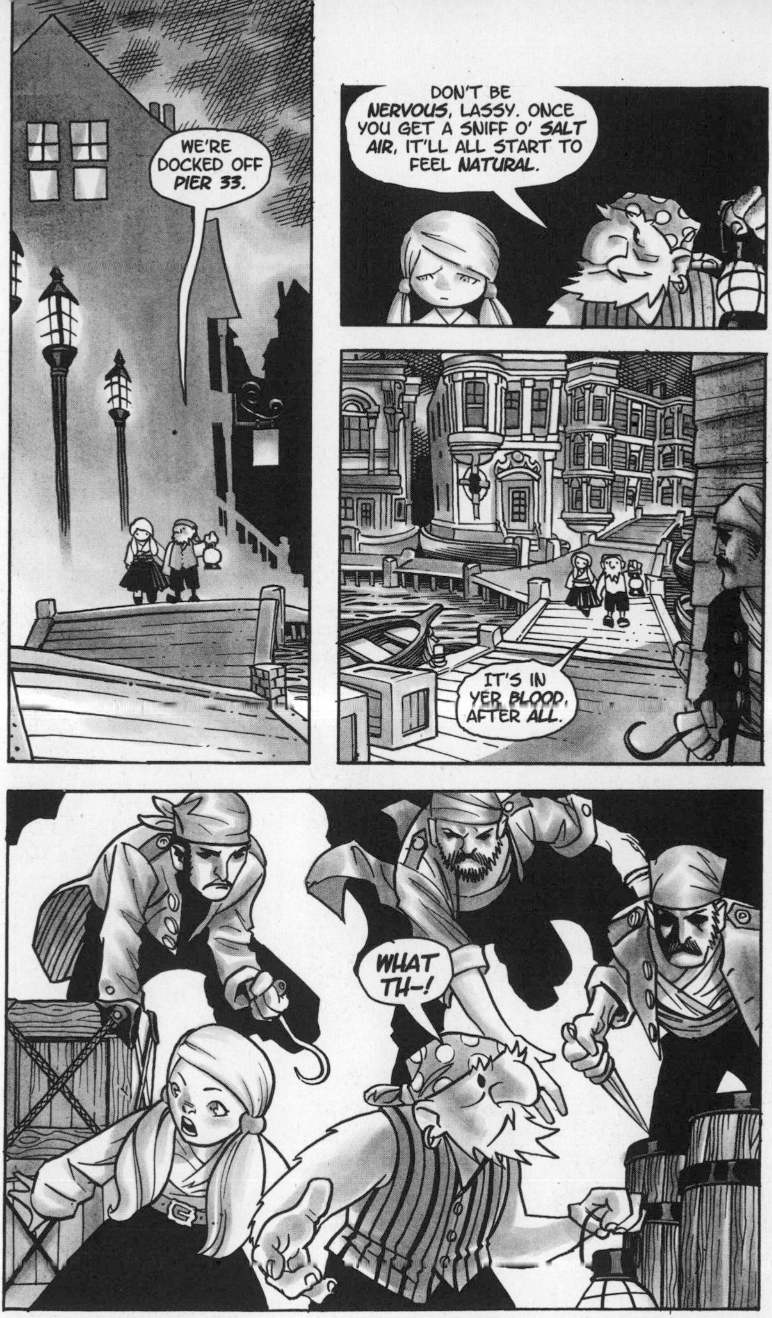
WE'RE DOCKED OFF PIER 33.
DON'T BE NERVOUS, LASSY. ONCE YOU GET A SNIFF O' SALT AIR, IT'LL ALL START TO FEEL NATURAL.
IT'S IN YER BLOOD, AFTER ALL.
WHAT TH-!

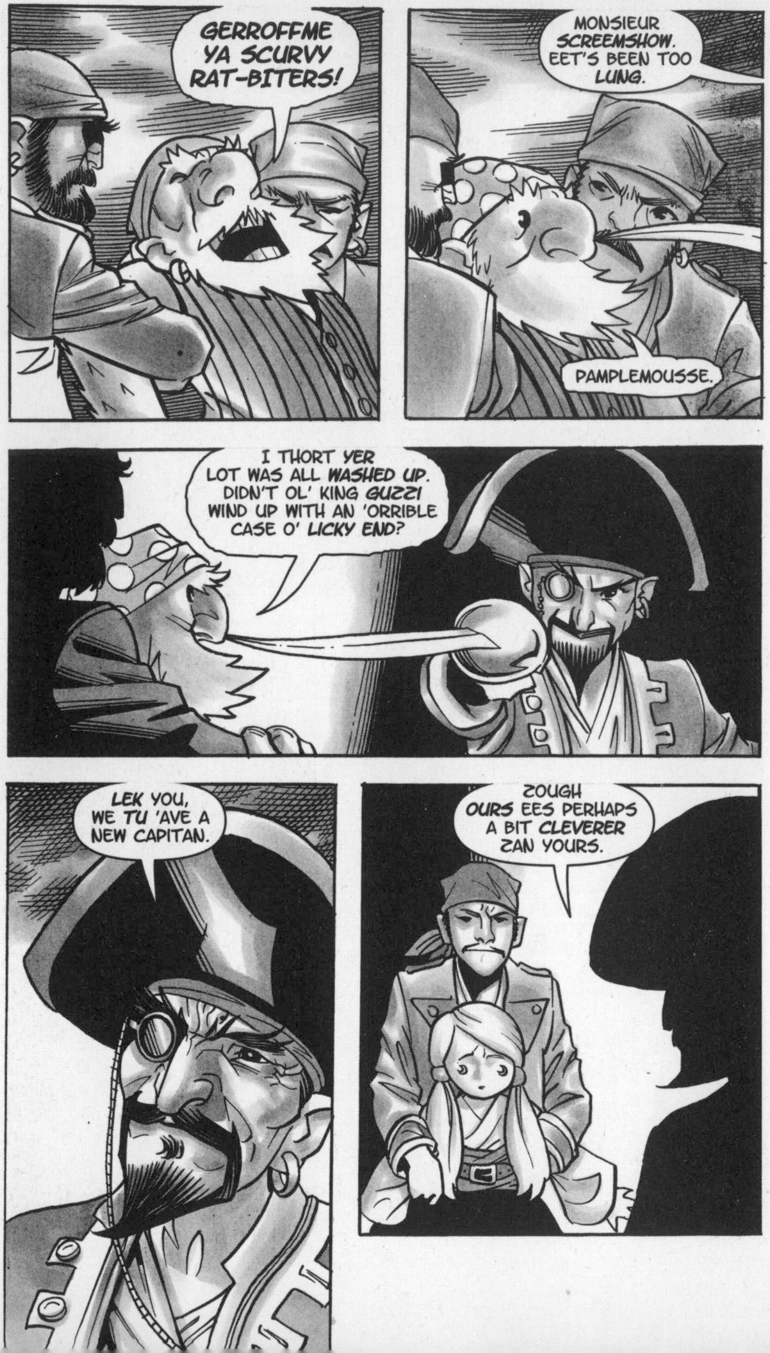
GERROFFME YA SCURVY RAT-BITERS!
MONSIEUR SCREEMSHOW. EET'S BEEN TOO LUNG.
PAMPLEMOUSSE.
I THORT YER LOT WAS ALL WASHED UP. DIDN'T OL' KING GUZZI WIND UP WITH AN 'ORRIBLE CASE O' LICKY END?
LEK YOU, WE TU 'AVE A NEW CAPITAN.
ZOUGH OURS EES PERHAPS A BIT CLEVERER ZAN YOURS.

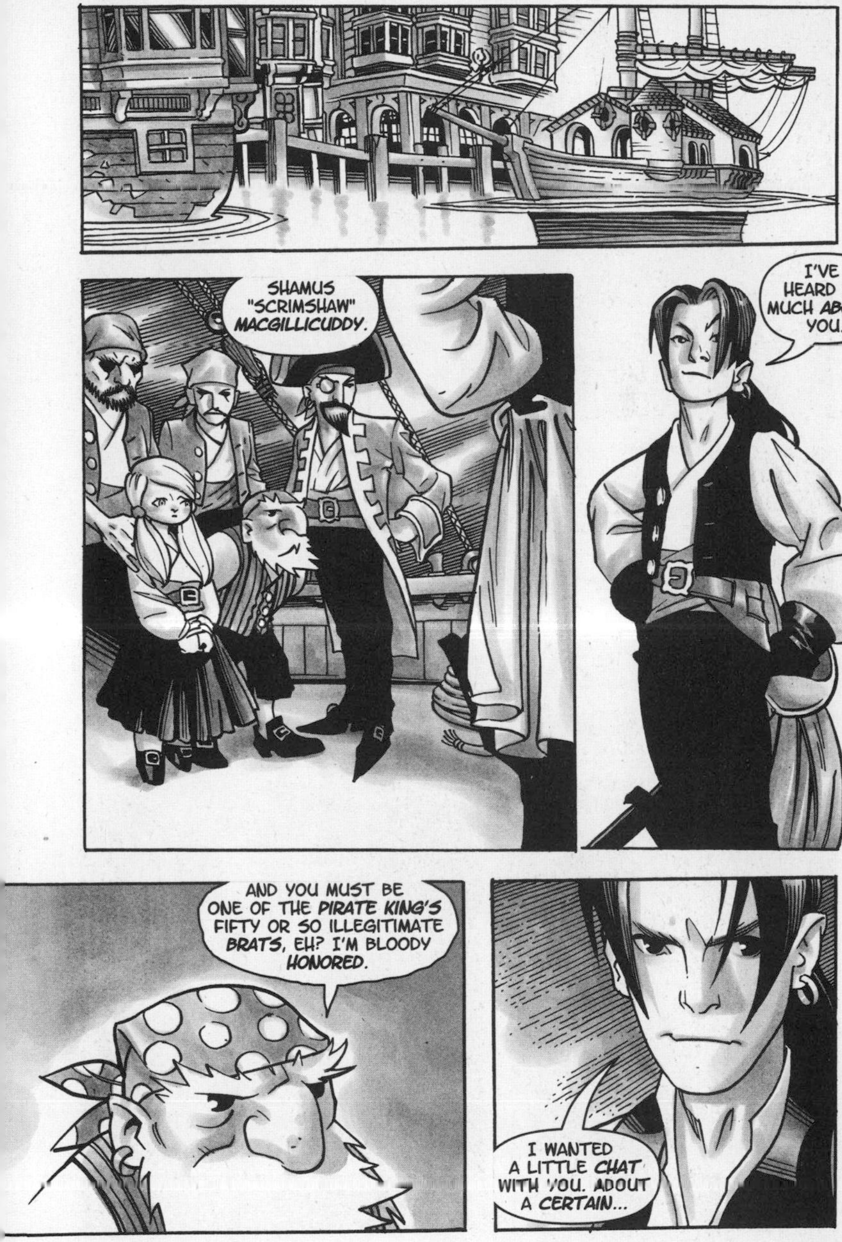
SHAMUS "SCRIMSHAW" MACGILLICUDDY.
I'VE HEARD SO MUCH ABOUT YOU.
AND YOU MUST BE ONE OF THE PIRATE KING'S FIFTY OR SO ILLEGITIMATE BRATS, EH? I'M BLOODY HONORED.
I WANTED A LITTLE CHAT WITH YOU. ABOUT A CERTAIN...

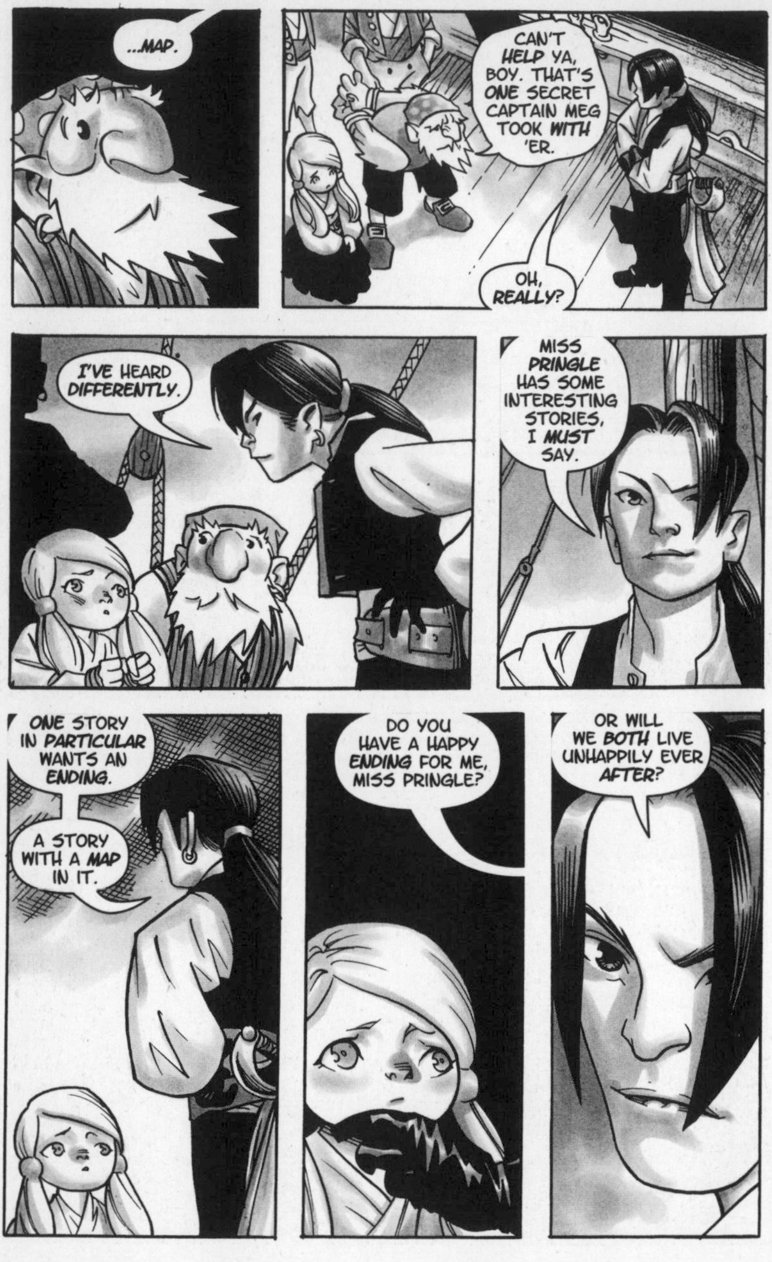
...MAP.
CAN'T HELP YA, BOY. THAT'S ONE SECRET CAPTAIN MEG TOOK WITH 'ER.
OH, REALLY?
I'VE HEARD DIFFERENTLY.
MISS PRINGLE HAS SOME INTERESTING STORIES, I MUST SAY.
ONE STORY IN PARTICULAR WANTS AN ENDING.
A STORY WITH A MAP IN IT.
DO YOU HAVE A HAPPY ENDING FOR ME, MISS PRINGLE?
OR WILL WE BOTH LIVE UNHAPPILY EVER AFTER?

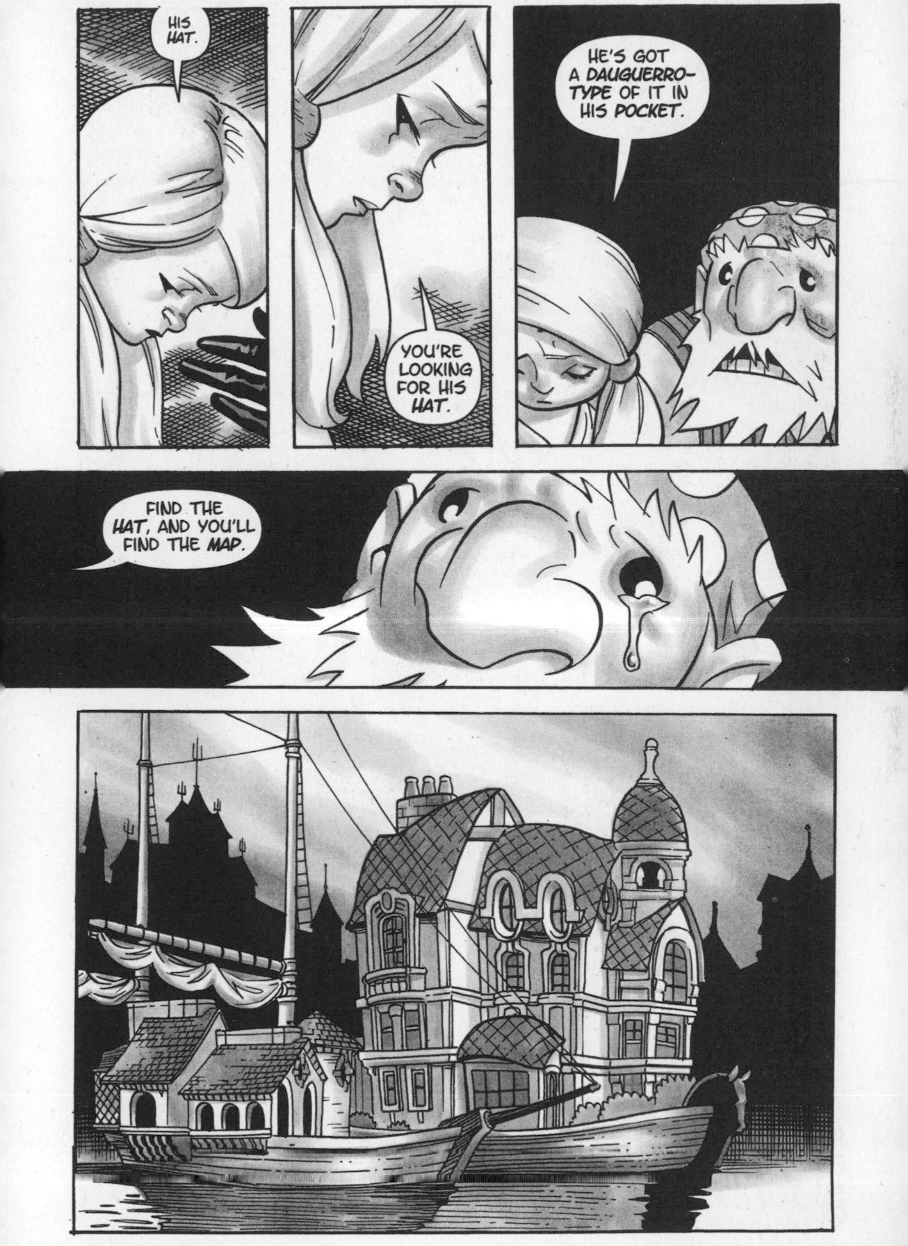
HIS HAT.
YOU'RE LOOKING FOR HIS HAT.
HE'S GOT A DAUGUERRO-TYPE OF IT IN HIS POCKET.
FIND THE HAT, AND YOU'LL FIND THE MAP.

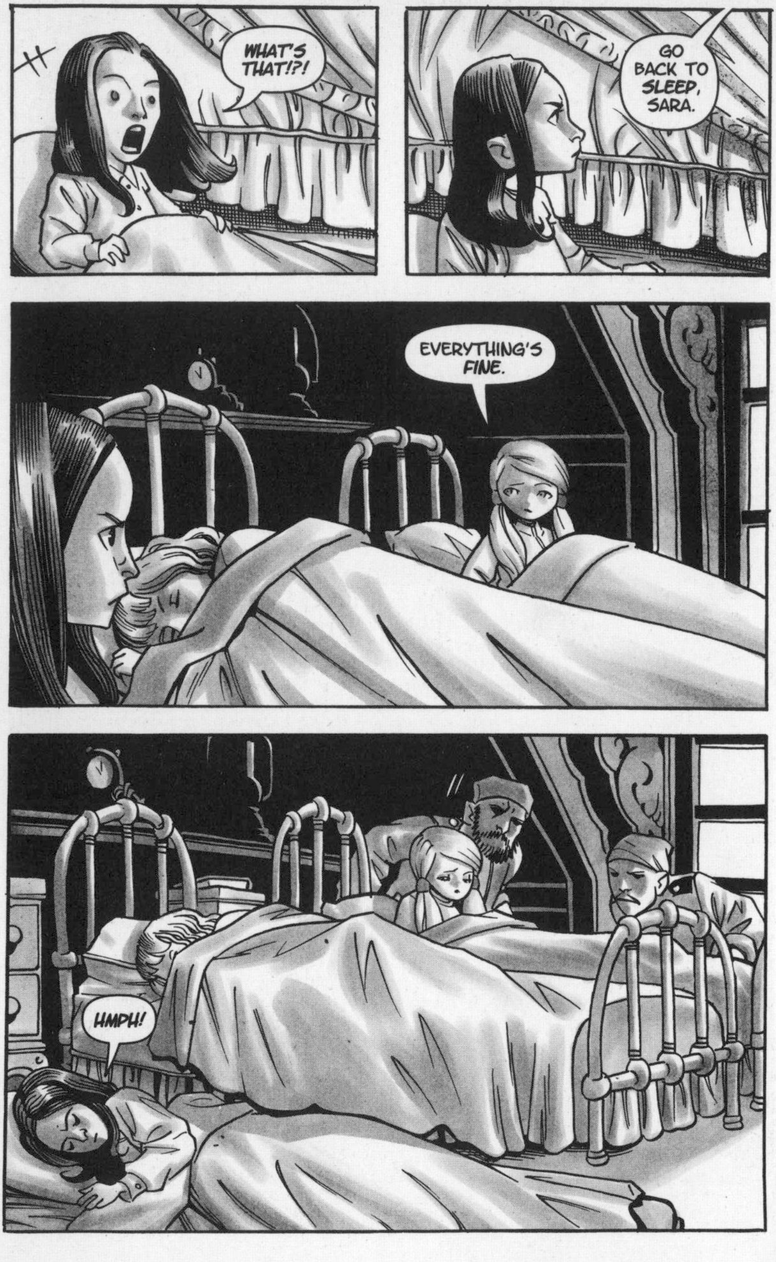
WHAT'S THAT!?!
GO BACK TO SLEEP, SARA.
EVERYTHING'S FINE.
HMPH!

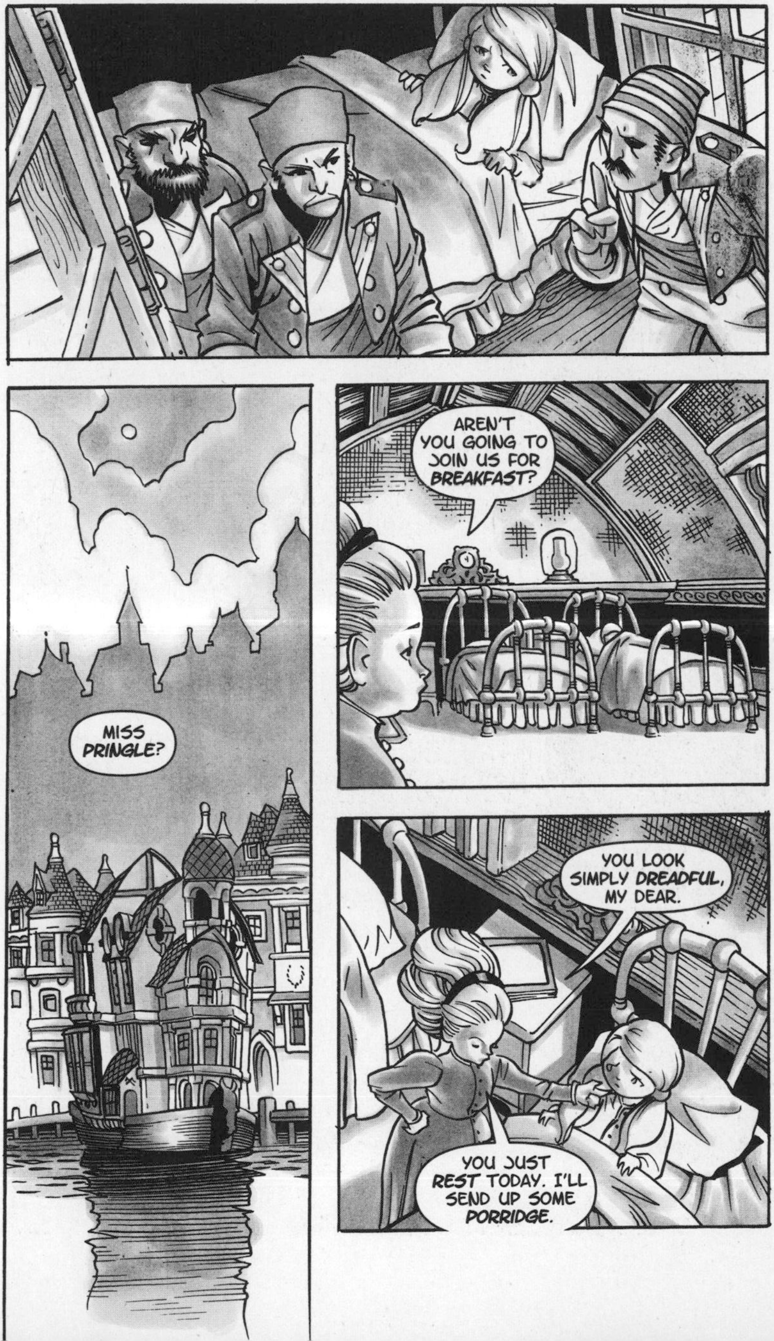
MISS PRINGLE?
AREN'T YOU GOING TO JOIN US FOR BREAKFAST?
YOU LOOK SIMPLY DREADFUL, MY DEAR.
YOU JUST REST TODAY. I'LL SEND UP SOME PORRIDGE.

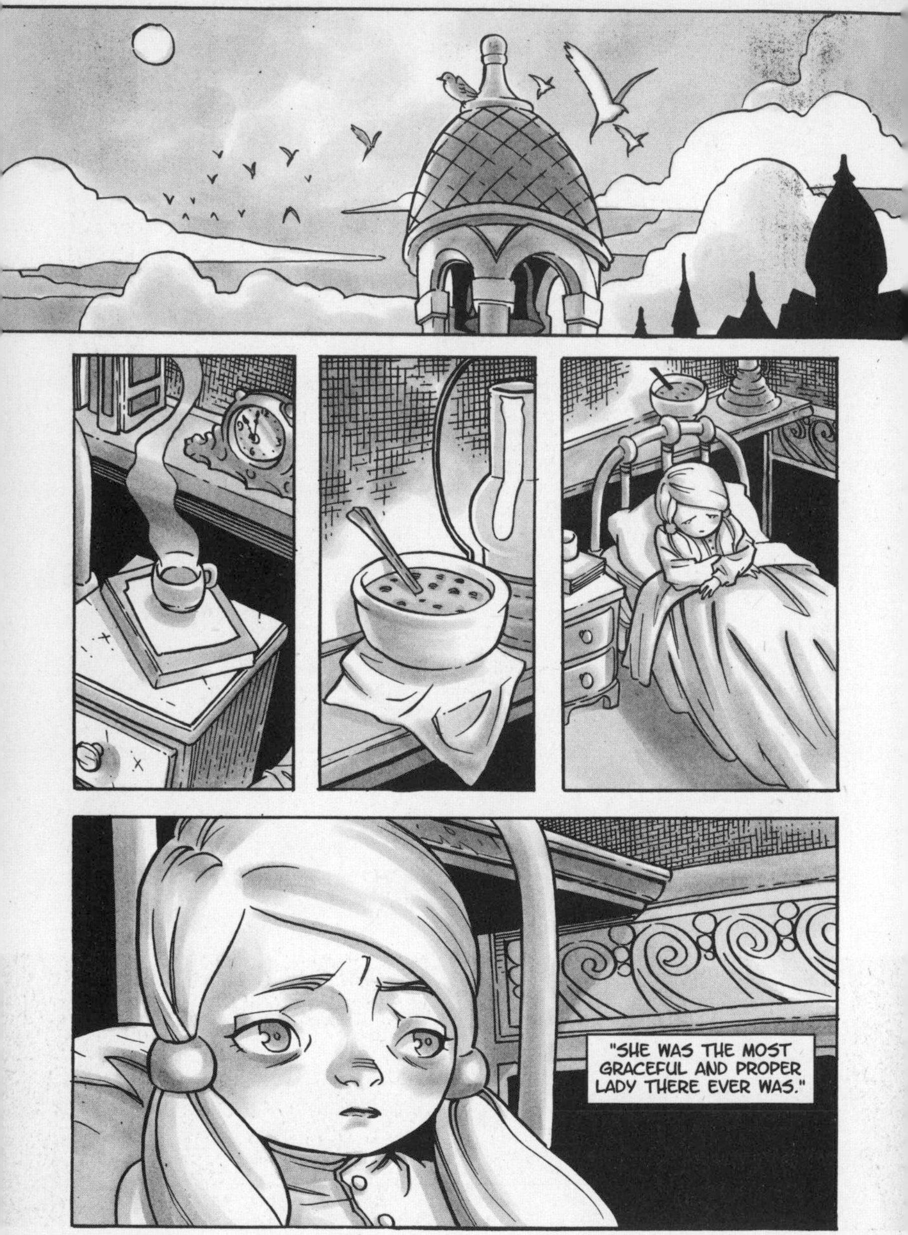
"SHE WAS THE MOST GRACEFUL AND PROPER LADY THERE EVER WAS."

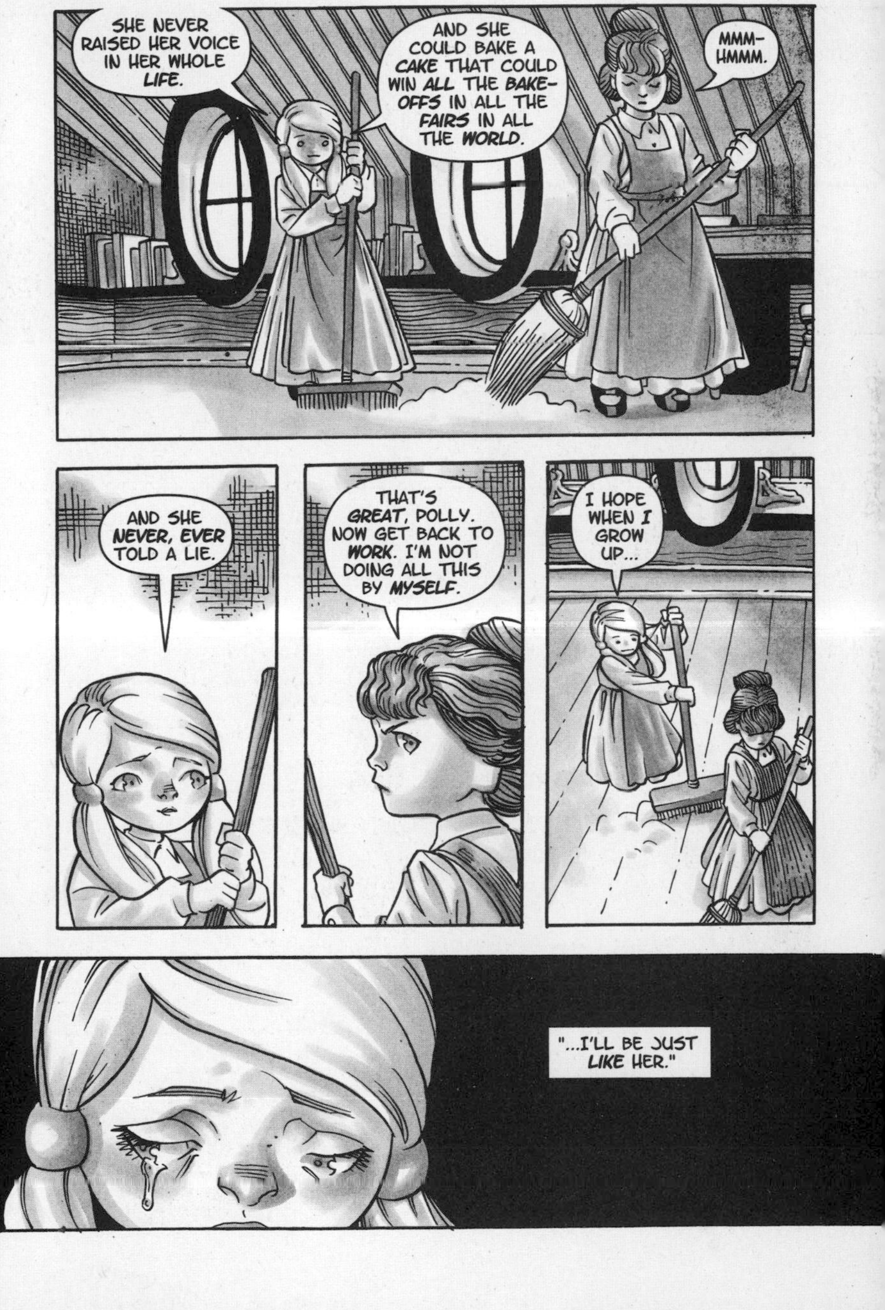
SHE NEVER RAISED HER VOICE IN HER WHOLE LIFE.
AND SHE COULD BAKE A CAKE THAT COULD WIN ALL THE BAKE-OFFS IN ALL THE FAIRS IN ALL THE WORLD.
MMM-HMMM.
AND SHE NEVER, EVER TOLD A LIE.
THAT'S GREAT, POLLY. NOW GET BACK TO WORK. I'M NOT DOING ALL THIS BY MYSELF.
I HOPE WHEN I GROW UP...
"...I'LL BE JUST LIKE HER."

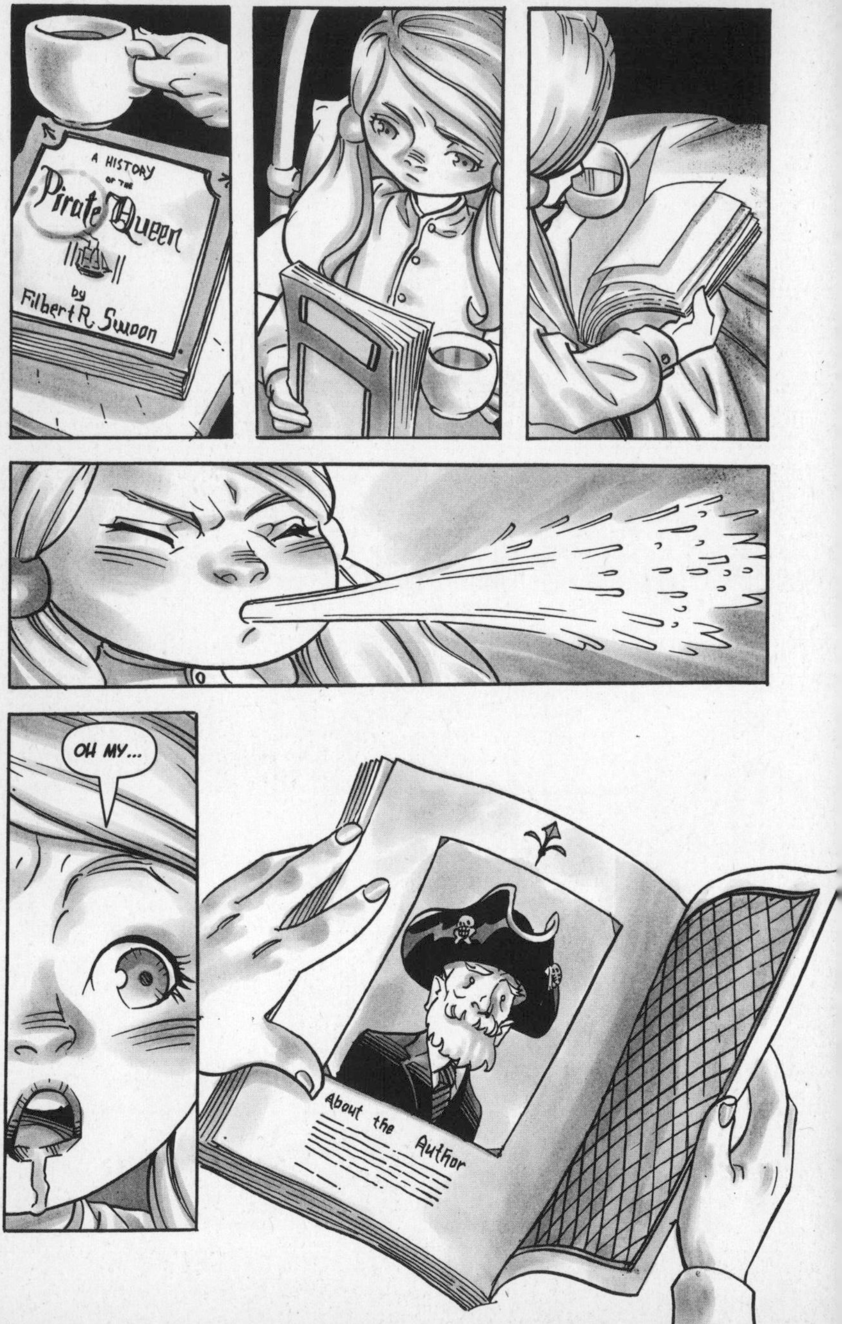
A HISTORY OF THE Pirate Queen
by Filbert R. Swoon
OH MY...
About the Author

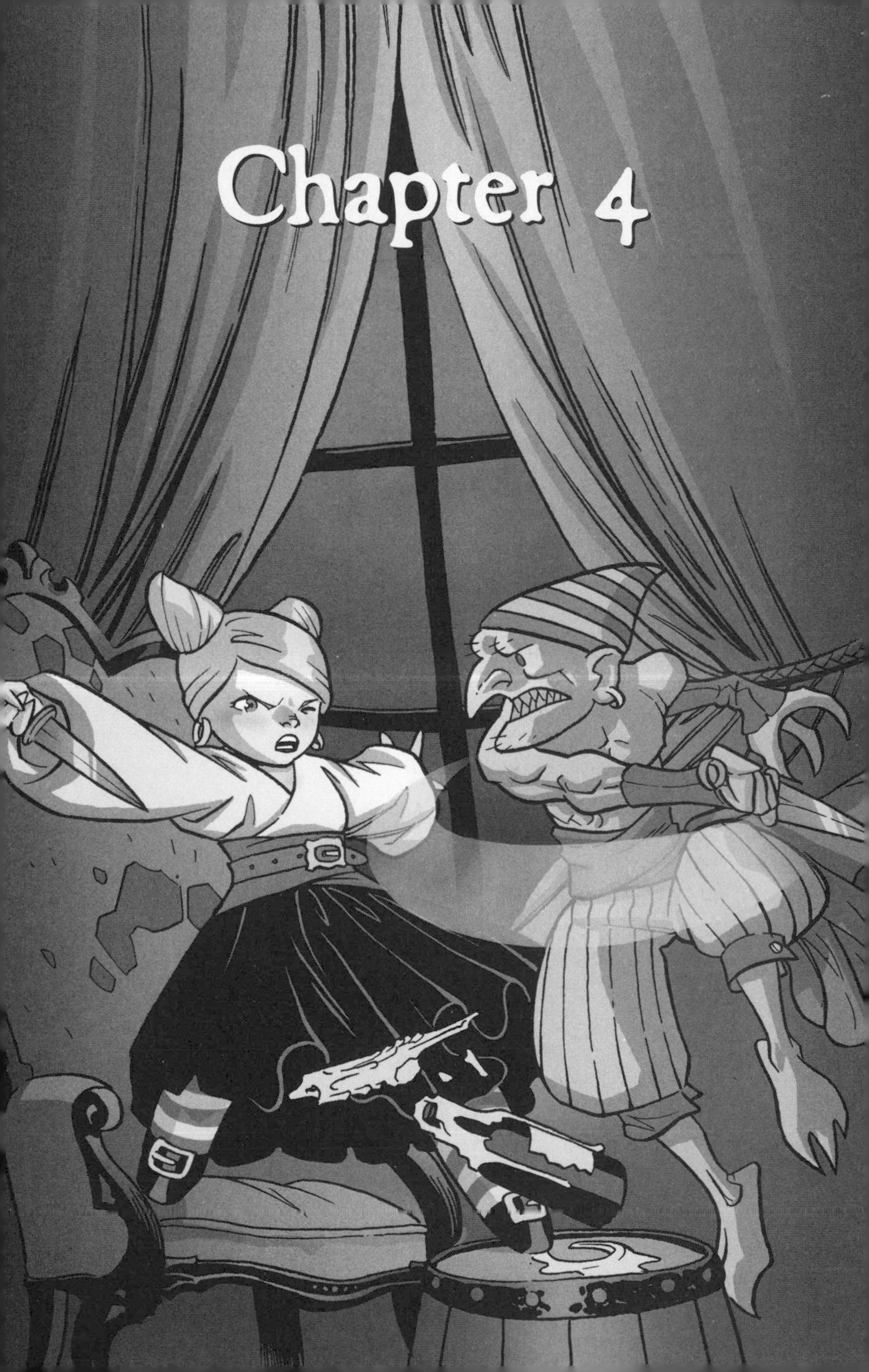
Chapter 4

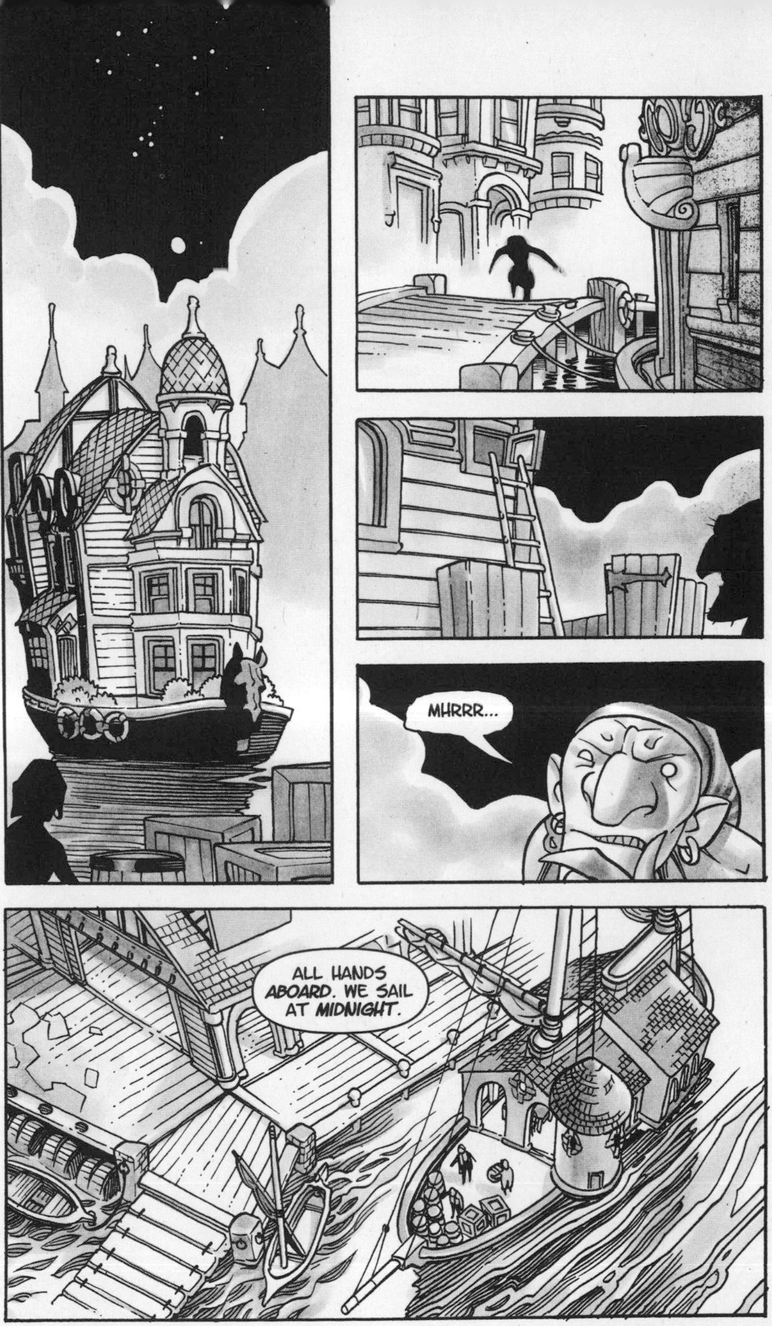
MHRRR...
ALL HANDS ABOARD. WE SAIL AT MIDNIGHT.

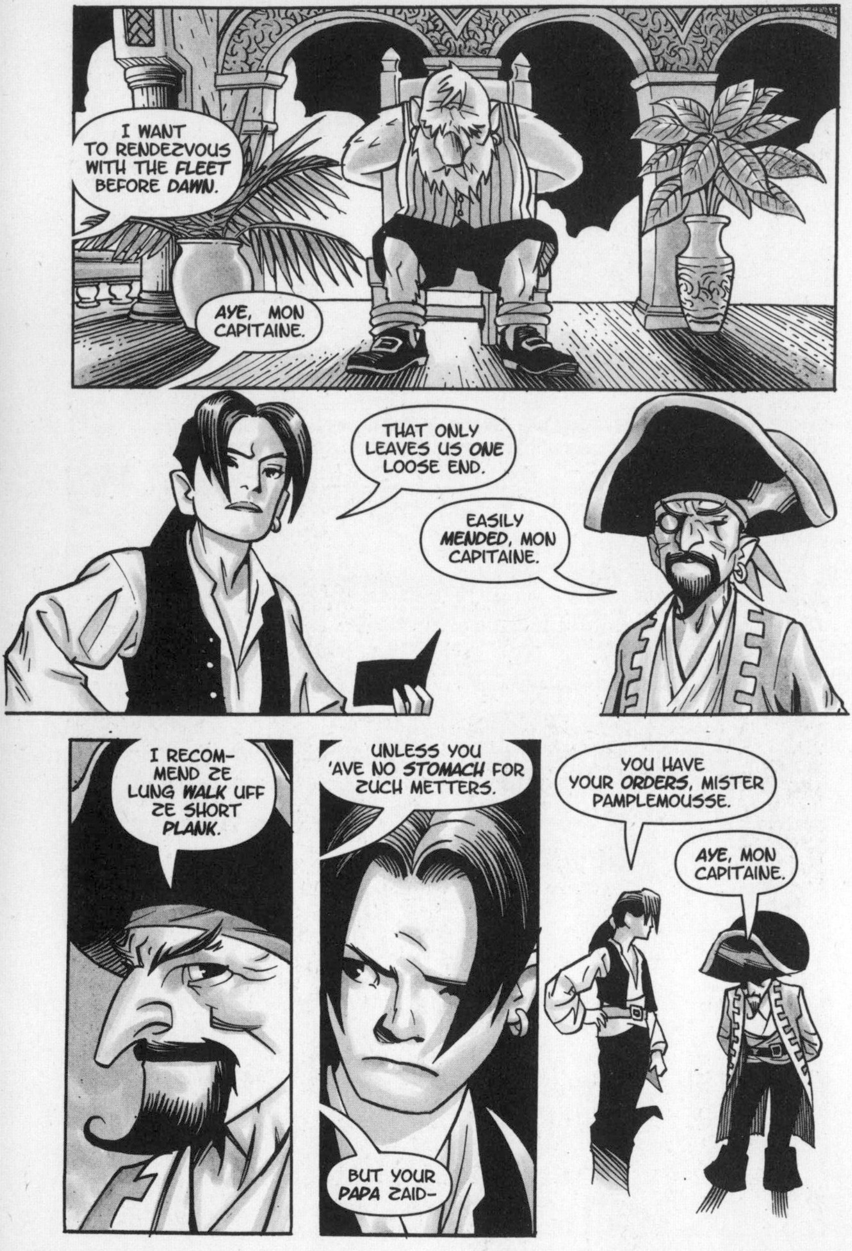
I WANT TO RENDEZVOUS WITH THE FLEET BEFORE DAWN.
AYE, MON CAPITAINE.
THAT ONLY LEAVES US ONE LOOSE END.
EASILY MENDED, MON CAPITAINE.
I RECOM-MEND ZE LUNG WALK UFF ZE SHORT PLANK.
UNLESS YOU 'AVE NO STOMACH FOR ZUCH METTERS.
BUT YOUR PAPA ZAID-
YOU HAVE YOUR ORDERS, MISTER PAMPLEMOUSSE.
AYE, MON CAPITAINE.

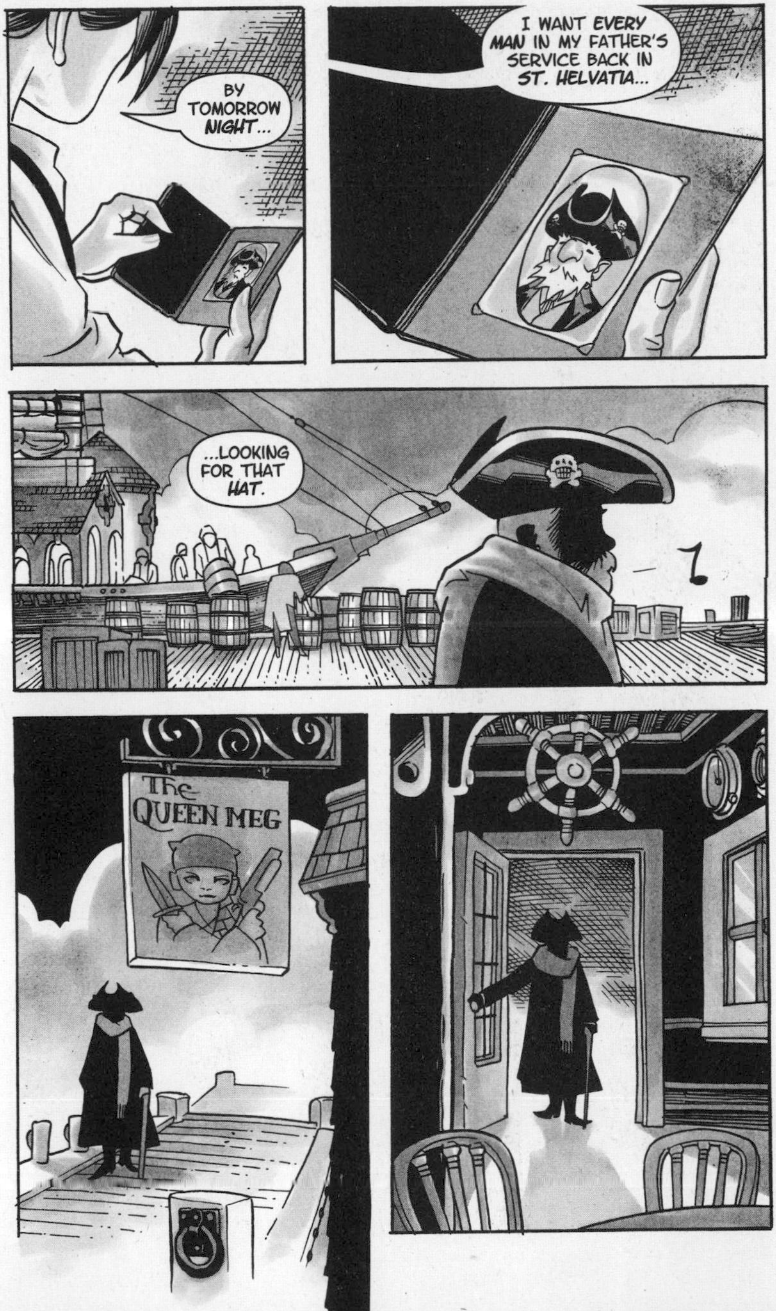
BY TOMORROW NIGHT...
I WANT EVERY MAN IN MY FATHER'S SERVICE BACK IN ST. HELVATIA...
...LOOKING FOR THAT HAT.
The QUEEN MEG

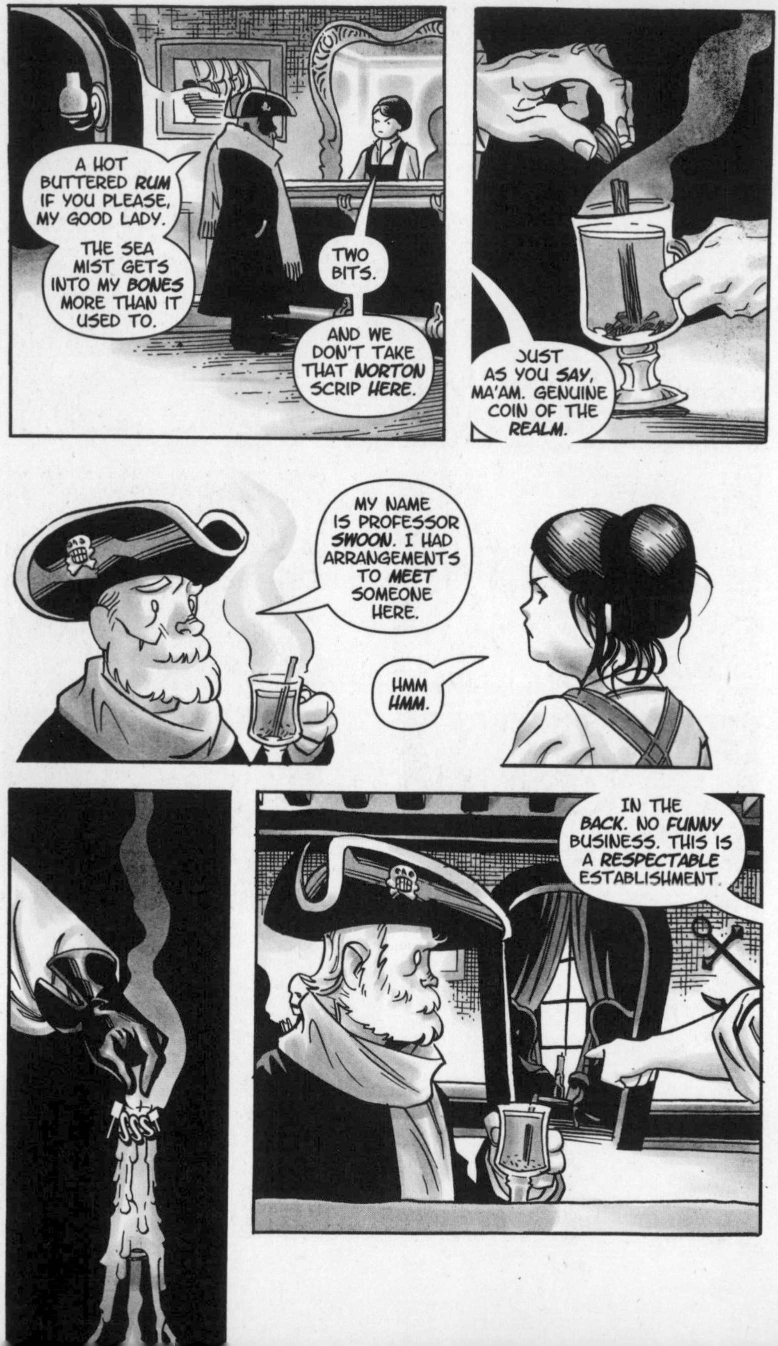
A HOT BUTTERED RUM IF YOU PLEASE, MY GOOD LADY.
THE SEA MIST GETS INTO MY BONES MORE THAN IT USED TO.
TWO BITS.
AND WE DON'T TAKE THAT NORTON SCRIP HERE.
JUST AS YOU SAY, MA'AM. GENUINE COIN OF THE REALM.
MY NAME IS PROFESSOR SWOON. I HAD ARRANGEMENTS TO MEET SOMEONE HERE.
HMM HMM.
IN THE BACK. NO FUNNY BUSINESS. THIS IS A RESPECTABLE ESTABLISHMENT.

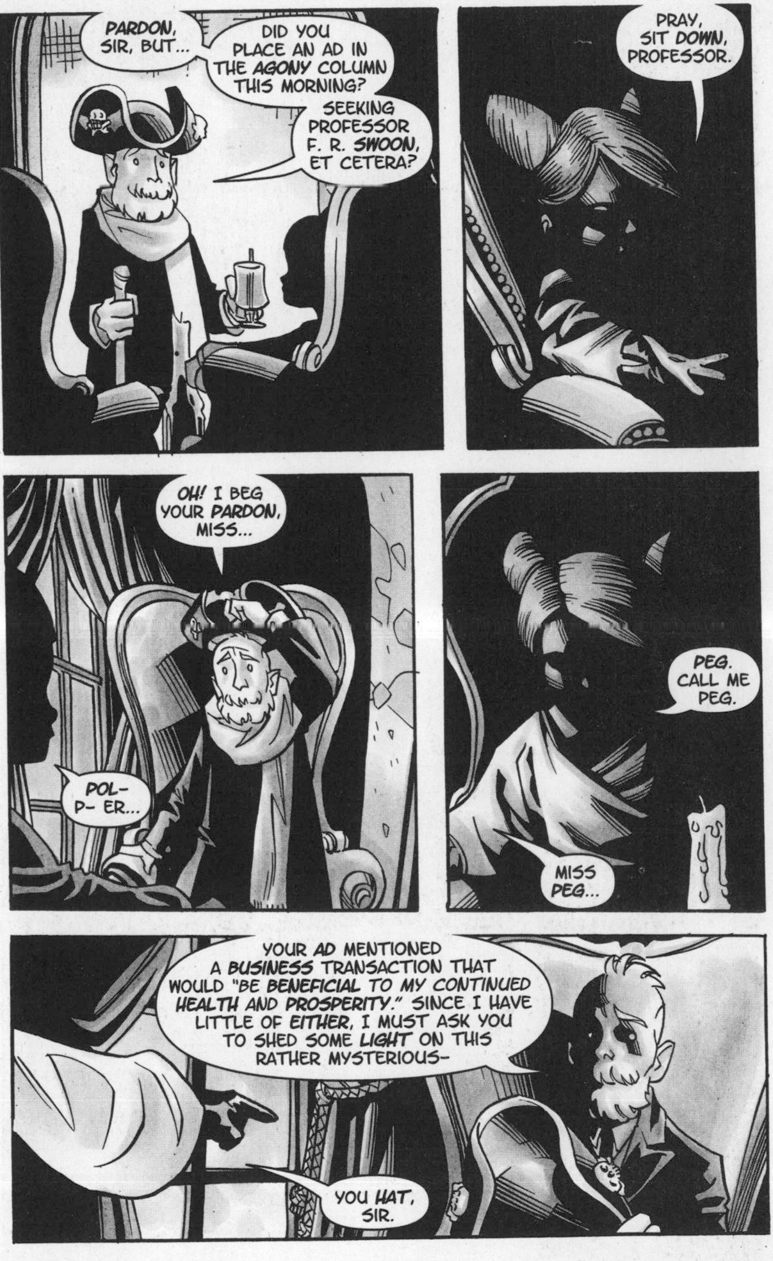
PARDON, SIR, BUT...
DID YOU PLACE AN AD IN THE AGONY COLUMN THIS MORNING?
SEEKING PROFESSOR F. R. SWOON, ET CETERA?
PRAY, SIT DOWN, PROFESSOR.
OH! I BEG YOUR PARDON, MISS...
POL- P- ER...
PEG. CALL ME PEG.
MISS PEG...
YOUR AD MENTIONED A BUSINESS TRANSACTION THAT WOULD "BE BENEFICIAL TO MY CONTINUED HEALTH AND PROSPERITY." SINCE I HAVE LITTLE OF EITHER, I MUST ASK YOU TO SHED SOME LIGHT ON THIS RATHER MYSTERIOUS-
YOU HAT, SIR.

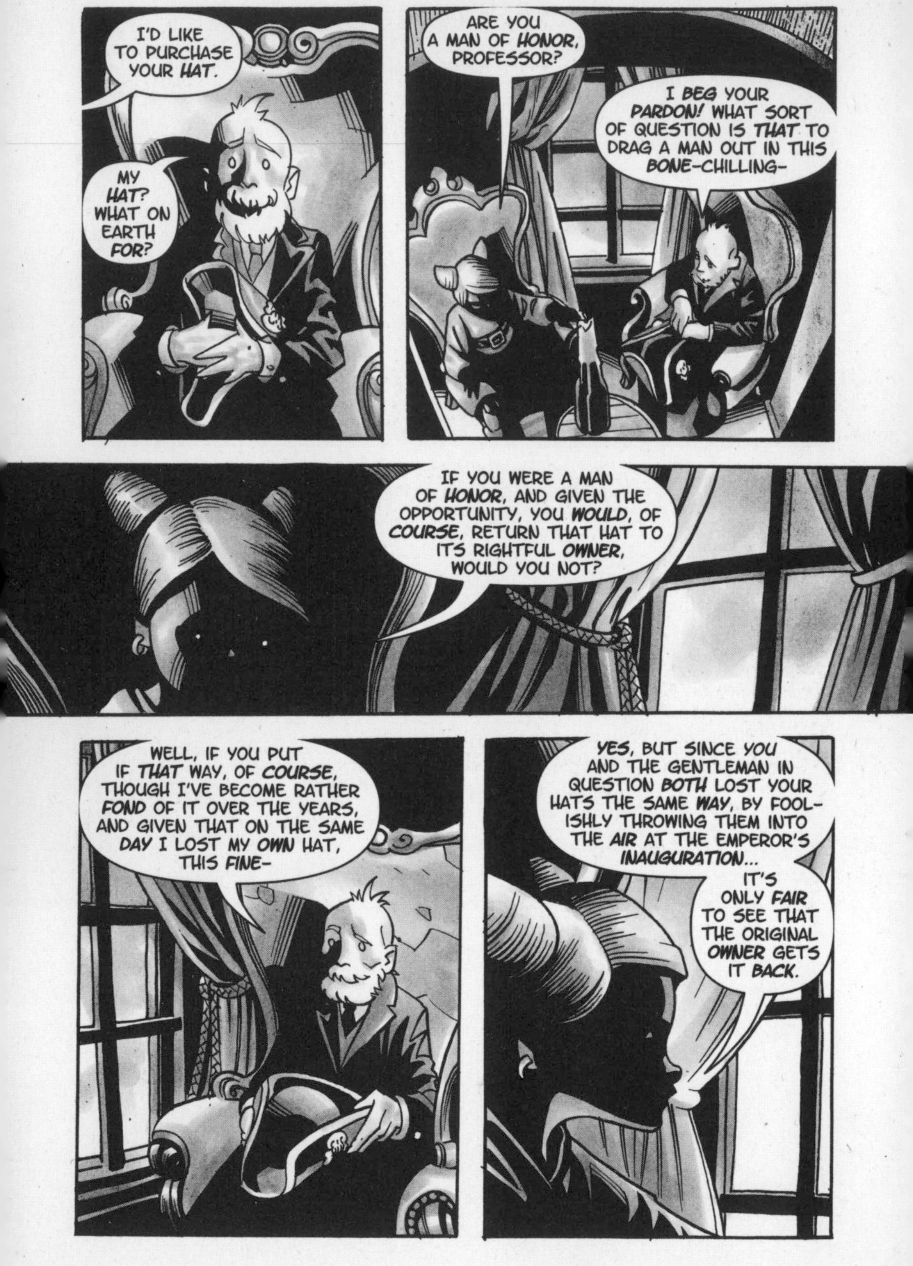
I'D LIKE TO PURCHASE YOUR HAT.
MY HAT? WHAT ON EARTH FOR?
ARE YOU A MAN OF HONOR, PROFESSOR?
I BEG YOUR PARDON! WHAT SORT OF QUESTION IS THAT TO DRAG A MAN OUT IN THIS BONE-CHILLING-
IF YOU WERE A MAN OF HONOR, AND GIVEN THE OPPORTUNITY, YOU WOULD, OF COURSE, RETURN THAT HAT TO ITS RIGHTFUL OWNER, WOULD YOU NOT?
WELL, IF YOU PUT IF THAT WAY, OF COURSE, THOUGH I'VE BECOME RATHER FOND OF IT OVER THE YEARS, AND GIVEN THAT ON THE SAME DAY I LOST MY OWN HAT, THIS FINE-
YES, BUT SINCE YOU AND THE GENTLEMAN IN QUESTION BOTH LOST YOUR HATS THE SAME WAY, BY FOOLISHLY THROWING THEM INTO THE AIR AT THE EMPEROR'S INAUGURATION...
IT'S ONLY FAIR TO SEE THAT THE ORIGINAL OWNER GETS IT BACK.

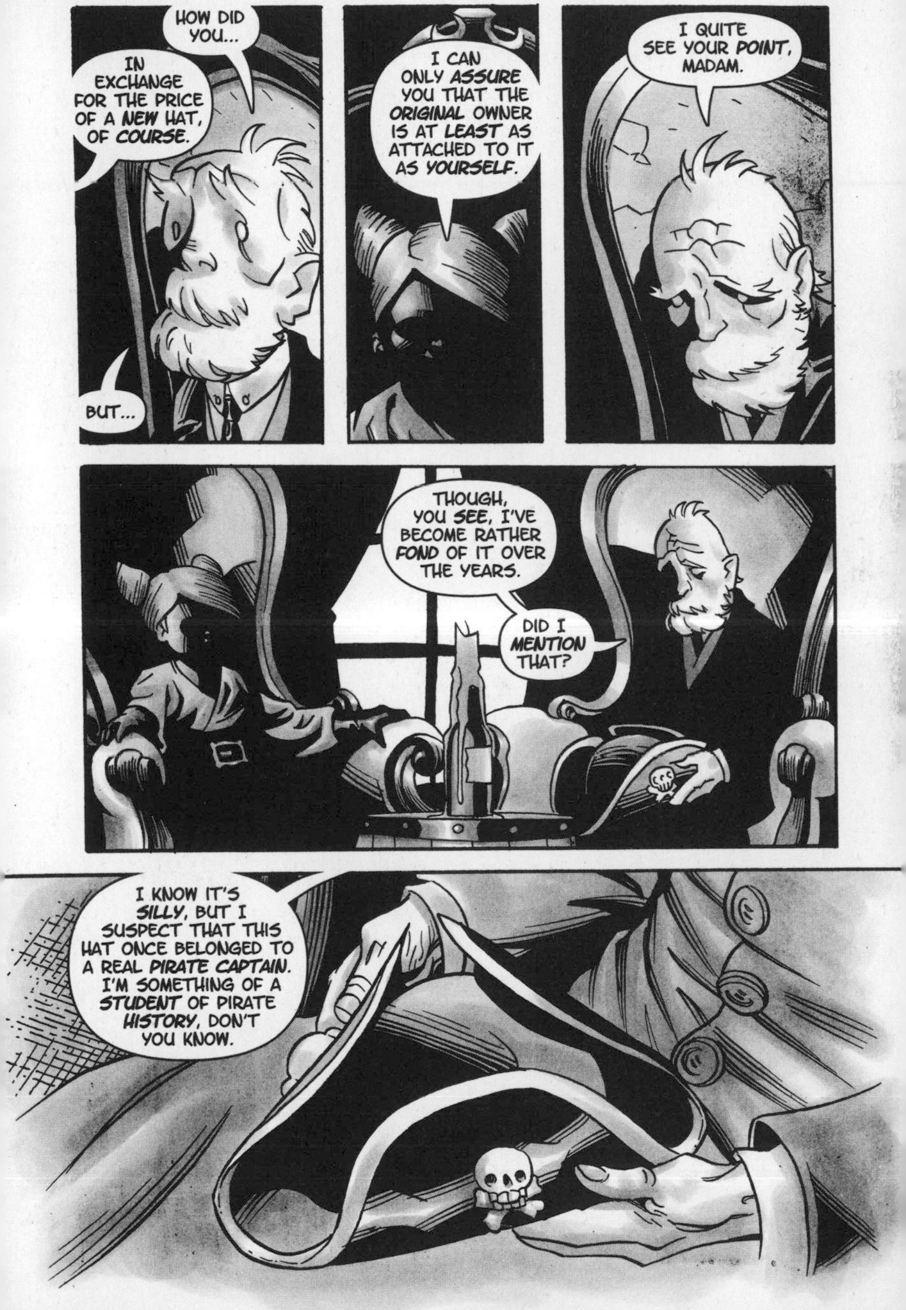

HOW DID YOU...
IN EXCHANGE FOR THE PRICE OF A NEW HAT, OF COURSE.
BUT...
I CAN ONLY ASSURE YOU THAT THE ORIGINAL OWNER IS AT LEAST AS ATTACHED TO IT AS YOURSELF.
I QUITE SEE YOUR POINT, MADAM.
THOUGH, YOU SEE, I'VE BECOME RATHER FOND OF IT OVER THE YEARS.
DID I MENTION THAT?
I KNOW IT'S SILLY, BUT I SUSPECT THAT THIS HAT ONCE BELONGED TO A REAL PIRATE CAPTAIN. I'M SOMETHING OF A STUDENT OF PIRATE HISTORY, DON'T YOU KNOW.

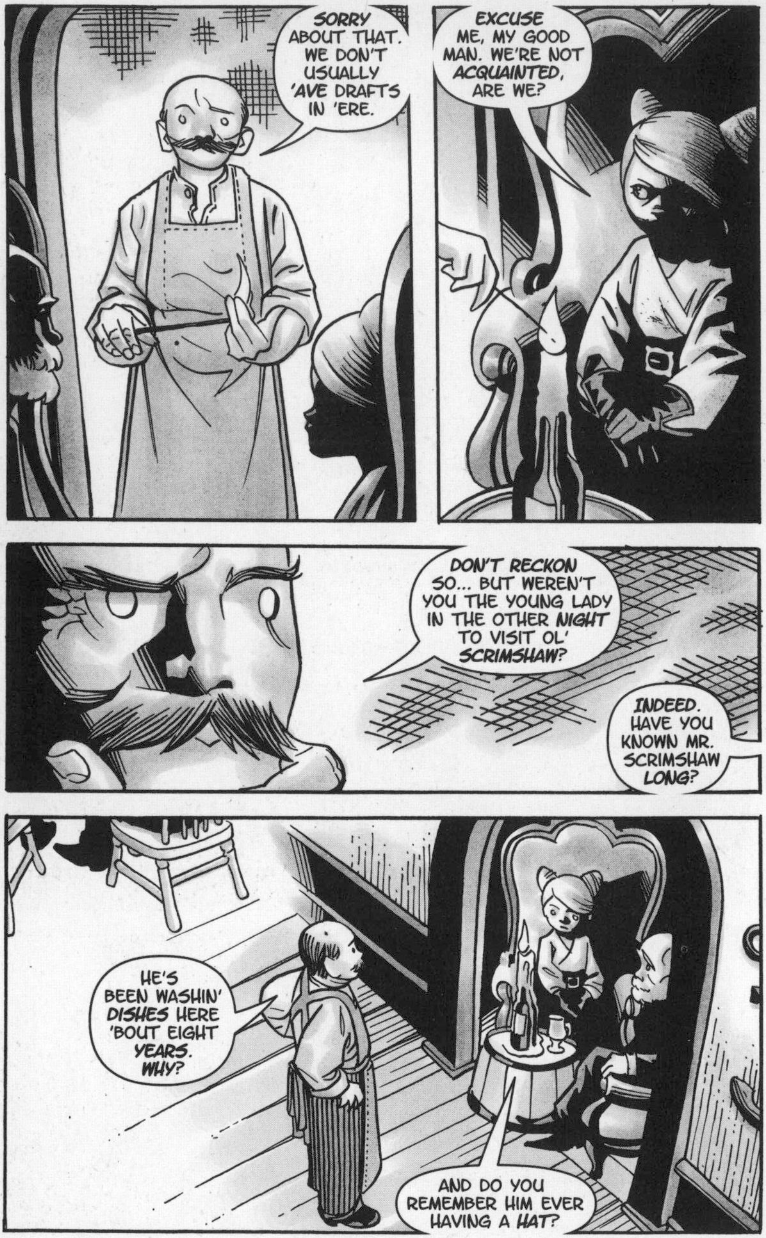
SORRY ABOUT THAT. WE DON'T USUALLY 'AVE DRAFTS IN 'ERE.
EXCUSE ME, MY GOOD MAN. WE'RE NOT ACQUAINTED, ARE WE?
DON'T RECKON SO... BUT WEREN'T YOU THE YOUNG LADY IN THE OTHER NIGHT TO VISIT OL' SCRIMSHAW?
INDEED. HAVE YOU KNOWN MR. SCRIMSHAW LONG?
HE'S BEEN WASHIN' DISHES HERE 'BOUT EIGHT YEARS. WHY?
AND DO YOU REMEMBER HIM EVER HAVING A HAT?

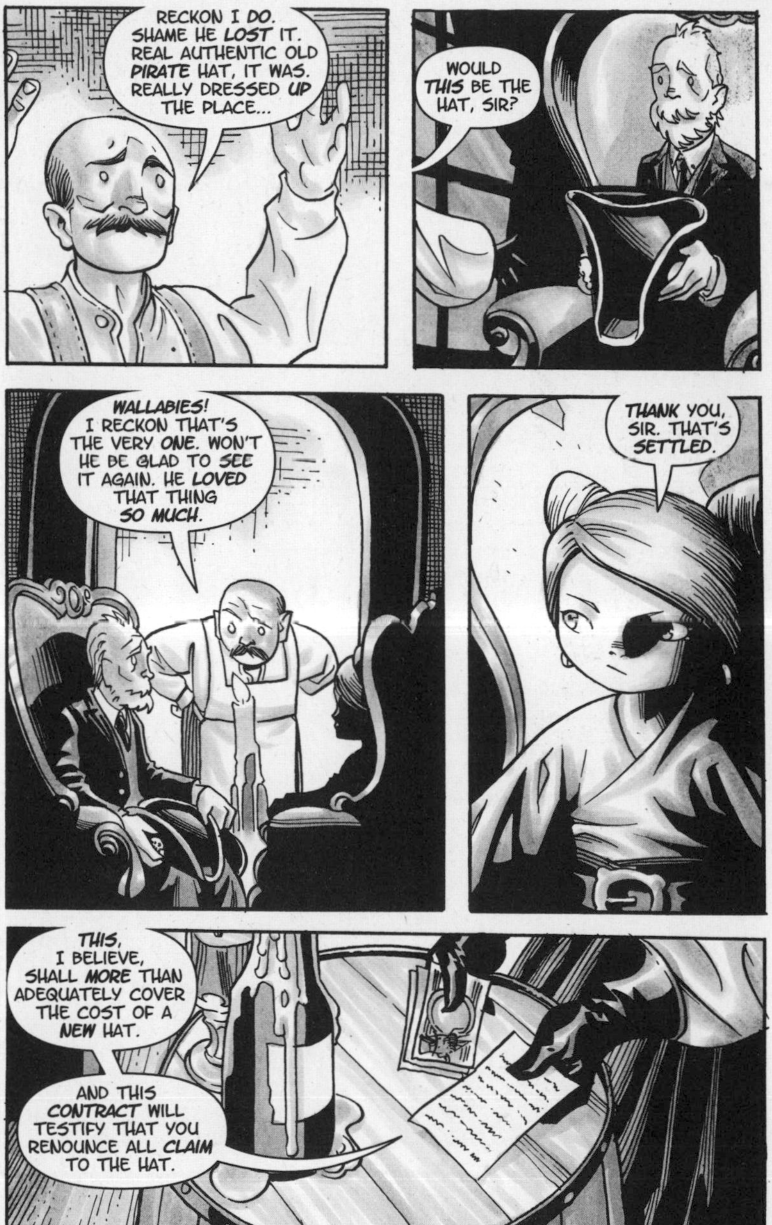
RECKON I DO. SHAME HE LOST IT. REAL AUTHENTIC OLD PIRATE HAT, IT WAS. REALLY DRESSED UP THE PLACE...
WOULD THIS BE THE HAT, SIR?
WALLABIES! I RECKON THAT'S THE VERY ONE. WON'T HE BE GLAD TO SEE IT AGAIN. HE LOVED THAT THING SO MUCH.
THANK YOU, SIR. THAT'S SETTLED.
THIS, I BELIEVE, SHALL MORE THAN ADEQUATELY COVER THE COST OF A NEW HAT.
AND THIS CONTRACT WILL TESTIFY THAT YOU RENOUNCE ALL CLAIM TO THE HAT.

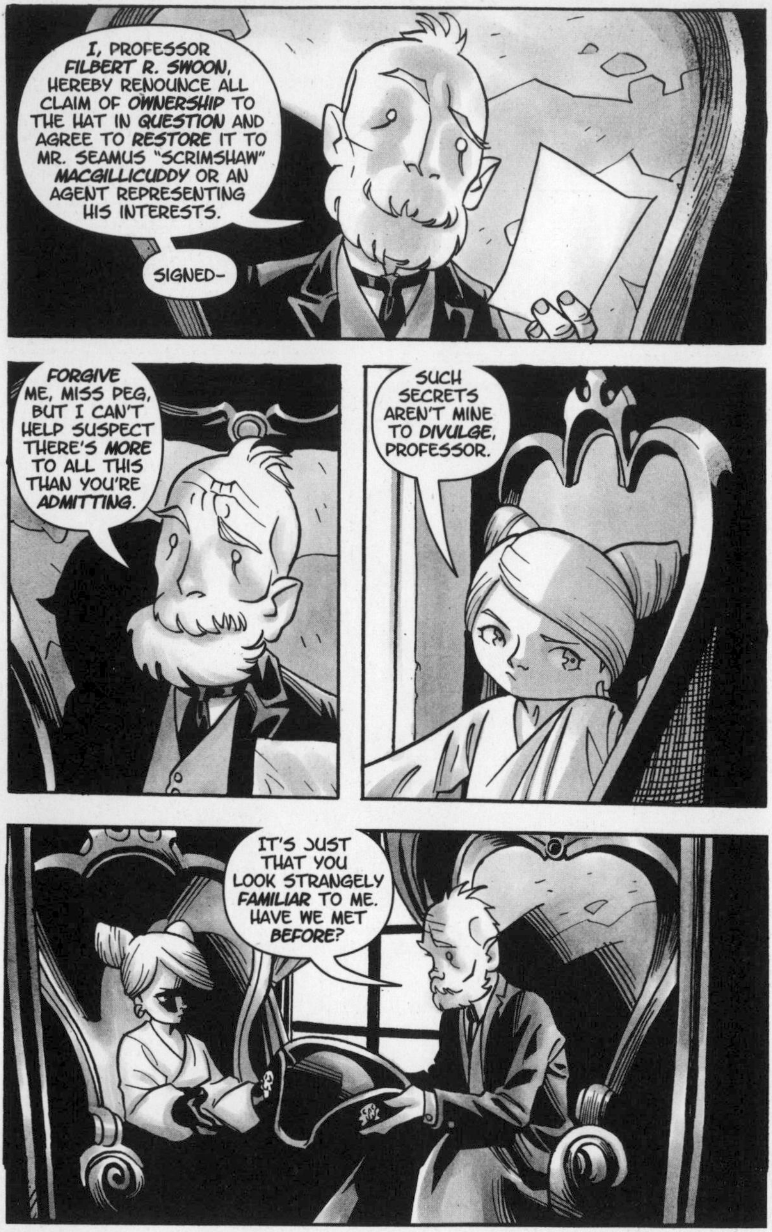
I, PROFESSOR FILBERT R. SWOON, HEREBY RENOUNCE ALL CLAIM OF OWNERSHIP TO THE HAT IN QUESTION AND AGREE TO RESTORE IT TO MR. SEAMUS "SCRIMSHAW" MACGILLICUDDY OR AN AGENT REPRESENTING HIS INTERESTS.
SIGNED-
FORGIVE ME, MISS PEG, BUT I CAN'T HELP SUSPECT THERE'S MORE TO ALL THIS THAN YOU'RE ADMITTING.
SUCH SECRETS AREN'T MINE TO DIVULGE, PROFESSOR.
IT'S JUST THAT YOU LOOK STRANGELY FAMILIAR TO ME. HAVE WE MET BEFORE?

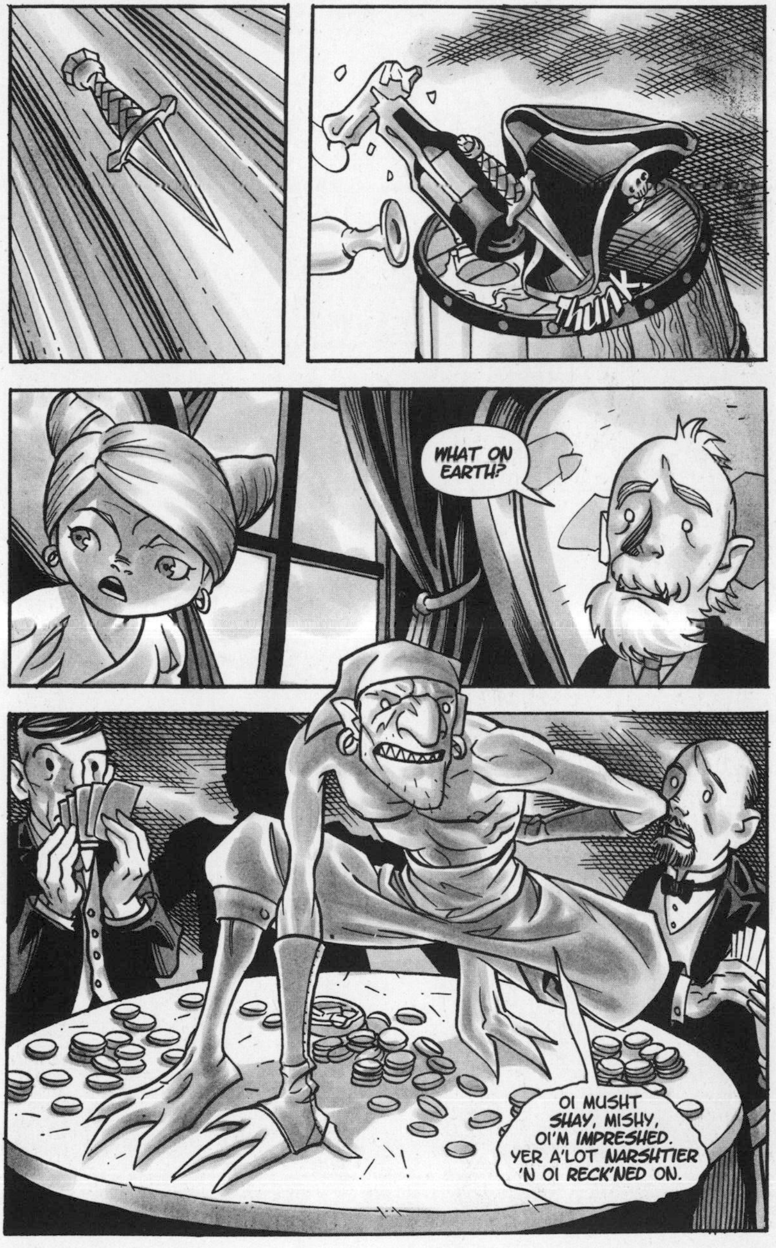
THUNK
WHAT ON EARTH?
OI MUSHT SHAY, MISHY, OI'M IMPRESHED. YER A'LOT NARSHTIER 'N OI RECK'NED ON.

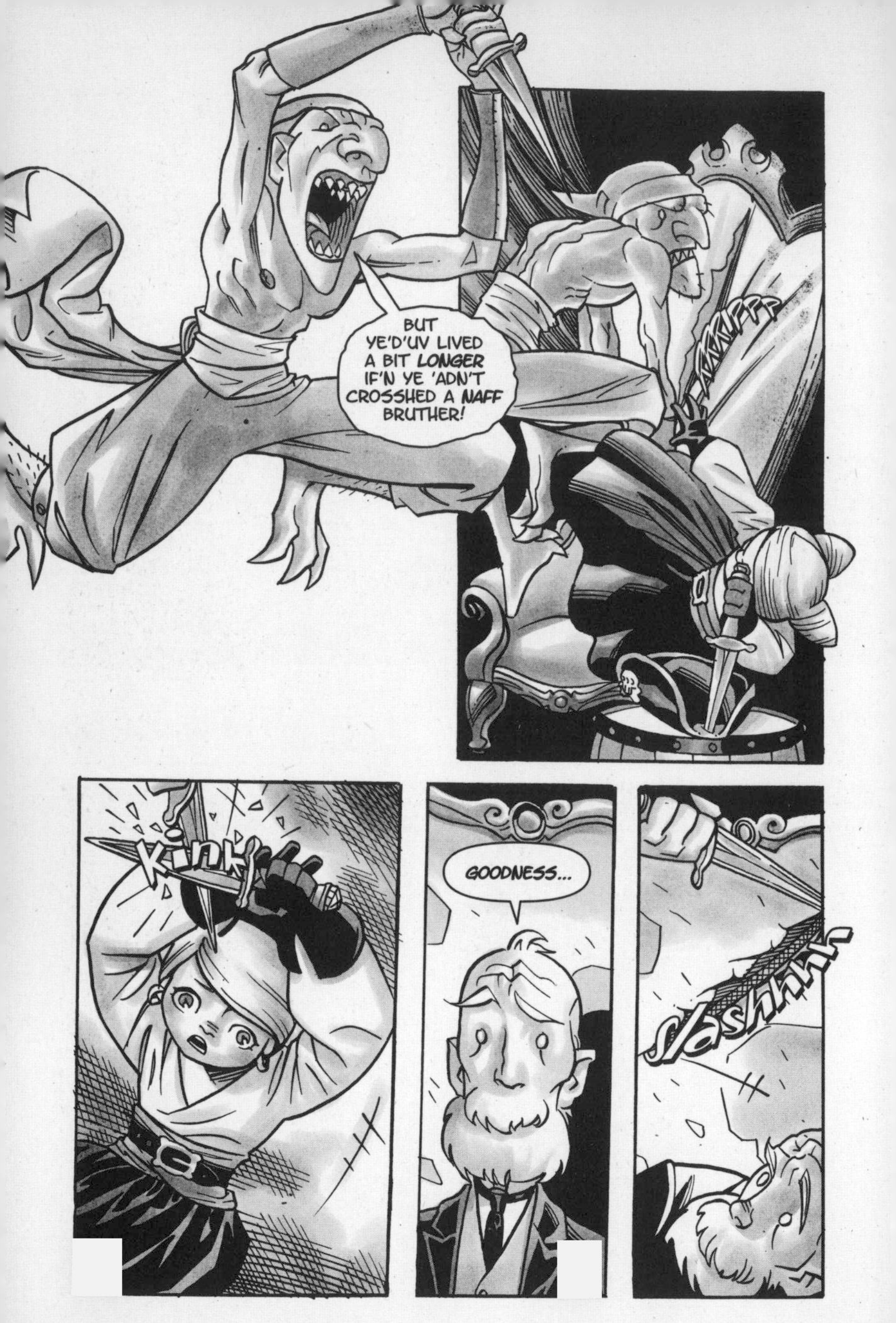
BUT YE'D'UV LIVED A BIT LONGER IF'N YE 'ADN'T CROSSHED A NAFF BRUTHER!
SKKRIPP
KINK
GOODNESS...
SLASHHHH

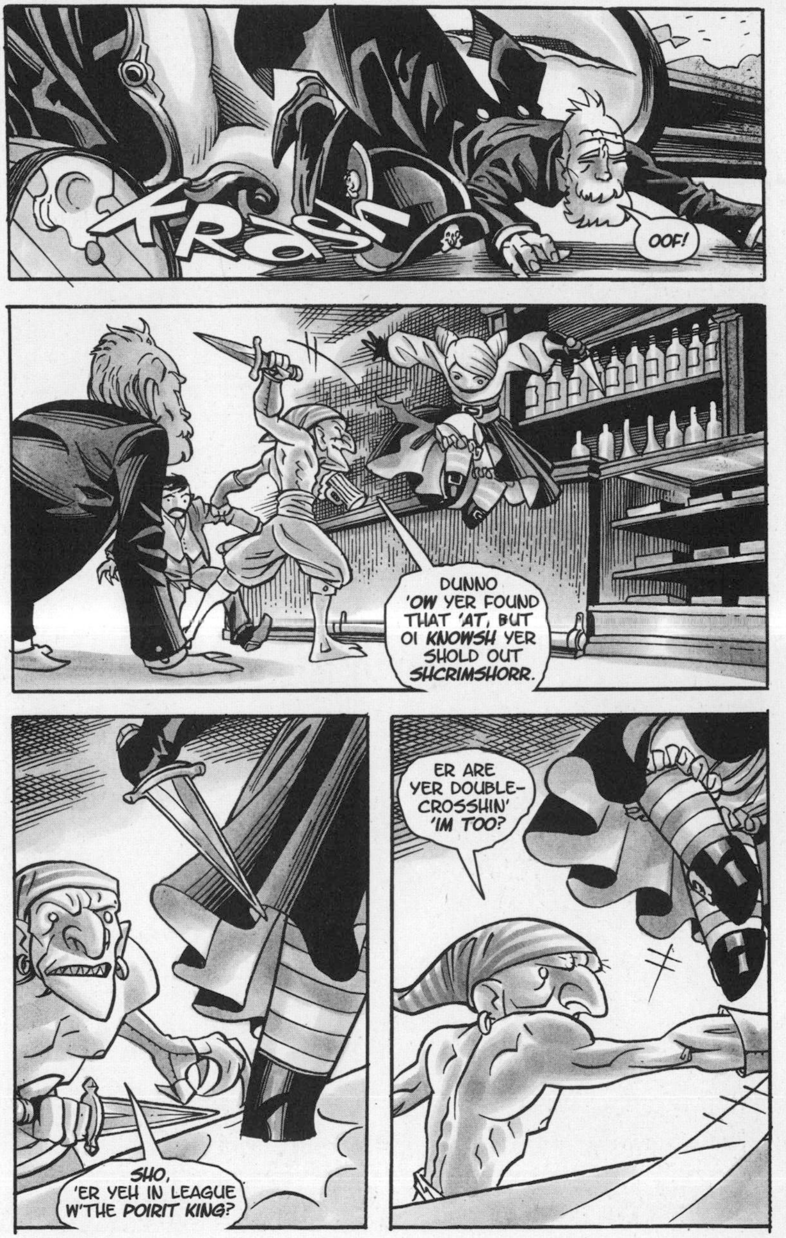
KRASH
OOF!
DUNNO 'OW YER FOUND THAT 'AT, BUT OI KNOWSH YER SHOLD OUT SHCRIMSHORR.
SHO, 'ER YEH IN LEAGUE W'THE POIRIT KING?
ER ARE YER DOUBLE-CROSSHIN' 'IM TOO?

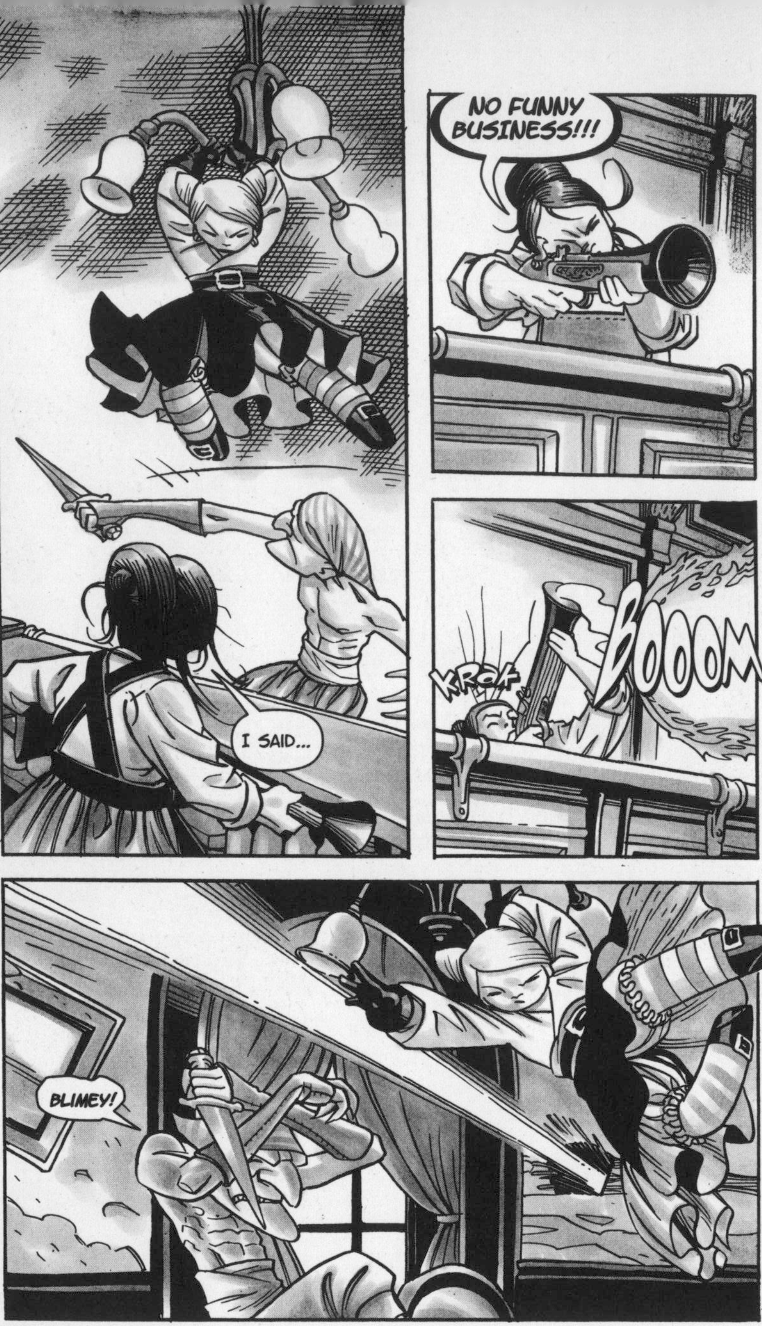
NO FUNNY BUSINESS!!!
I SAID...
KROK
BOOOM
BLIMEY!

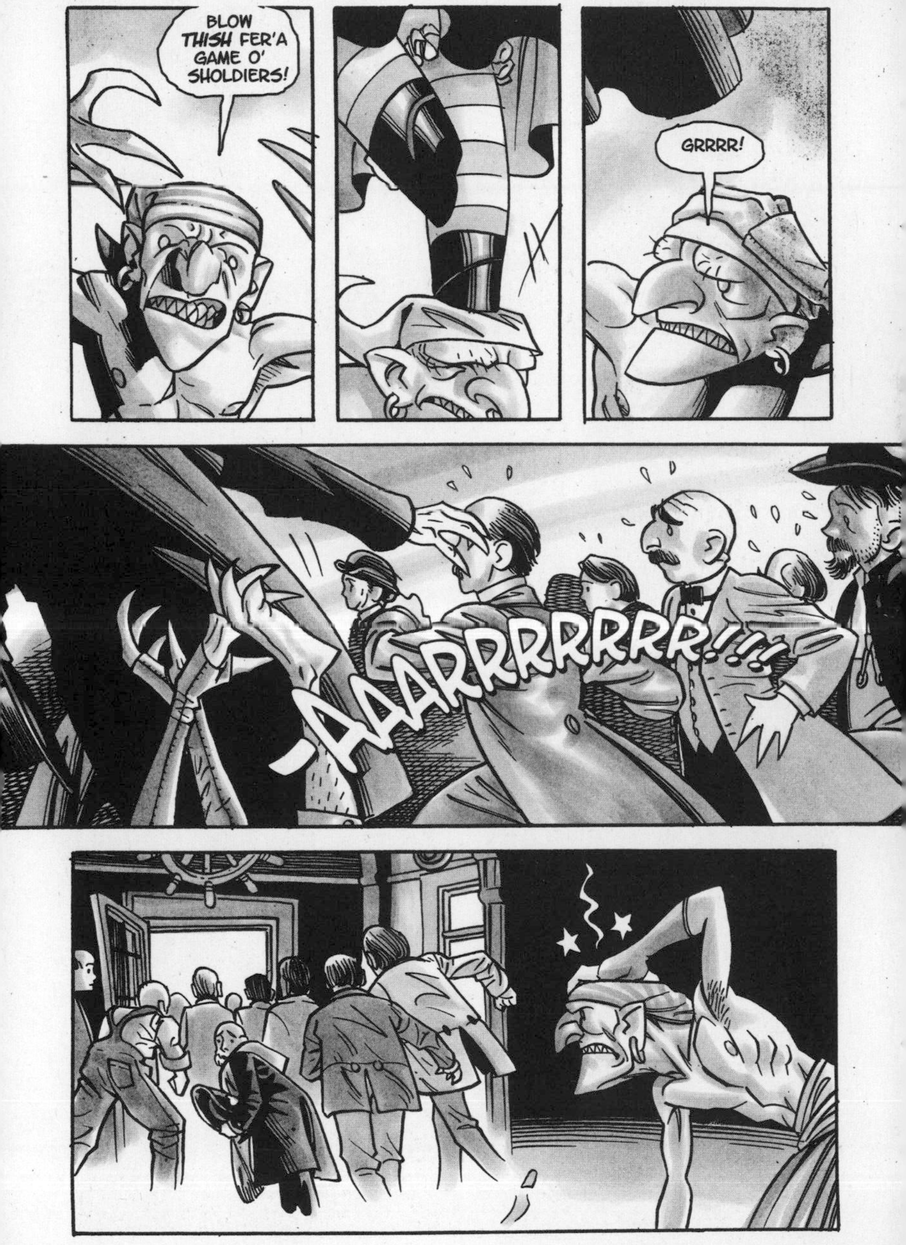
BLOW THISH FER'A GAME O' SHOLDIERS!
GRRRR!
AAARRRRRRRR!!!!

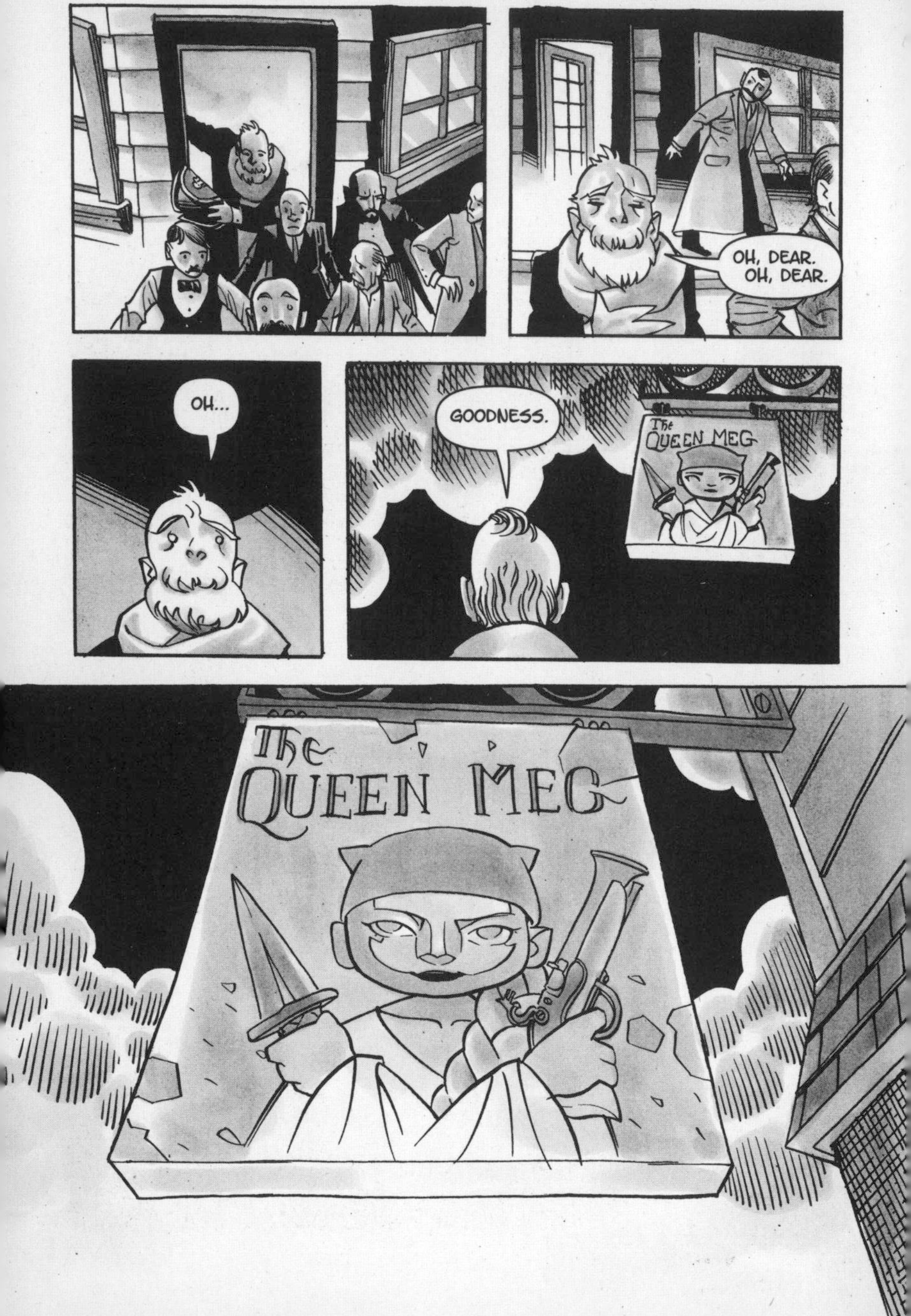
OH, DEAR.
OH, DEAR.
OH...
GOODNESS.
The QUEEN MEG
The QUEEN MEG

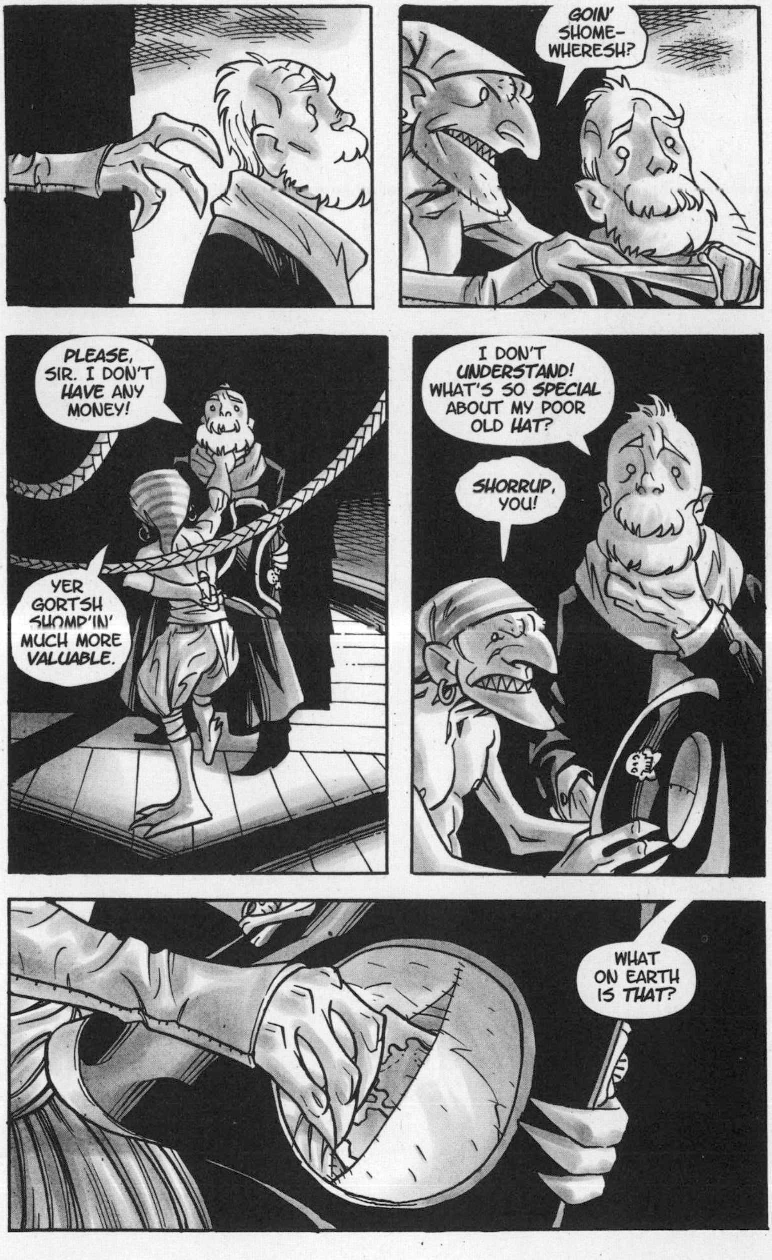
GOIN' SHOME-WHERESH?
PLEASE, SIR. I DON'T HAVE ANY MONEY!
YER GORTSH SHOMP'IN' MUCH MORE VALUABLE.
I DON'T UNDERSTAND! WHAT'S SO SPECIAL ABOUT MY POOR OLD HAT?
SHORRUP, YOU!
WHAT ON EARTH IS THAT?

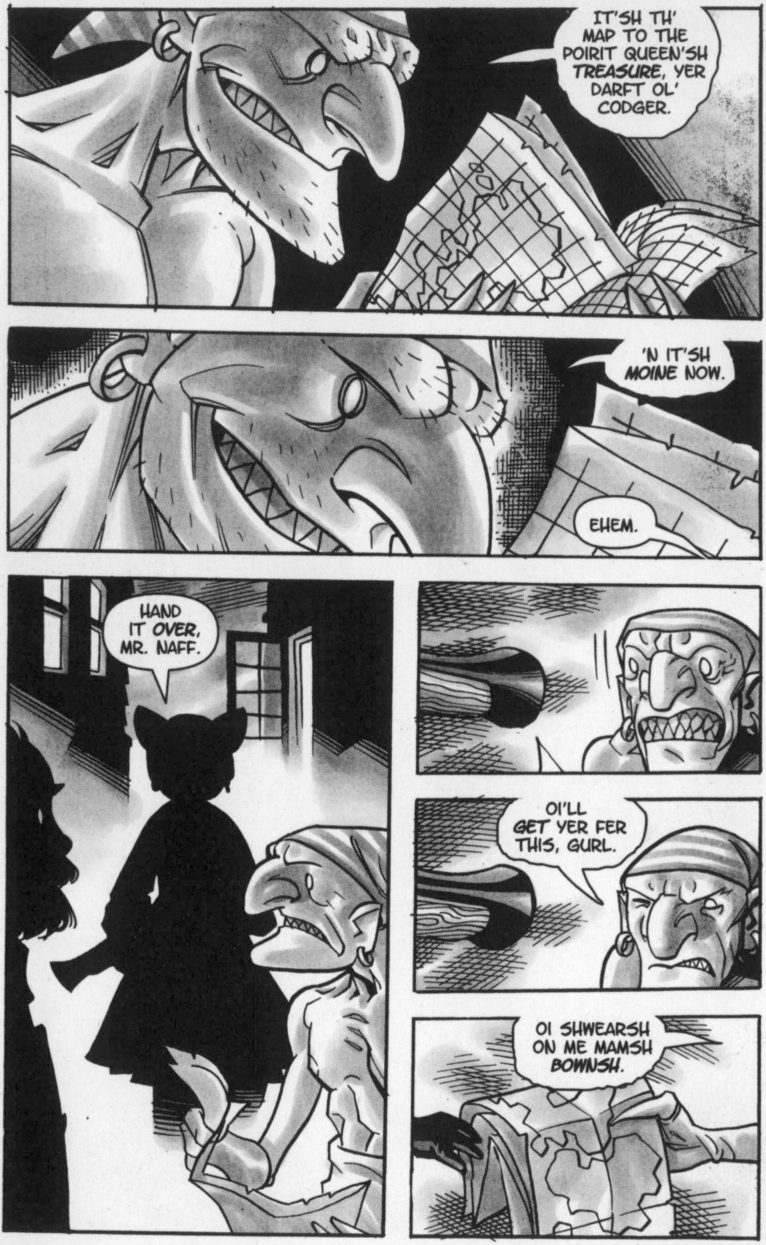
IT'SH TH' MAP TO THE POIRIT QUEEN'SH TREASURE, YER DARFT OL' CODGER.
'N IT'SH MOINE NOW.
EHEM.
HAND IT OVER, MR. NAFF.
OI'LL GET YER FER THIS, GURL.
OI SHWEARSH ON ME MAMSH BOWNSH.

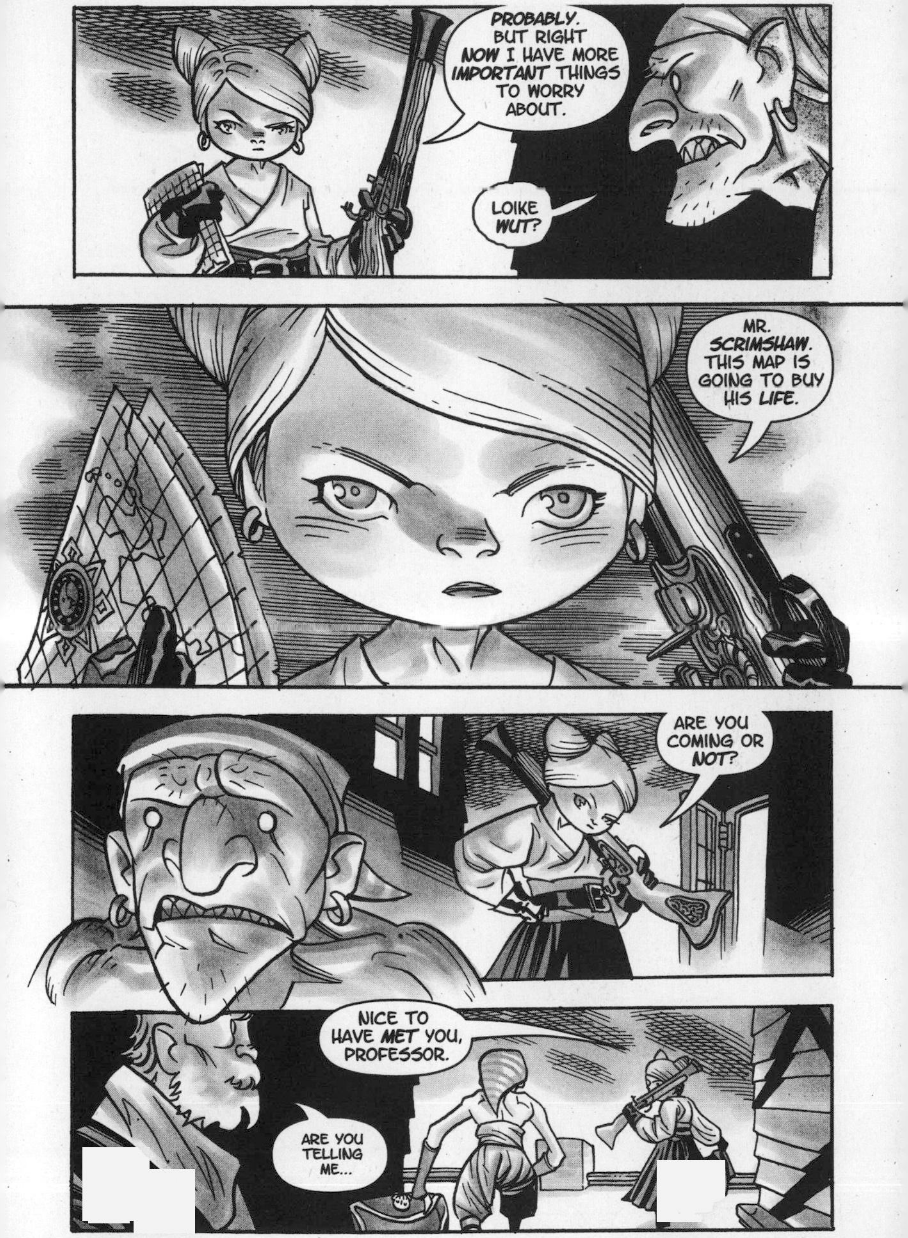
PROBABLY. BUT RIGHT NOW I HAVE MORE IMPORTANT THINGS TO WORRY ABOUT.
LOIKE WUT?
MR. SCRIMSHAW. THIS MAP IS GOING TO BUY HIS LIFE.
ARE YOU COMING OR NOT?
NICE TO HAVE MET YOU, PROFESSOR.
ARE YOU TELLING ME...

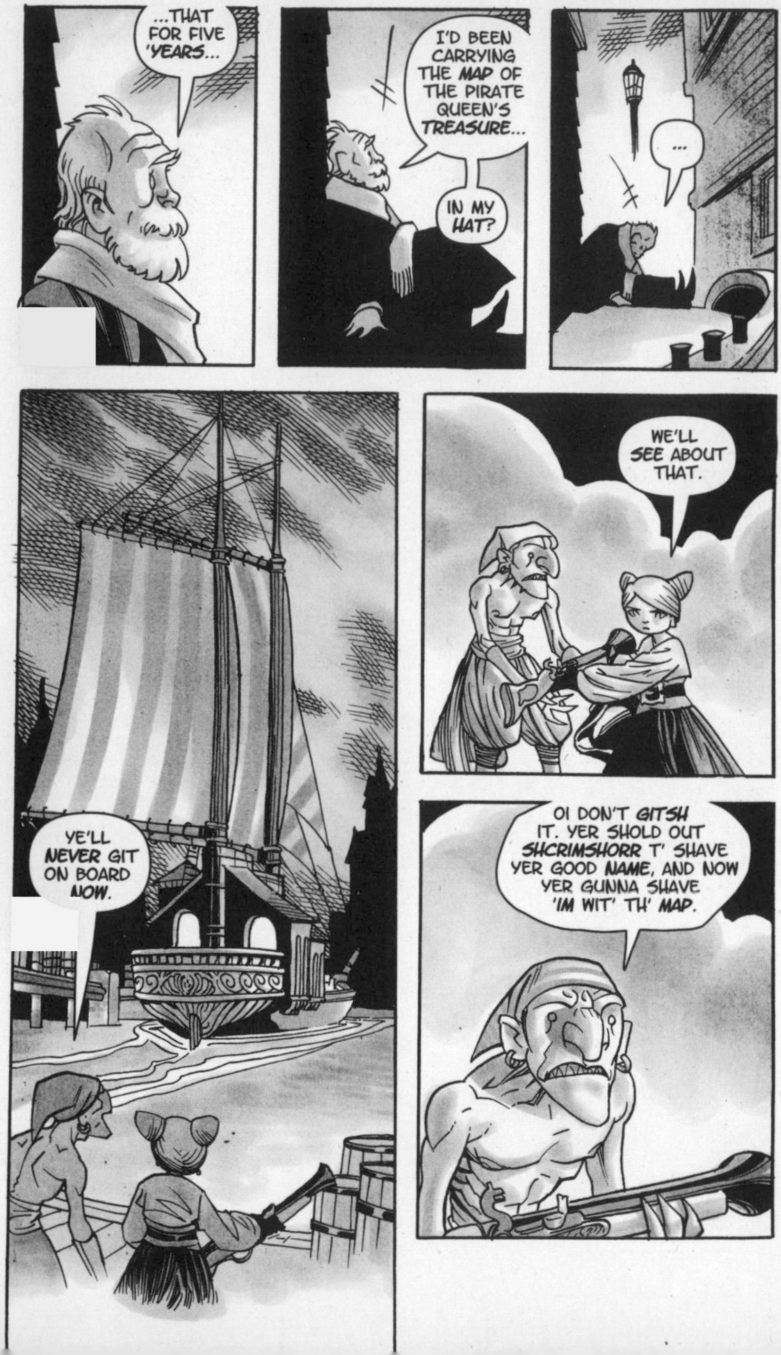
...THAT FOR FIVE 'YEARS...
I'D BEEN CARRYING THE MAP OF THE PIRATE QUEEN'S TREASURE...
IN MY HAT?
...
WE'LL SEE ABOUT THAT.
YE'LL NEVER GIT ON BOARD NOW.
OI DON'T GITSH IT. YER SHOLD OUT SHCRIMSHORR T' SHAVE YER GOOD NAME, AND NOW YER GUNNA SHAVE 'IM WIT' TH' MAP.

WUT'SH IT ALL FOR, THEN? YER LOIKE ENUFF TEH LOSE YER GOOD NAME ANYWAYS.

BUT I'LL HAVE MY HONOR.

AIN'T THEY TH' SHAME FING?

I THOUGHT SO...

UNTIL I SOLD MY HONOR FOR THE SAKE OF MY COMFORTABLE LITTLE LIFE.

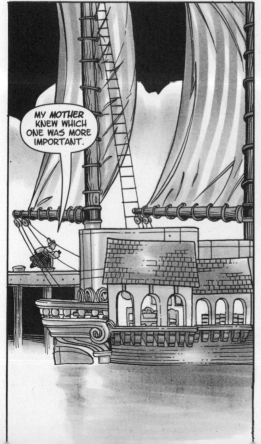

MY MOTHER KNEW WHICH ONE WAS MORE IMPORTANT.

WHOEVER SHE WAS.

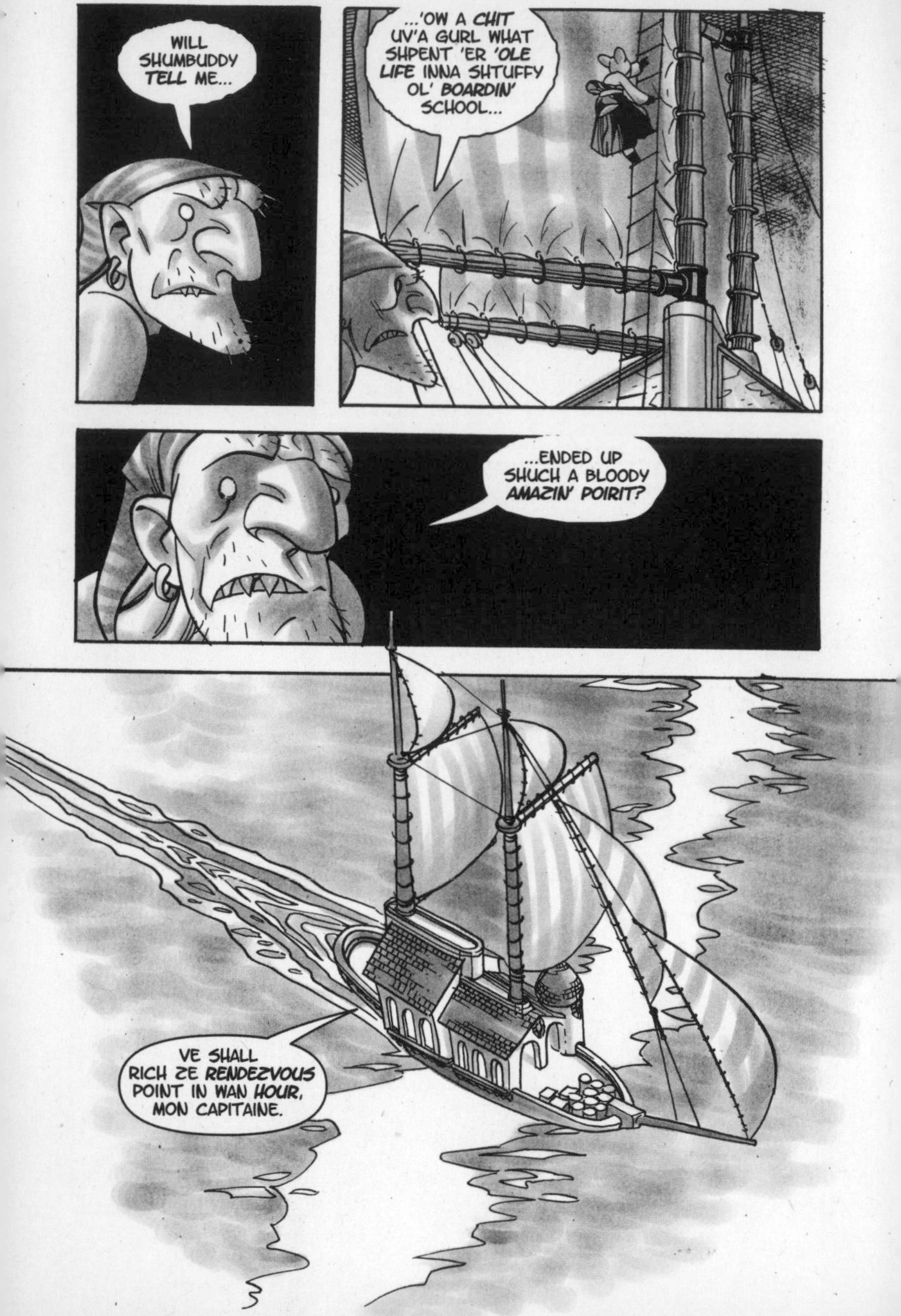
WILL SHUMBUDDY TELL ME...
...'OW A CHIT UV'A GURL WHAT SHPENT 'ER 'OLE LIFE INNA SHTUFFY OL' BOARDIN' SCHOOL...
...ENDED UP SHUCH A BLOODY AMAZIN' POIRIT?
VE SHALL RICH ZE RENDEZVOUS POINT IN WAN HOUR, MON CAPITAINE.

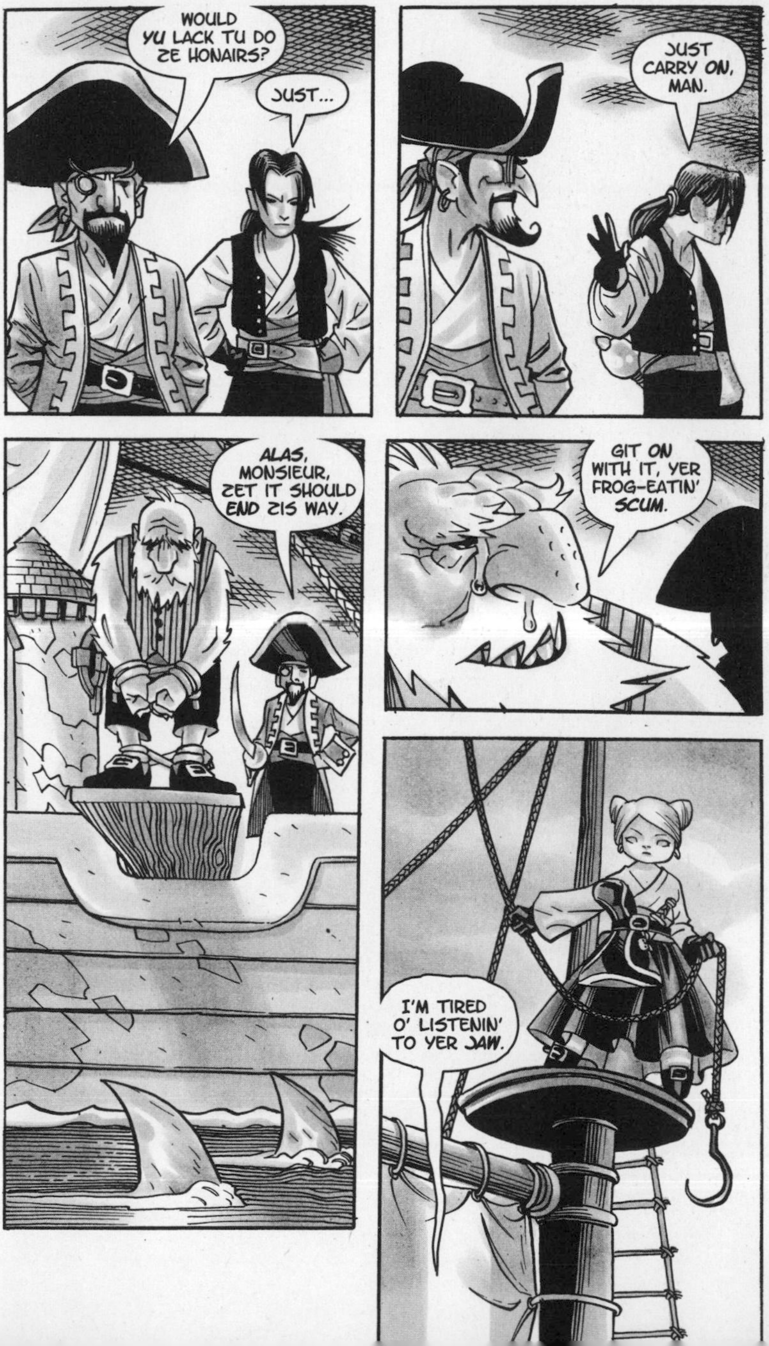
WOULD YU LACK TU DO ZE HONAIRS?
JUST...
JUST CARRY ON, MAN.
ALAS, MONSIEUR, ZET IT SHOULD END ZIS WAY.
GIT ON WITH IT, YER FROG-EATIN' SCUM.
I'M TIRED O' LISTENIN' TO YER JAW.

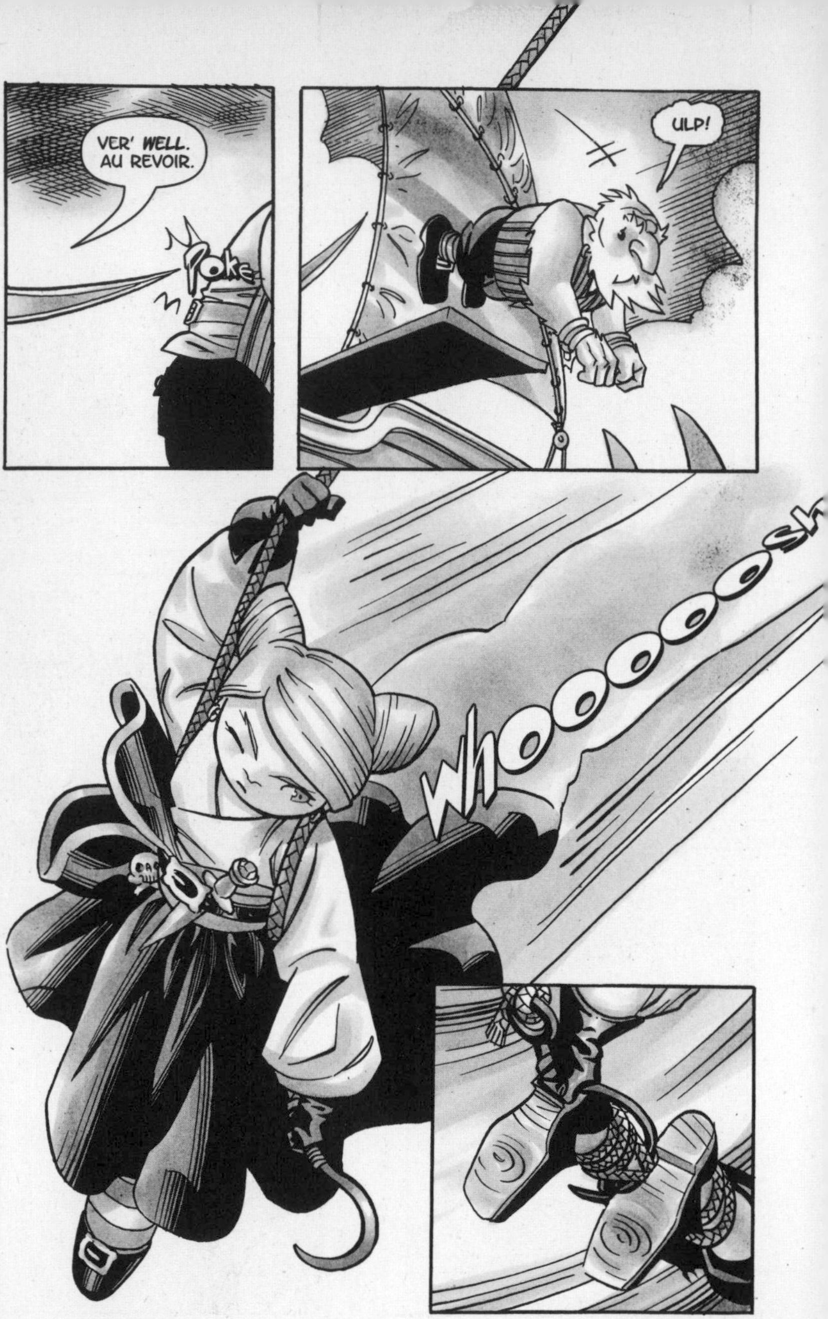
VER' WELL. AU REVOIR.
POKE
ULP!
WHOOOOOOSH

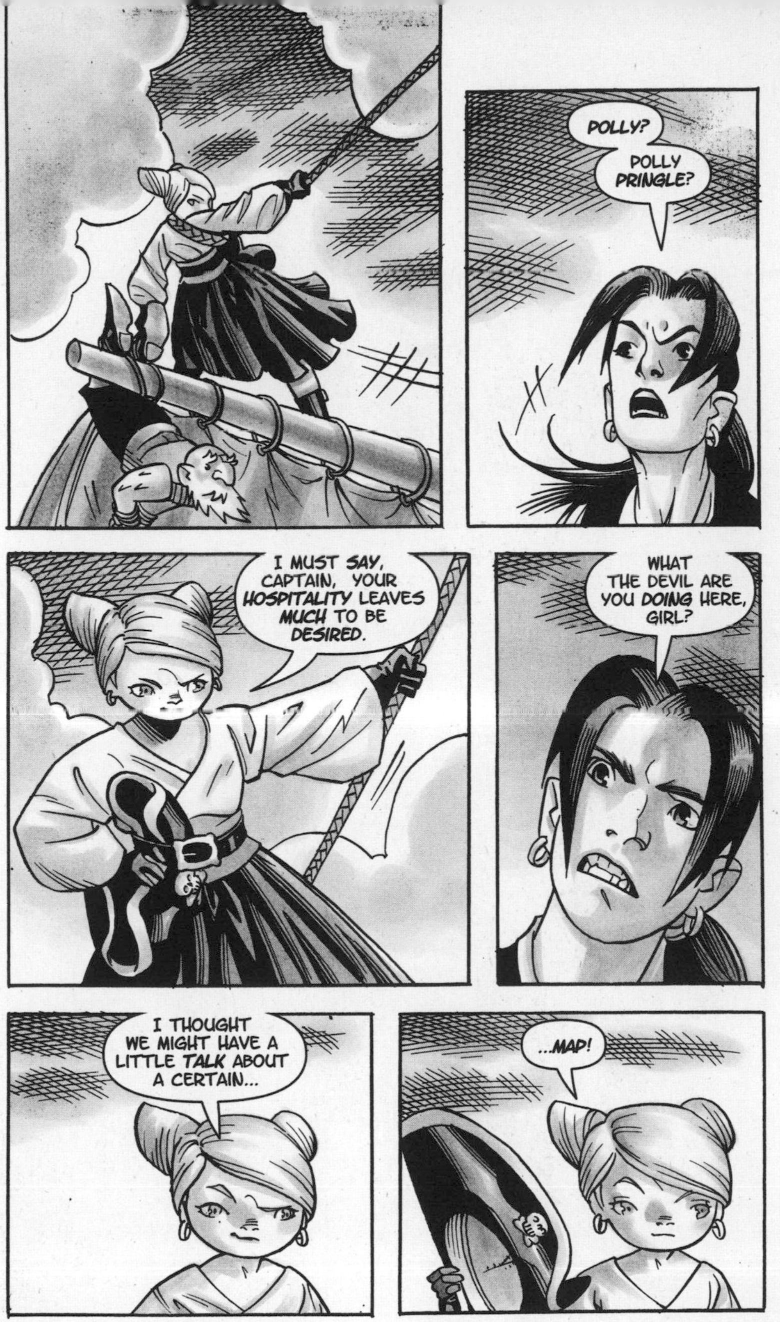
POLLY?
POLLY PRINGLE?
I MUST SAY, CAPTAIN, YOUR HOSPITALITY LEAVES MUCH TO BE DESIRED.
WHAT THE DEVIL ARE YOU DOING HERE, GIRL?
I THOUGHT WE MIGHT HAVE A LITTLE TALK ABOUT A CERTAIN...
...MAP!

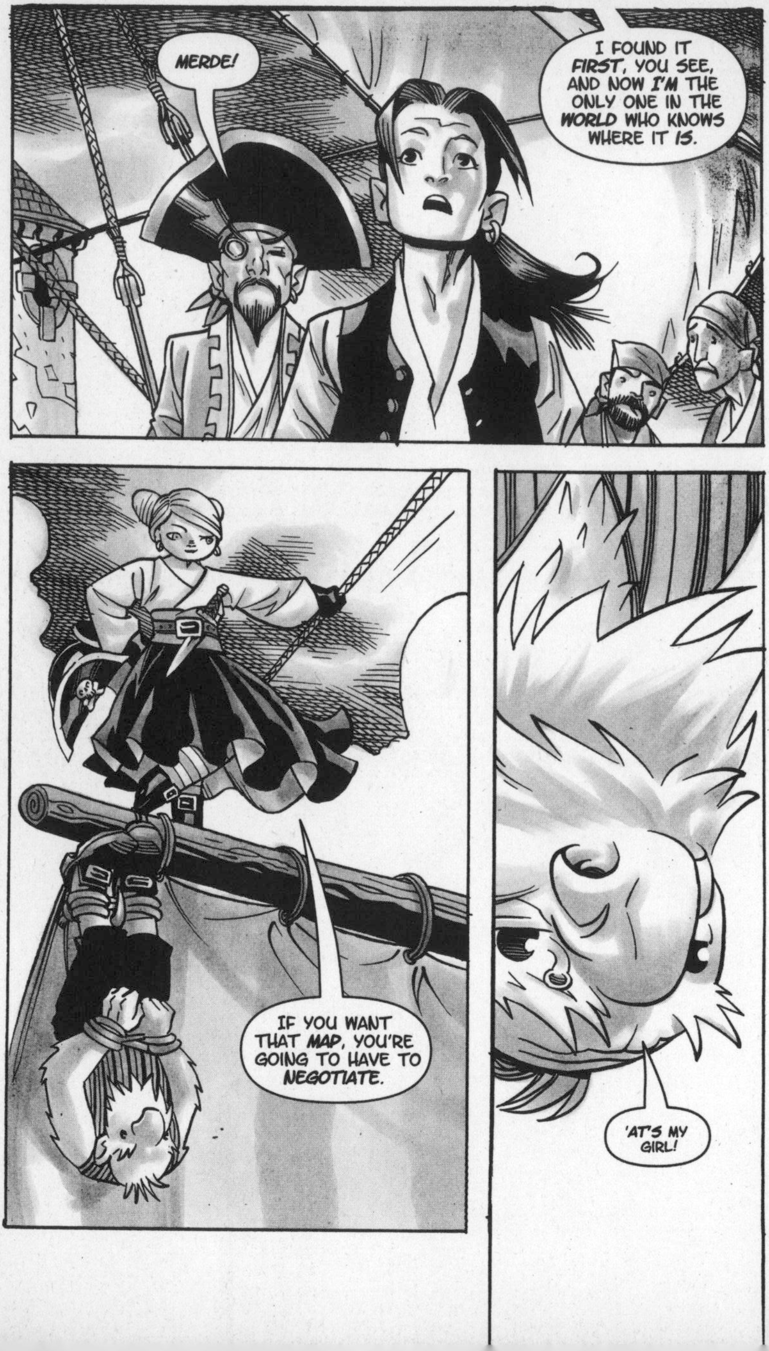
MERDE!
I FOUND IT FIRST, YOU SEE, AND NOW I'M THE ONLY ONE IN THE WORLD WHO KNOWS WHERE IT IS.
IF YOU WANT THAT MAP, YOU'RE GOING TO HAVE TO NEGOTIATE.
'AT'S MY GIRL!

Chapter 5

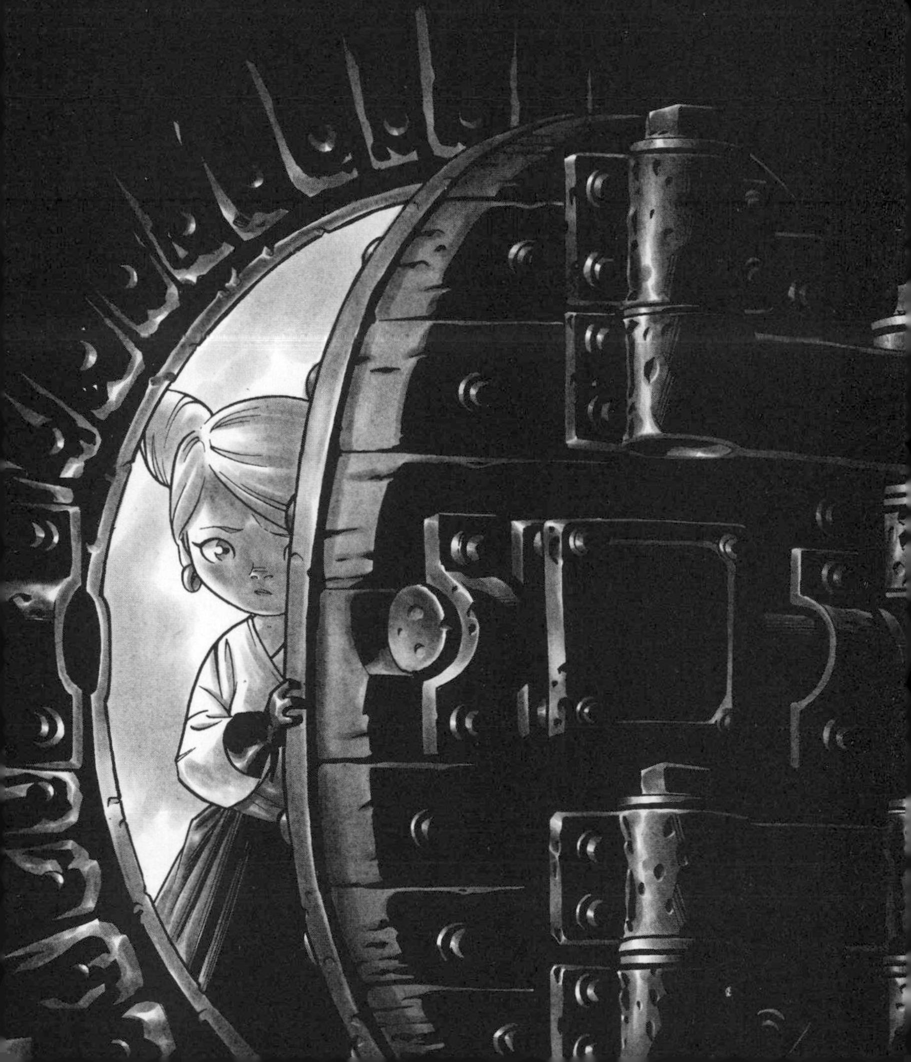

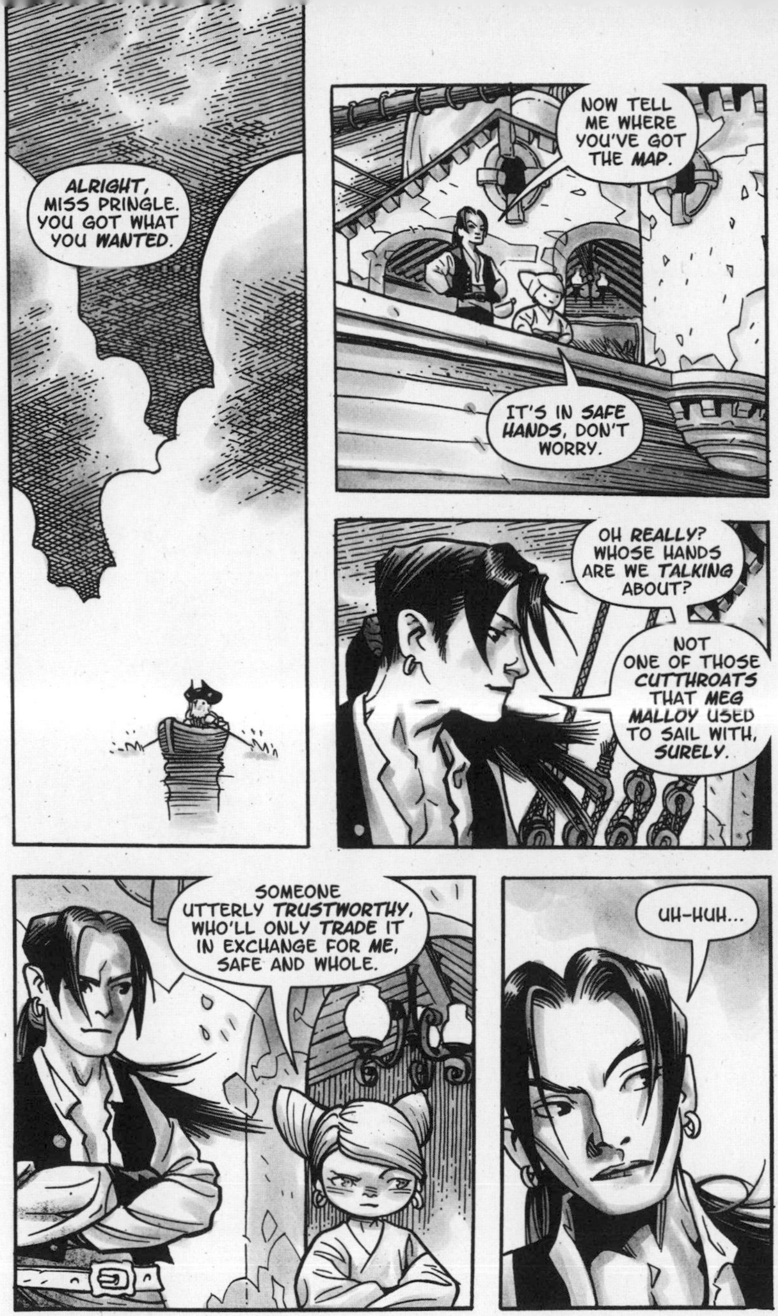
ALRIGHT, MISS PRINGLE. YOU GOT WHAT YOU WANTED.
NOW TELL ME WHERE YOU'VE GOT THE MAP.
IT'S IN SAFE HANDS, DON'T WORRY.
OH REALLY? WHOSE HANDS ARE WE TALKING ABOUT?
NOT ONE OF THOSE CUTTHROATS THAT MEG MALLOY USED TO SAIL WITH, SURELY.
SOMEONE UTTERLY TRUSTWORTHY, WHO'LL ONLY TRADE IT IN EXCHANGE FOR ME, SAFE AND WHOLE.
UH-HUH...

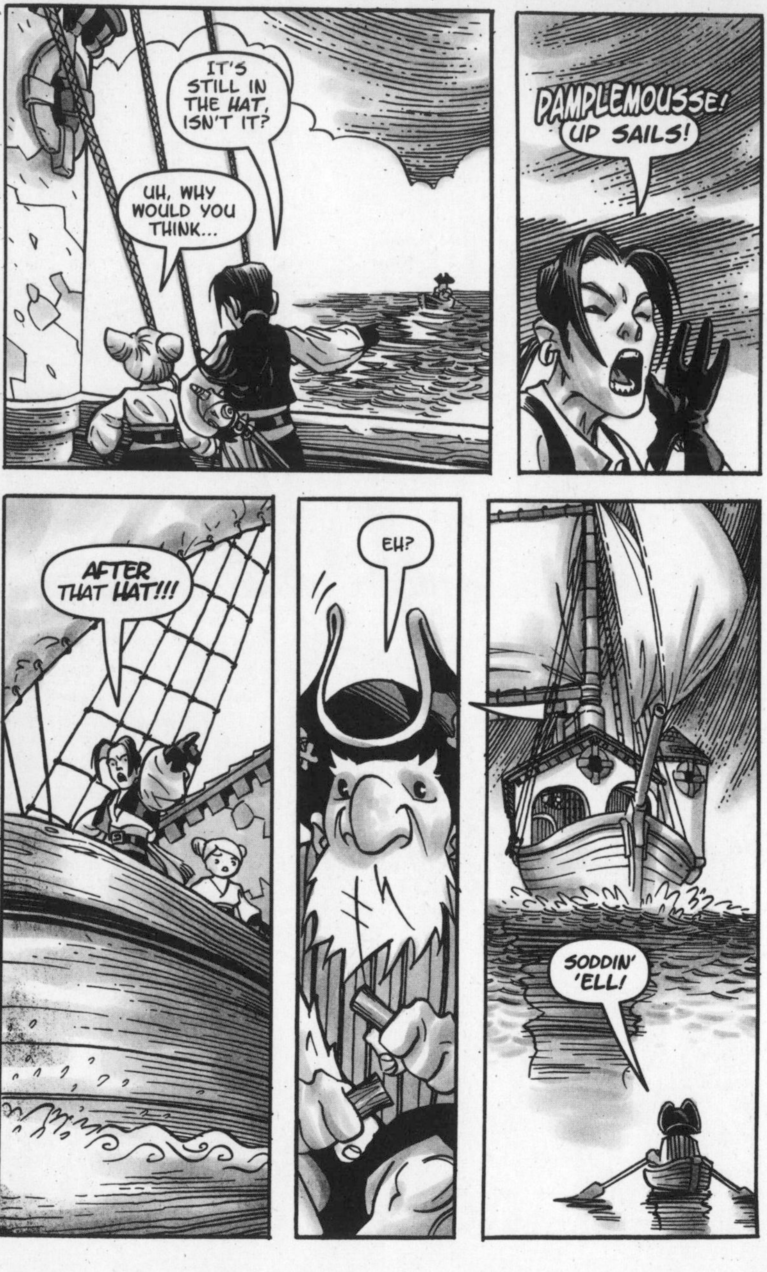
IT'S STILL IN THE HAT, ISN'T IT?
UH, WHY WOULD YOU THINK...
PAMPLEMOUSSE! UP SAILS!
AFTER THAT HAT!!!
EH?
SODDIN' 'ELL!

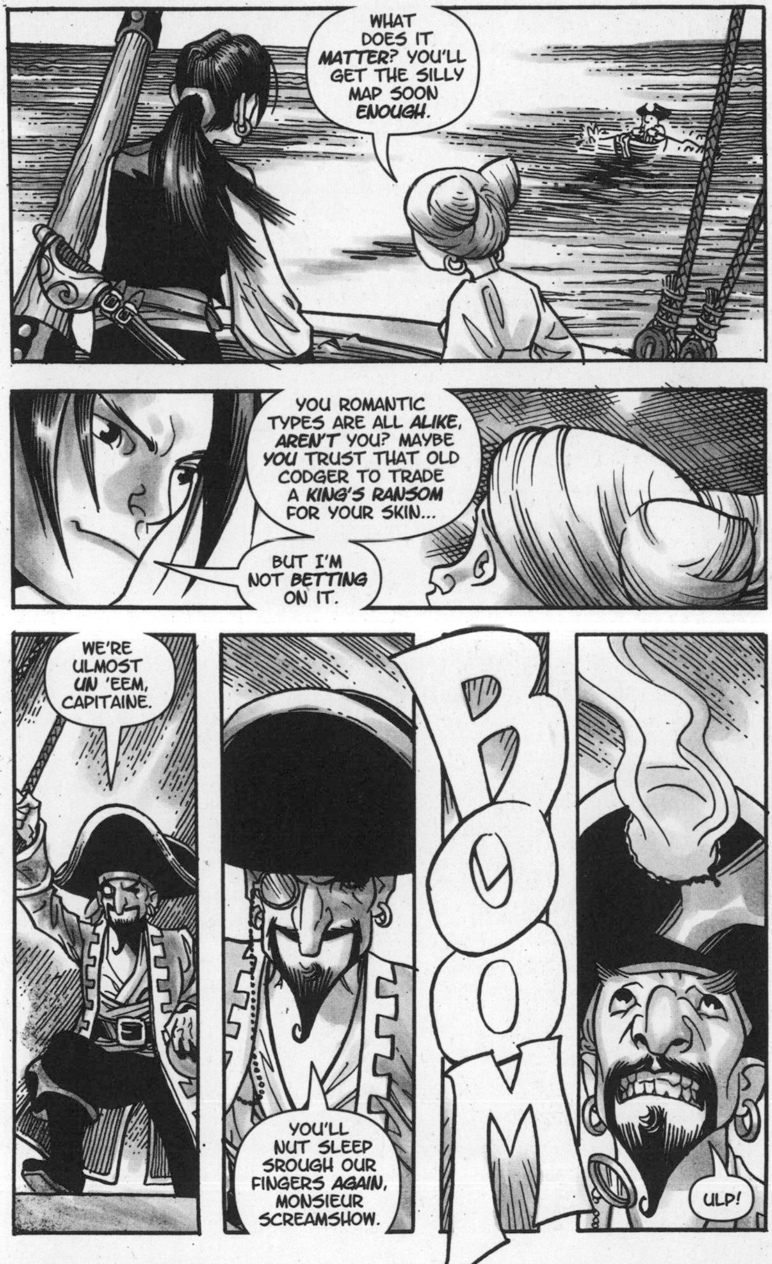
WHAT DOES IT MATTER? YOU'LL GET THE SILLY MAP SOON ENOUGH.
YOU ROMANTIC TYPES ARE ALL ALIKE, AREN'T YOU? MAYBE YOU TRUST THAT OLD CODGER TO TRADE A KING'S RANSOM FOR YOUR SKIN...
BUT I'M NOT BETTING ON IT.
WE'RE ULMOST UN 'EEM, CAPITAINE.
YOU'LL NUT SLEEP SROUGH OUR FINGERS AGAIN, MONSIEUR SCREAMSHOW.
BOOM
ULP!

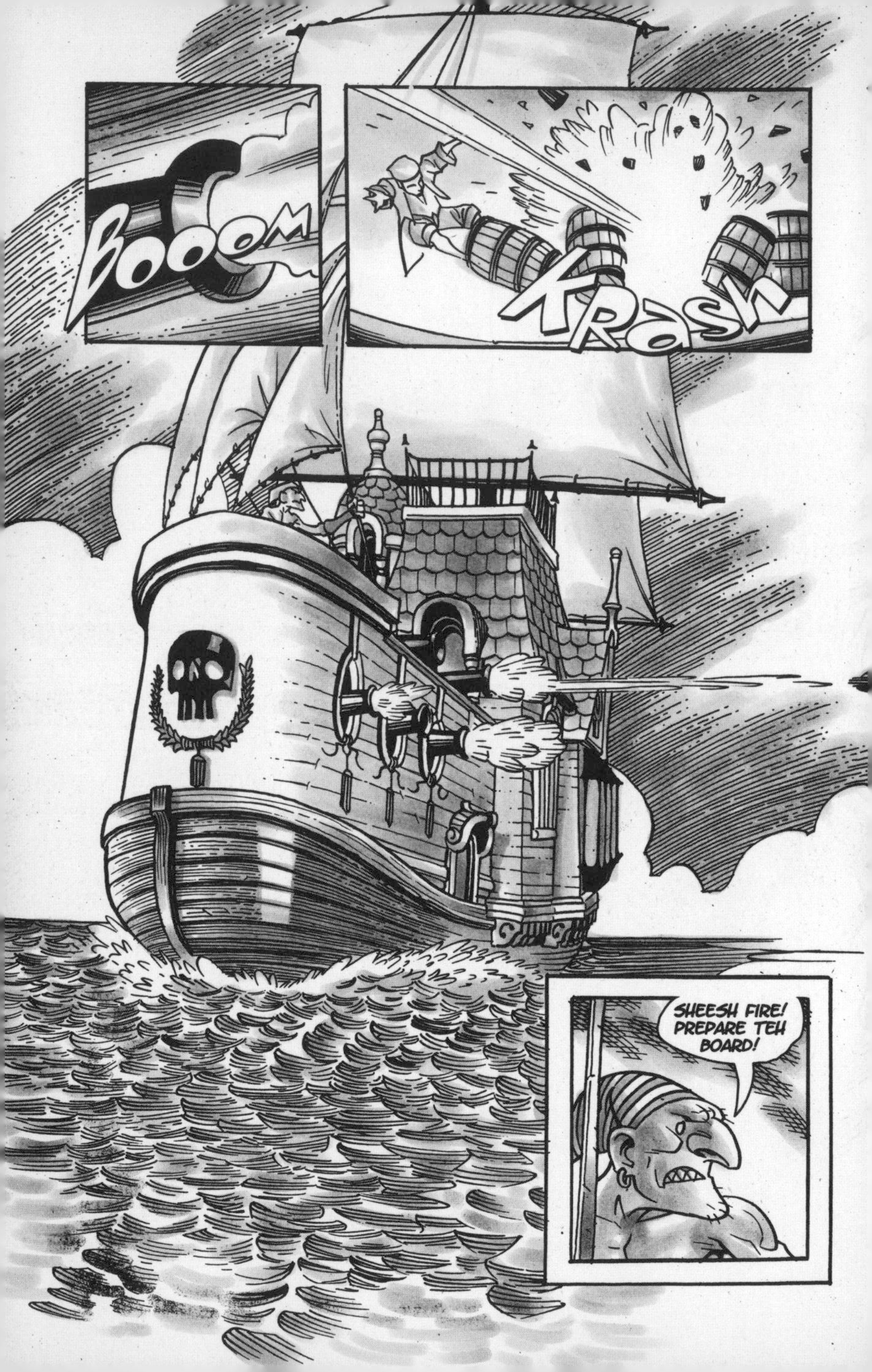
BOOOM
KRASH
SHEESH FIRE! PREPARE TEH BOARD!

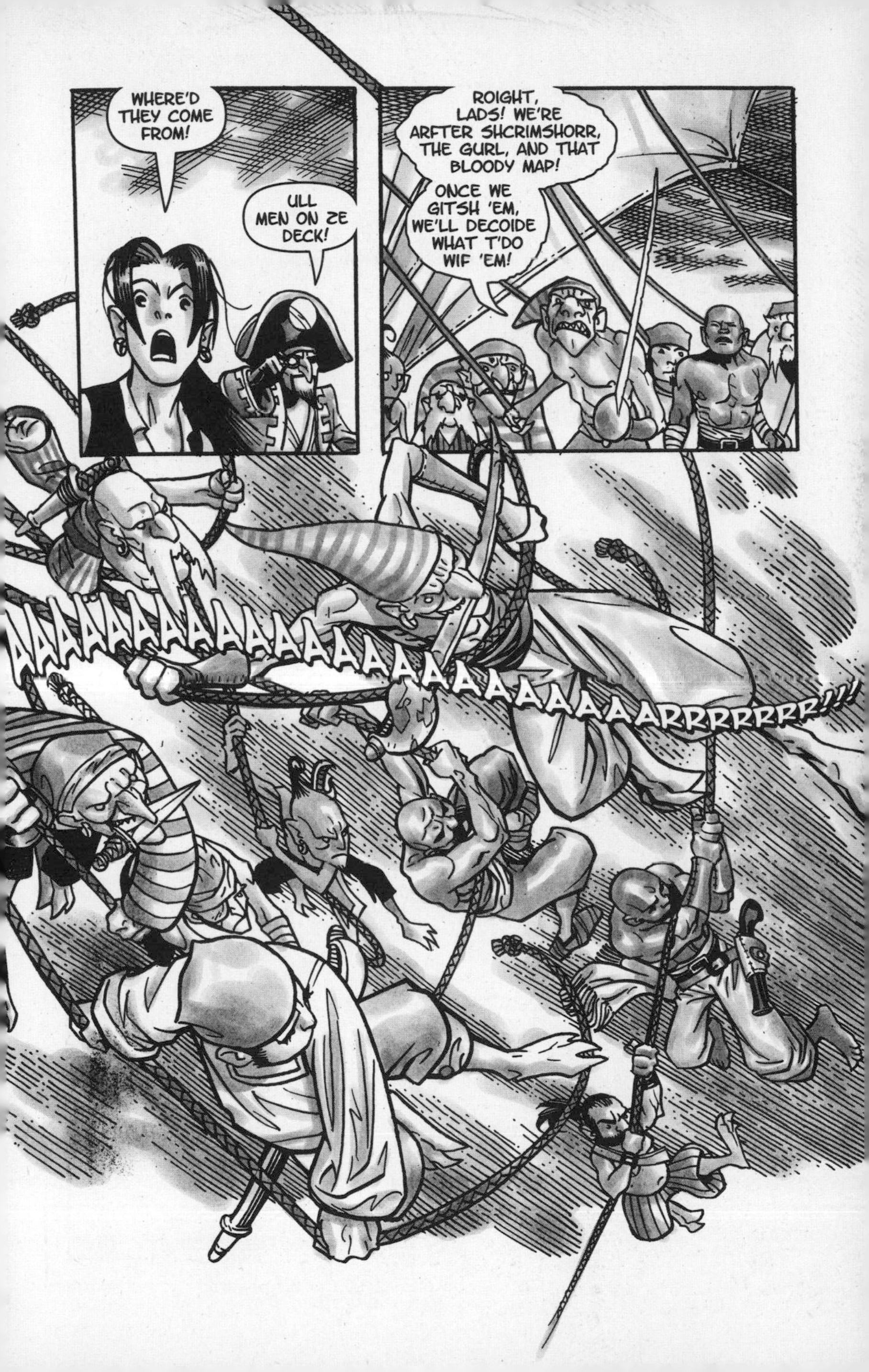
WHERE'D THEY COME FROM!
ULL MEN ON ZE DECK!
ROIGHT, LADS! WE'RE ARFTER SHCRIMSHORR, THE GURL, AND THAT BLOODY MAP!
ONCE WE GITSH 'EM, WE'LL DECOIDE WHAT T'DO WIF 'EM!
AAAAAAAAAAAAAAAAAAAAAAAAAAAAAAARRRRRRR!!!

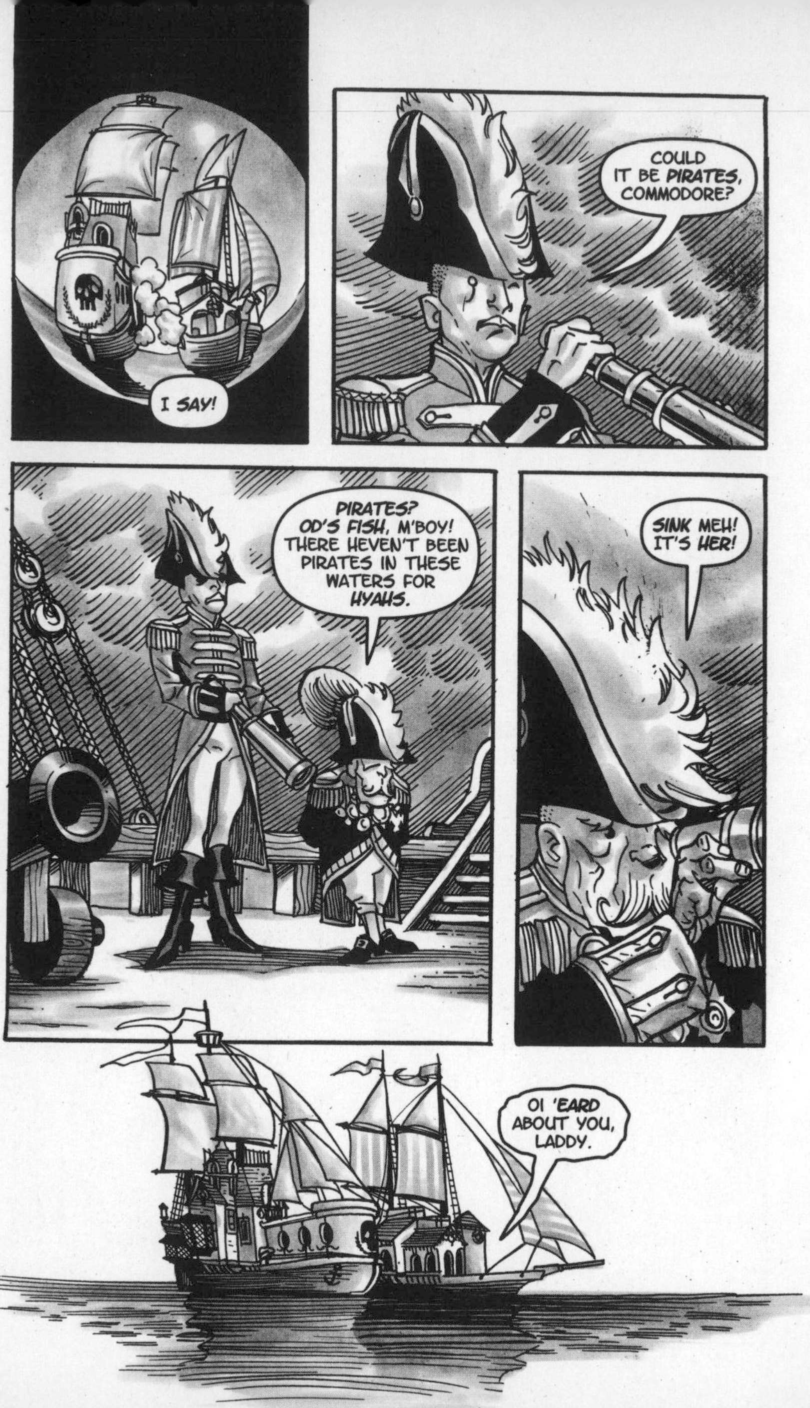
I SAY!
COULD IT BE PIRATES, COMMODORE?
PIRATES? OD'S FISH, M'BOY! THERE HEVEN'T BEEN PIRATES IN THESE WATERS FOR HYAHS.
SINK MEH! IT'S HER!
OI 'EARD ABOUT YOU, LADDY.

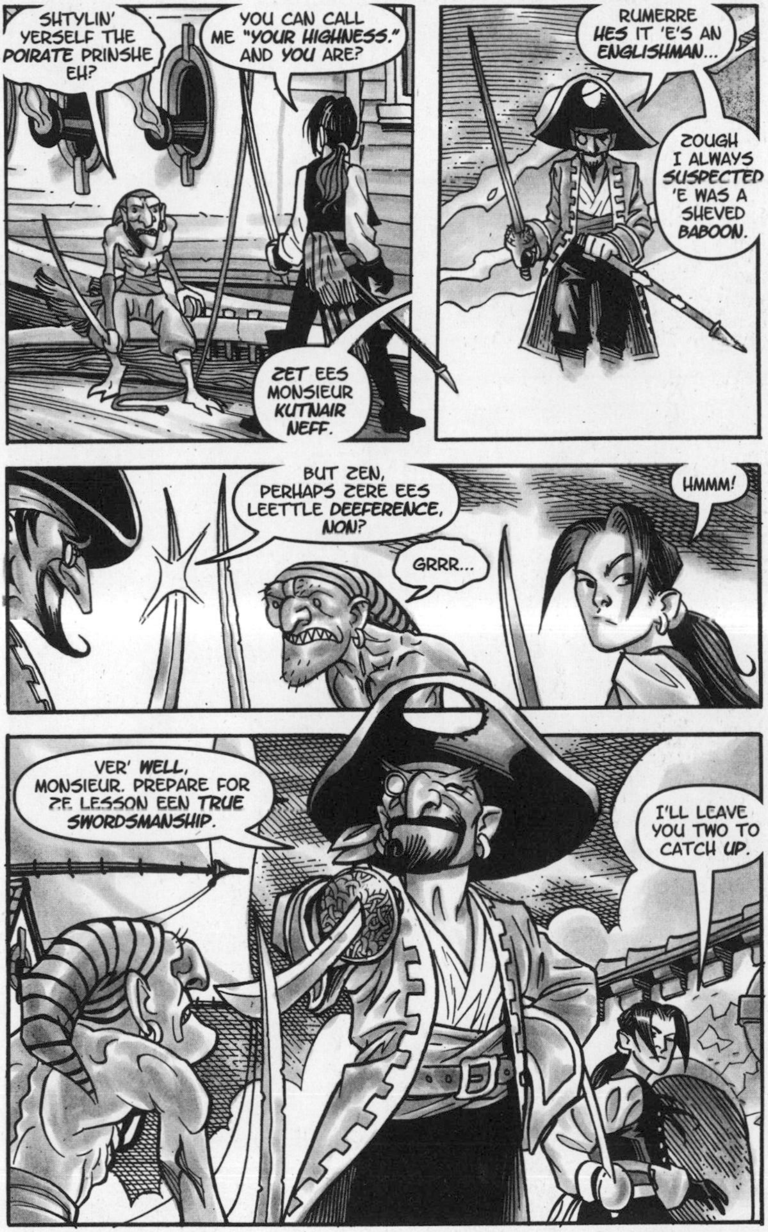
SHTYLIN' YERSELF THE POIRATE PRINSHE EH?
YOU CAN CALL ME "YOUR HIGHNESS." AND YOU ARE?
ZET EES MONSIEUR KUTNAIR NEFF.
RUMERRE HES IT 'E'S AN ENGLISHMAN...
ZOUGH I ALWAYS SUSPECTED 'E WAS A SHEVED BABOON.
BUT ZEN, PERHAPS ZERE EES LEETTLE DEEFERENCE, NON?
GRRR...
HMMM!
VER' WELL, MONSIEUR. PREPARE FOR ZE LESSON EEN TRUE SWORDSMANSHIP.
I'LL LEAVE YOU TWO TO CATCH UP.

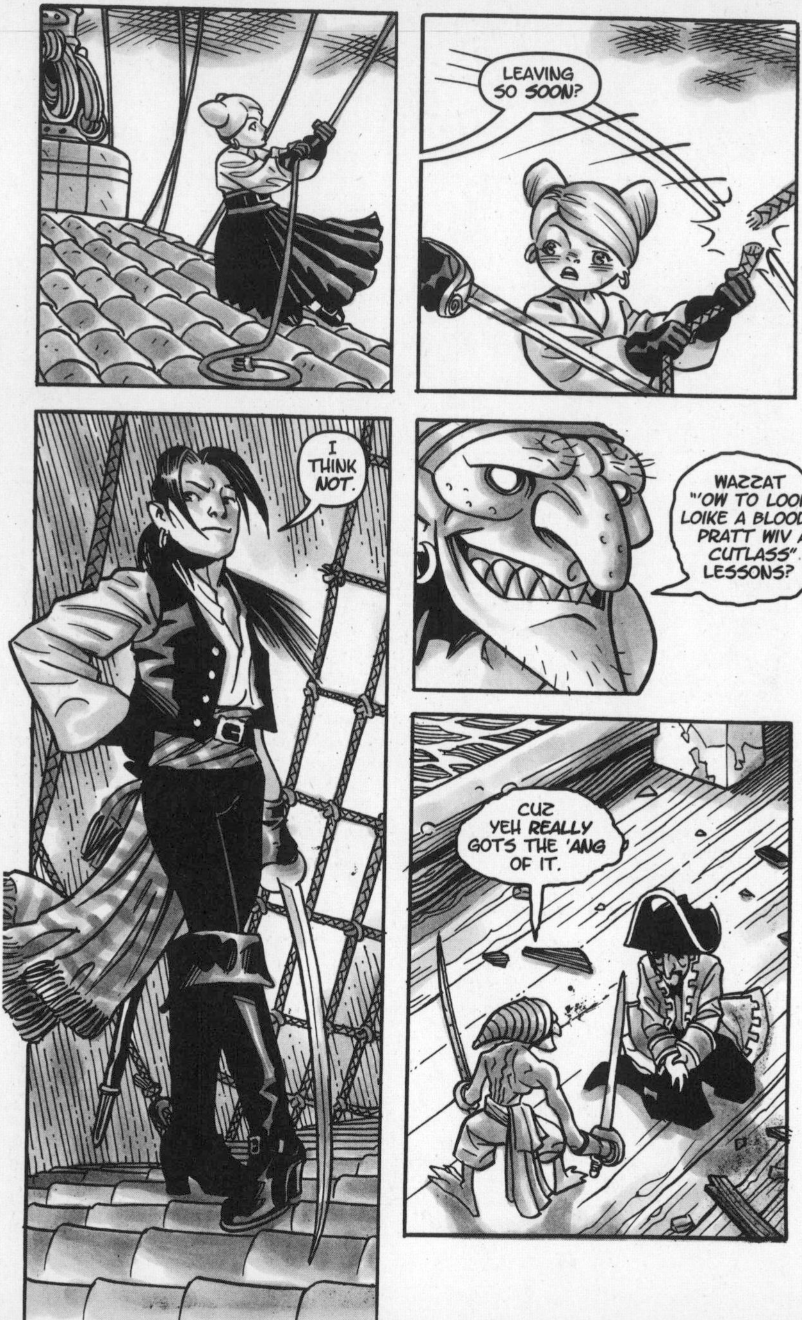
LEAVING SO SOON?
I THINK NOT.
WAZZAT "'OW TO LOOK LOIKE A BLOODY PRATT WIV A CUTLASS" LESSONS?
CUZ YEH REALLY GOTS THE 'ANG OF IT.

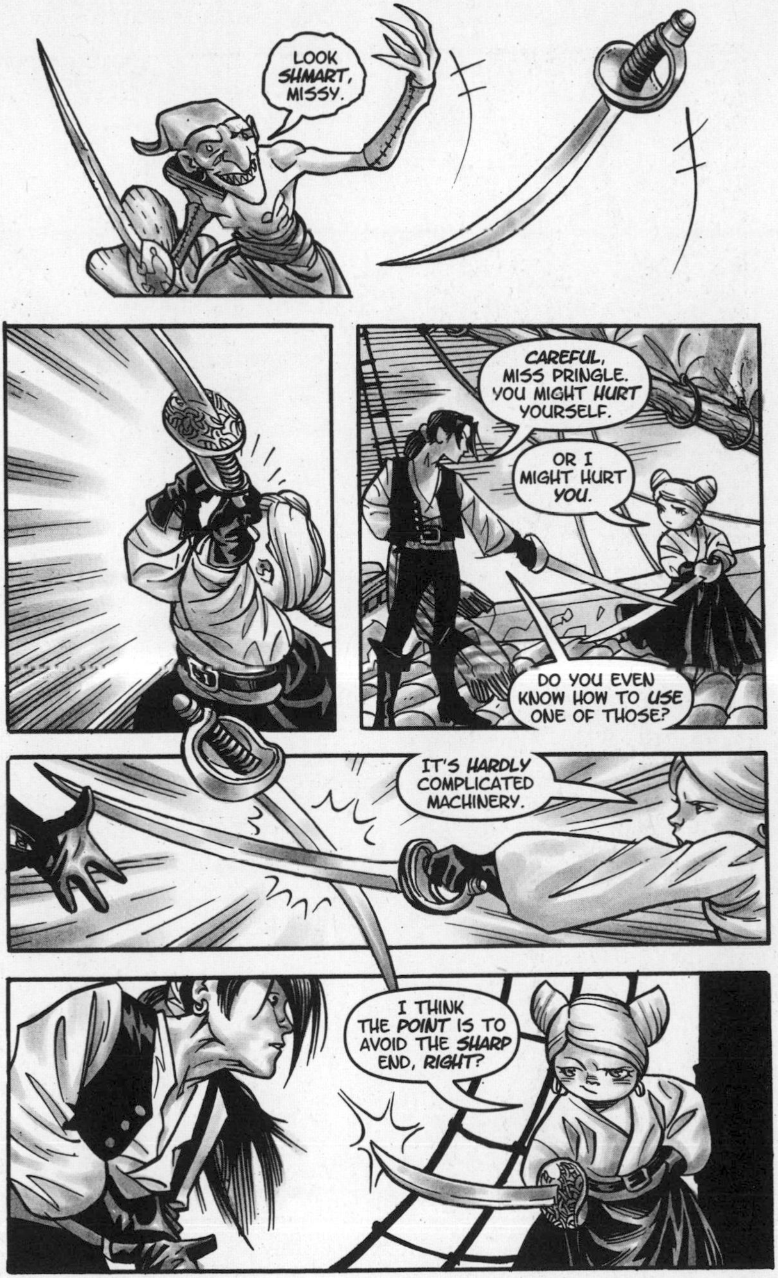
LOOK SHMART, MISSY.
CAREFUL, MISS PRINGLE. YOU MIGHT HURT YOURSELF.
OR I MIGHT HURT YOU.
DO YOU EVEN KNOW HOW TO USE ONE OF THOSE?
IT'S HARDLY COMPLICATED MACHINERY.
I THINK THE POINT IS TO AVOID THE SHARP END, RIGHT?

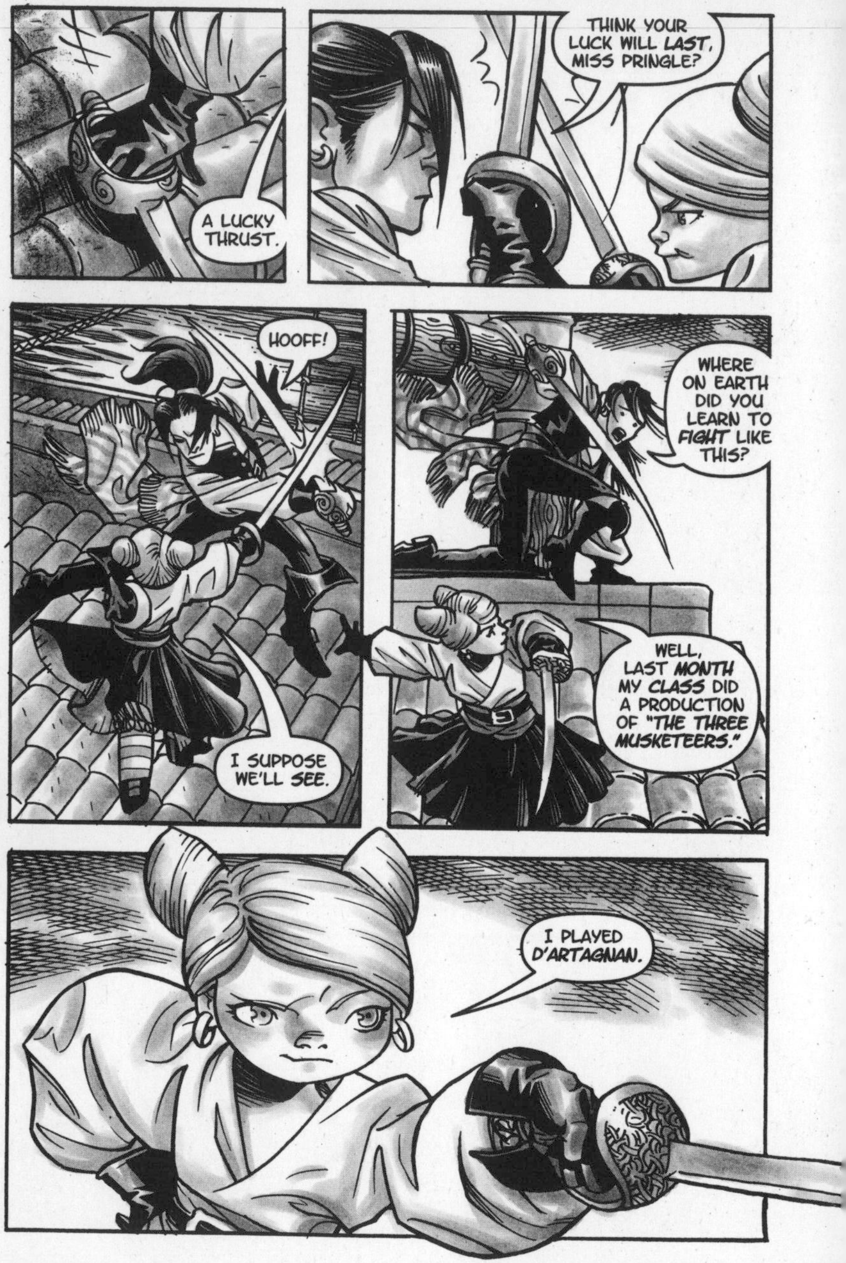
A LUCKY THRUST.
THINK YOUR LUCK WILL LAST, MISS PRINGLE?
HOOFF!
I SUPPOSE WE'LL SEE.
WHERE ON EARTH DID YOU LEARN TO FIGHT LIKE THIS?
WELL, LAST MONTH MY CLASS DID A PRODUCTION OF "THE THREE MUSKETEERS."
I PLAYED D'ARTAGNAN.

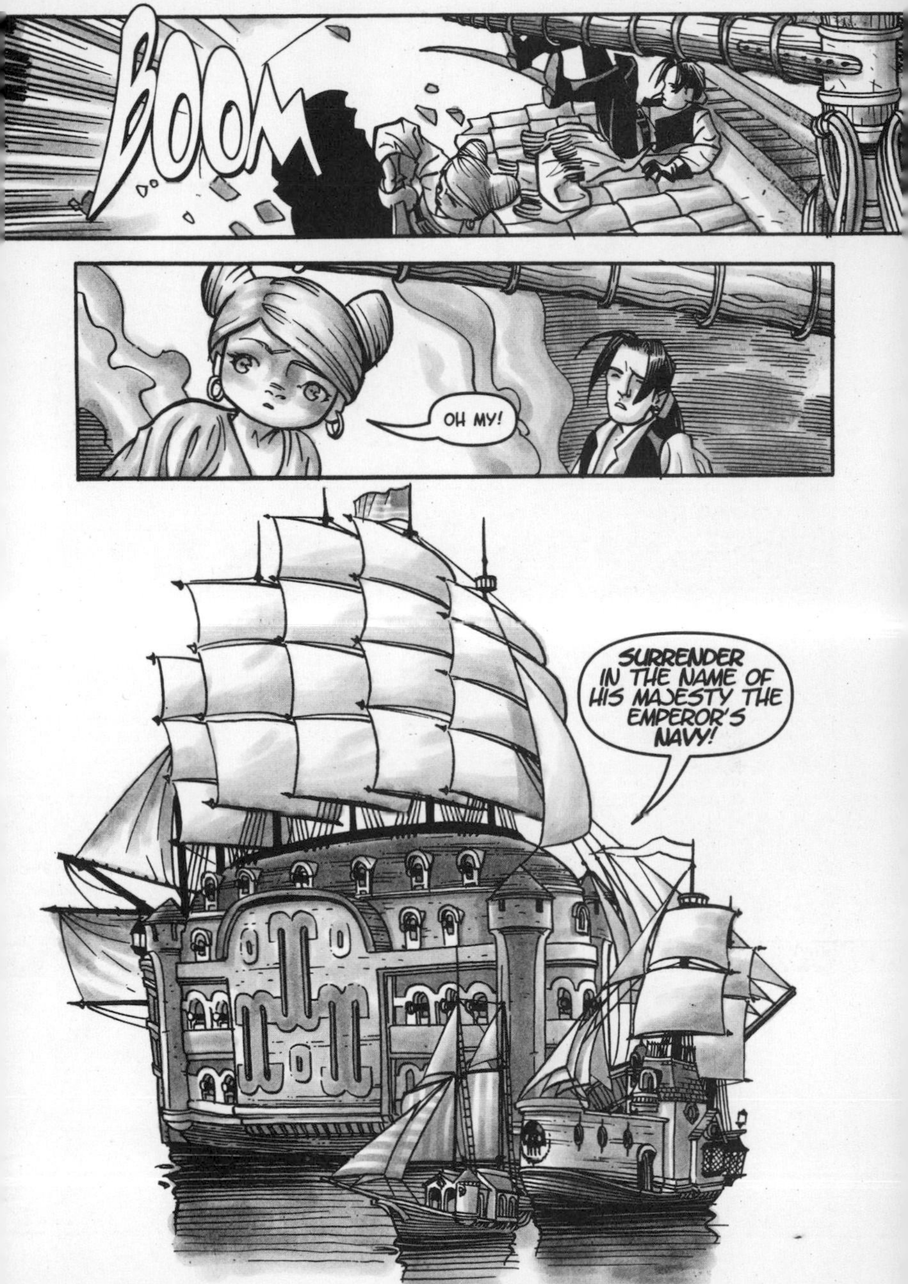
BOOM
OH MY!
SURRENDER IN THE NAME OF HIS MAJESTY THE EMPEROR'S NAVY!

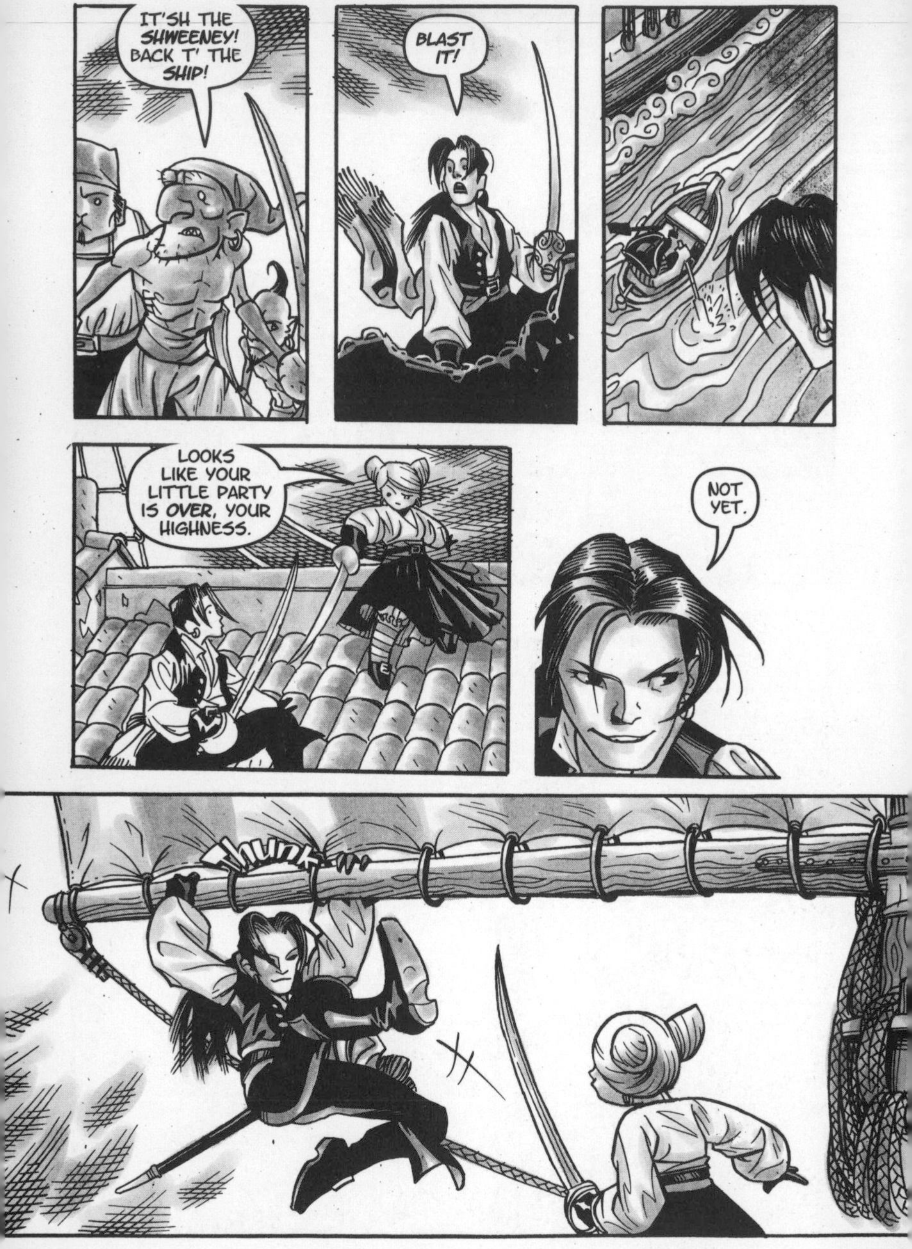
IT'SH THE SHWEENEY! BACK T' THE SHIP!
BLAST IT!
LOOKS LIKE YOUR LITTLE PARTY IS OVER, YOUR HIGHNESS.
NOT YET.
thunk

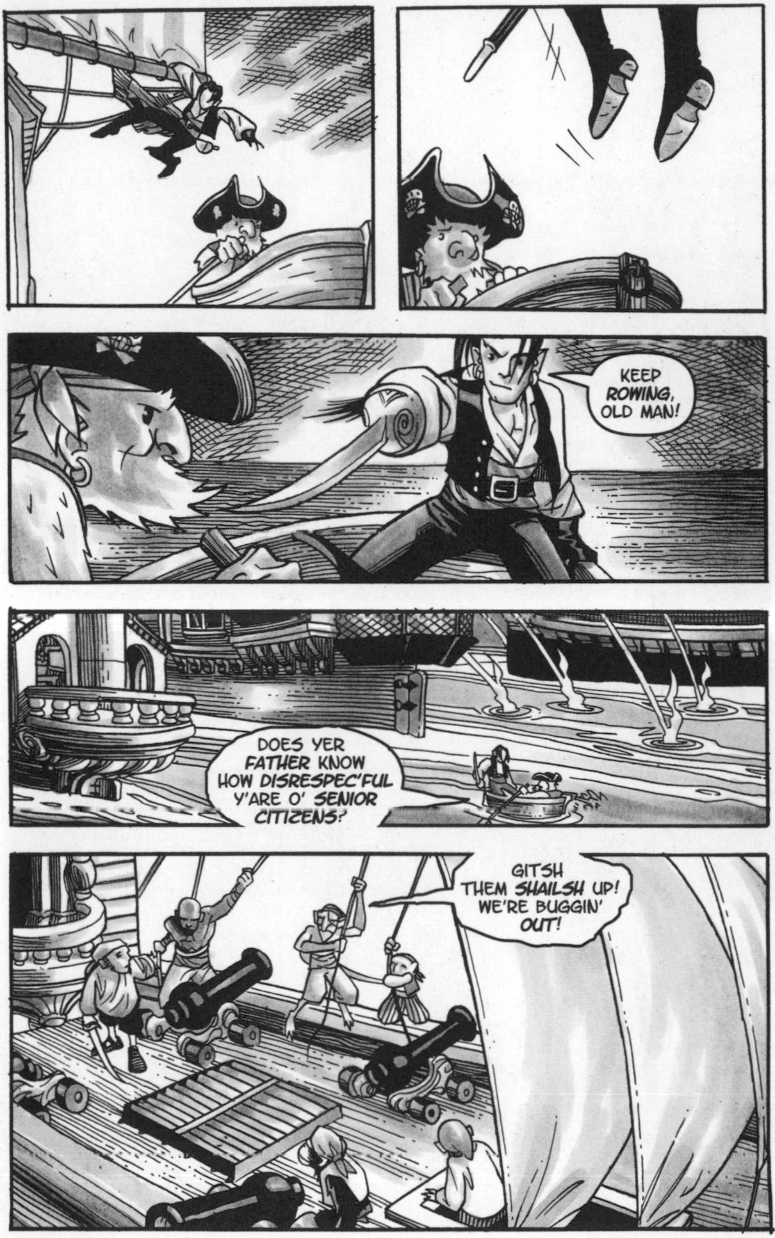
KEEP ROWING, OLD MAN!
DOES YER FATHER KNOW HOW DISRESPEC'FUL Y'ARE O' SENIOR CITIZENS?
GITSH THEM SHAILSH UP! WE'RE BUGGIN' OUT!

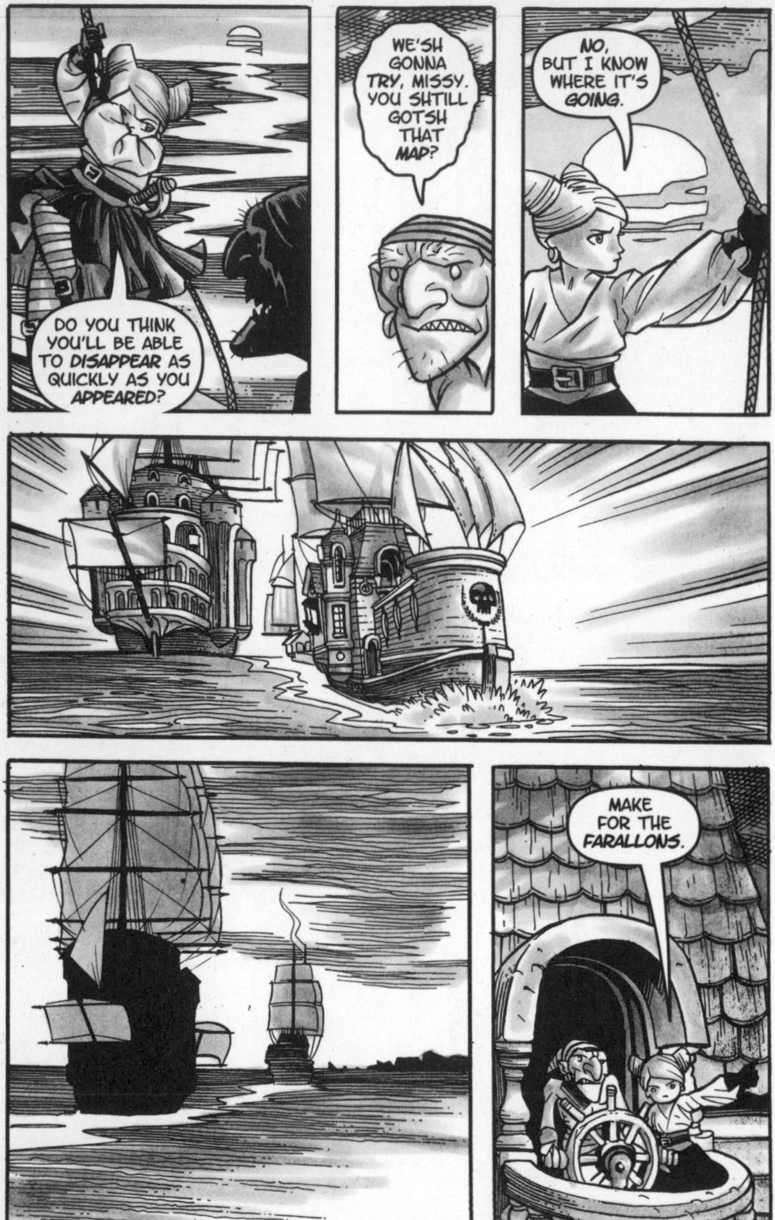
DO YOU THINK YOU'LL BE ABLE TO DISAPPEAR AS QUICKLY AS YOU APPEARED?
WE'SH GONNA TRY, MISSY. YOU SHTILL GOTSH THAT MAP?
NO, BUT I KNOW WHERE IT'S GOING.
MAKE FOR THE FARALLONS.

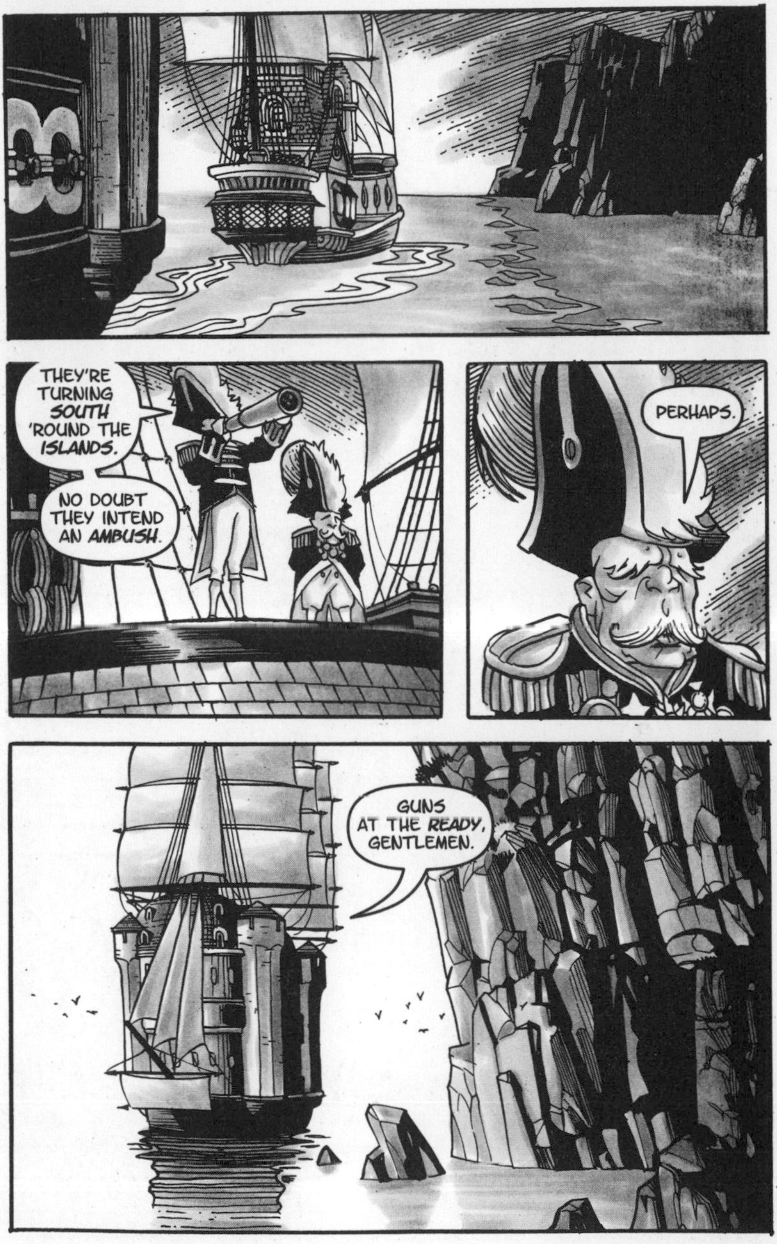
THEY'RE TURNING SOUTH 'ROUND THE ISLANDS.
NO DOUBT THEY INTEND AN AMBUSH.
PERHAPS.
GUNS AT THE READY, GENTLEMEN.

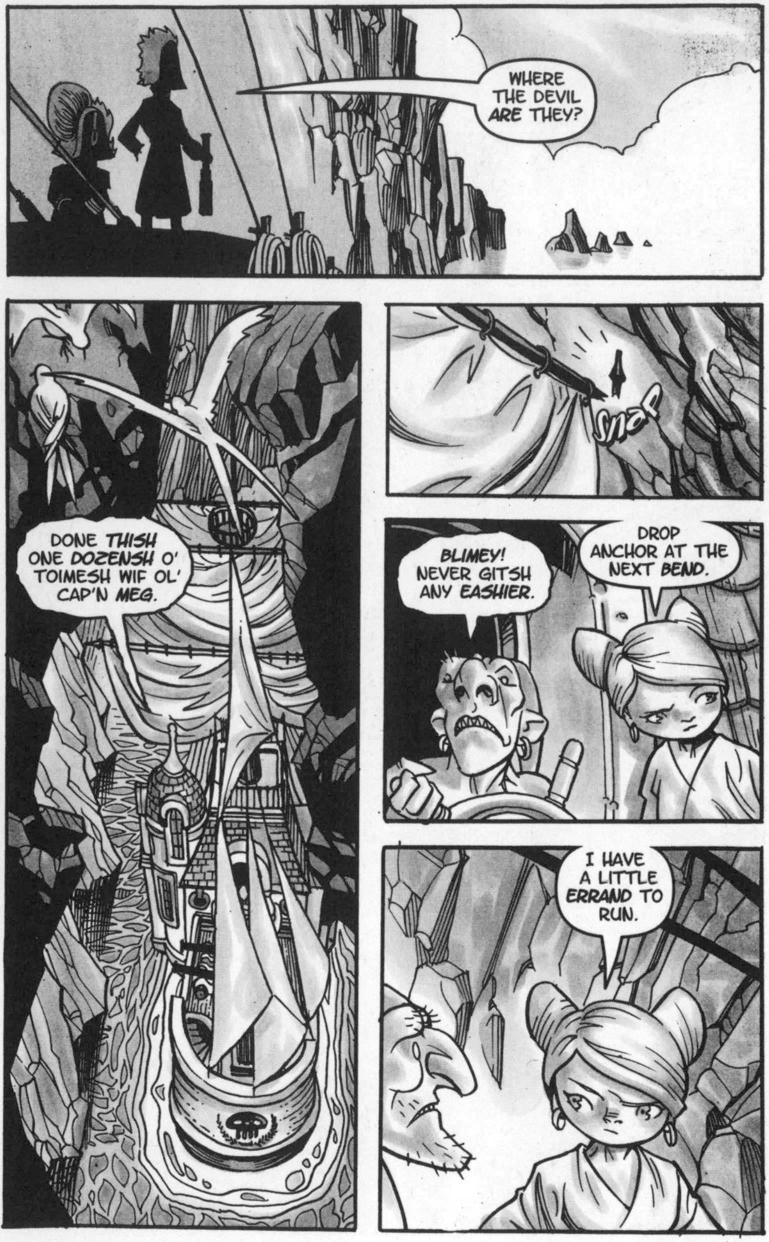
WHERE THE DEVIL ARE THEY?
DONE THISH ONE DOZENSH O' TOIMESH WIF OL' CAP'N MEG.
SNAP
DROP ANCHOR AT THE NEXT BEND.
BLIMEY! NEVER GITSH ANY EASHIER.
I HAVE A LITTLE ERRAND TO RUN.

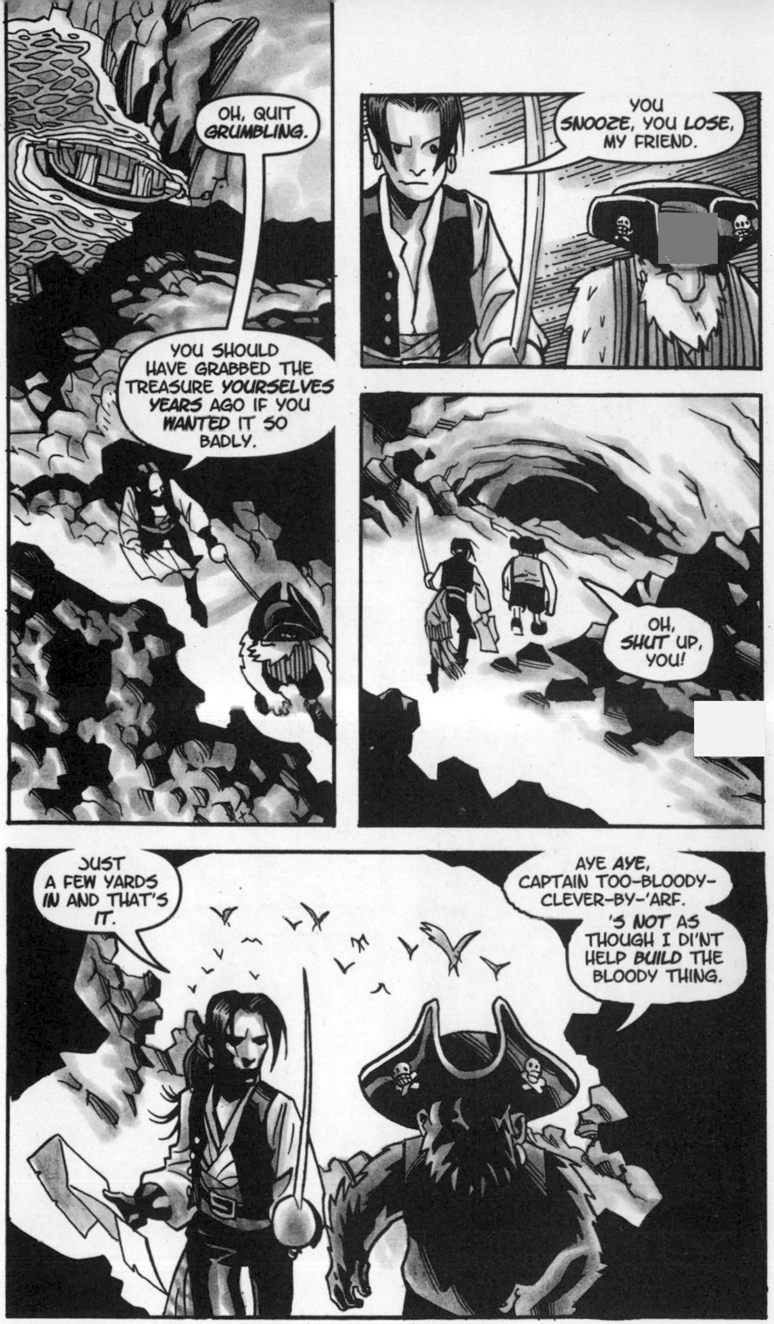
OH, QUIT GRUMBLING.
YOU SHOULD HAVE GRABBED THE TREASURE YOURSELVES YEARS AGO IF YOU WANTED IT SO BADLY.
YOU SNOOZE, YOU LOSE, MY FRIEND.
OH, SHUT UP, YOU!
JUST A FEW YARDS IN AND THAT'S IT.
AYE AYE, CAPTAIN TOO-BLOODY-CLEVER-BY-'ARF.
'S NOT AS THOUGH I DI'NT HELP BUILD THE BLOODY THING.

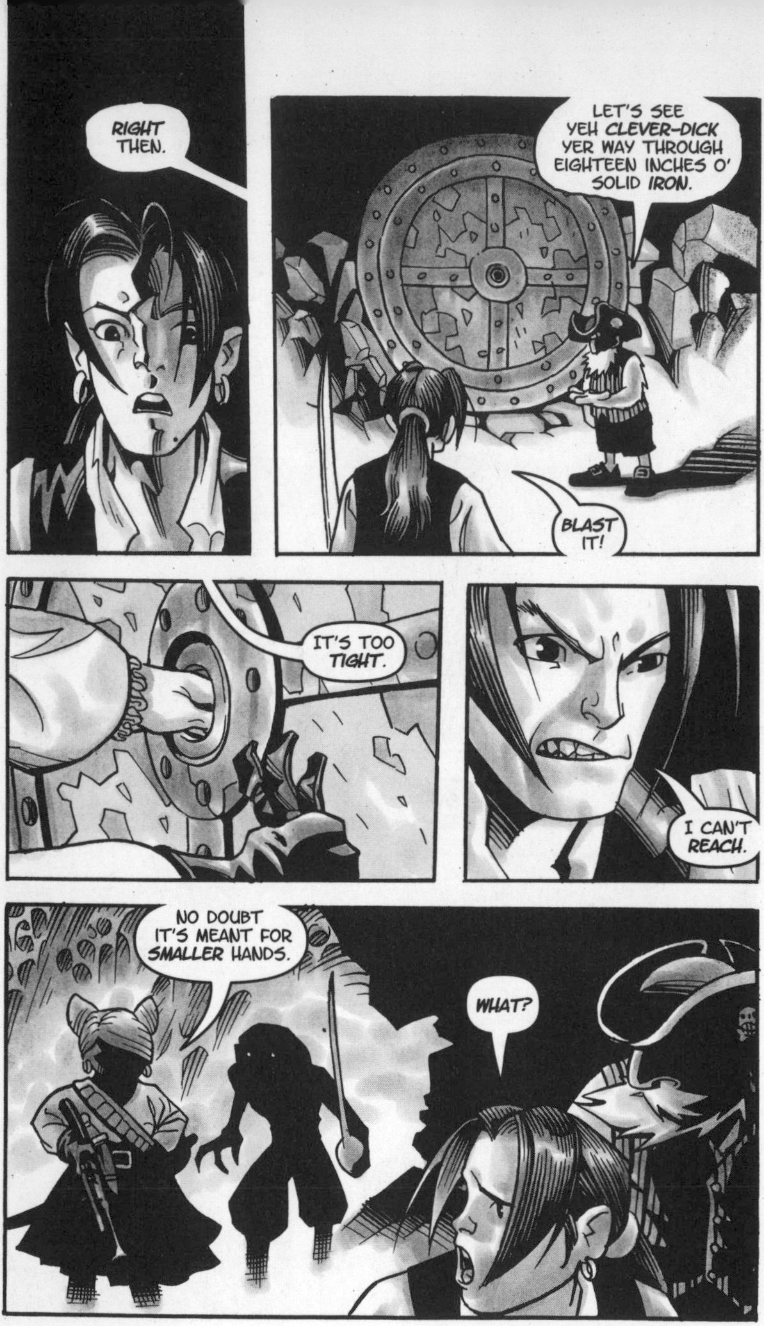
RIGHT THEN.
LET'S SEE YEH CLEVER-DICK YER WAY THROUGH EIGHTEEN INCHES O' SOLID IRON.
BLAST IT!
IT'S TOO TIGHT.
I CAN'T REACH.
NO DOUBT IT'S MEANT FOR SMALLER HANDS.
WHAT?

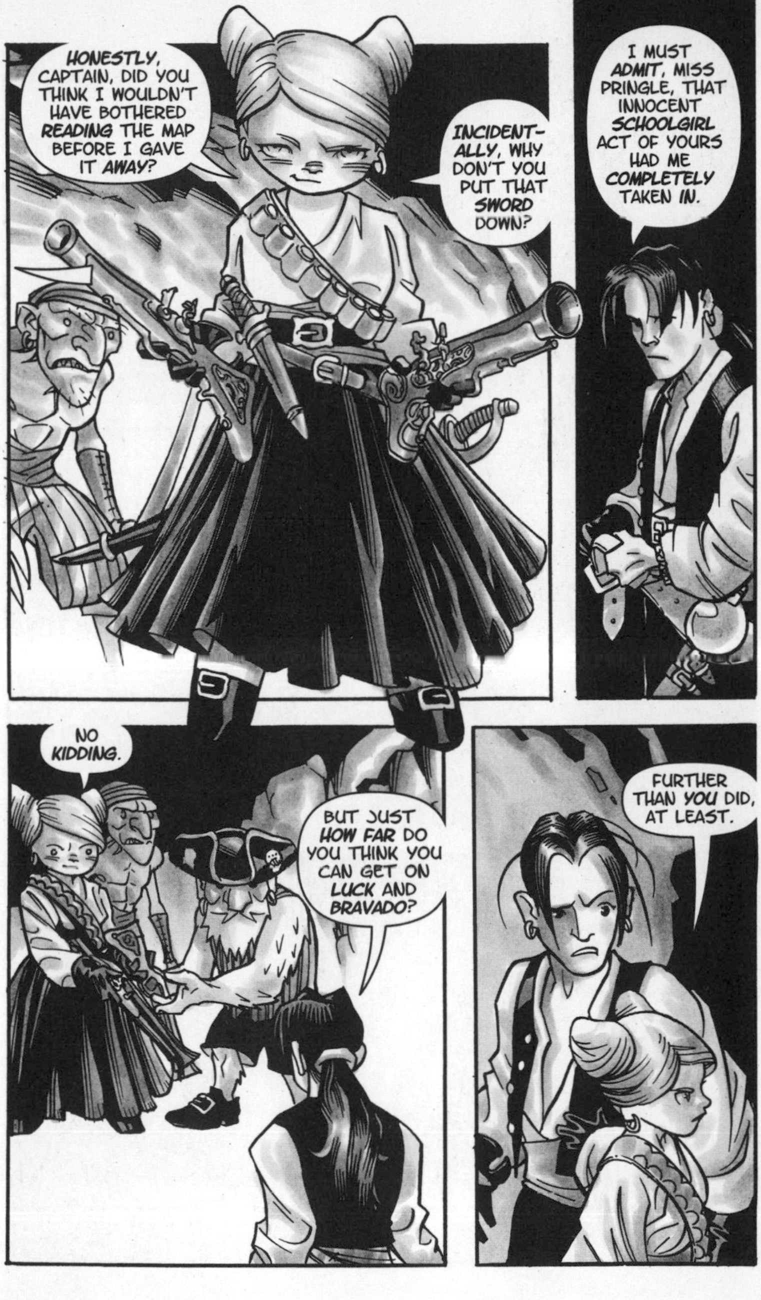
HONESTLY, CAPTAIN, DID YOU THINK I WOULDN'T HAVE BOTHERED READING THE MAP BEFORE I GAVE IT AWAY?
INCIDENT-ALLY, WHY DON'T YOU PUT THAT SWORD DOWN?
I MUST ADMIT, MISS PRINGLE, THAT INNOCENT SCHOOLGIRL ACT OF YOURS HAD ME COMPLETELY TAKEN IN.
NO KIDDING.
BUT JUST HOW FAR DO YOU THINK YOU CAN GET ON LUCK AND BRAVADO?
FURTHER THAN YOU DID, AT LEAST.

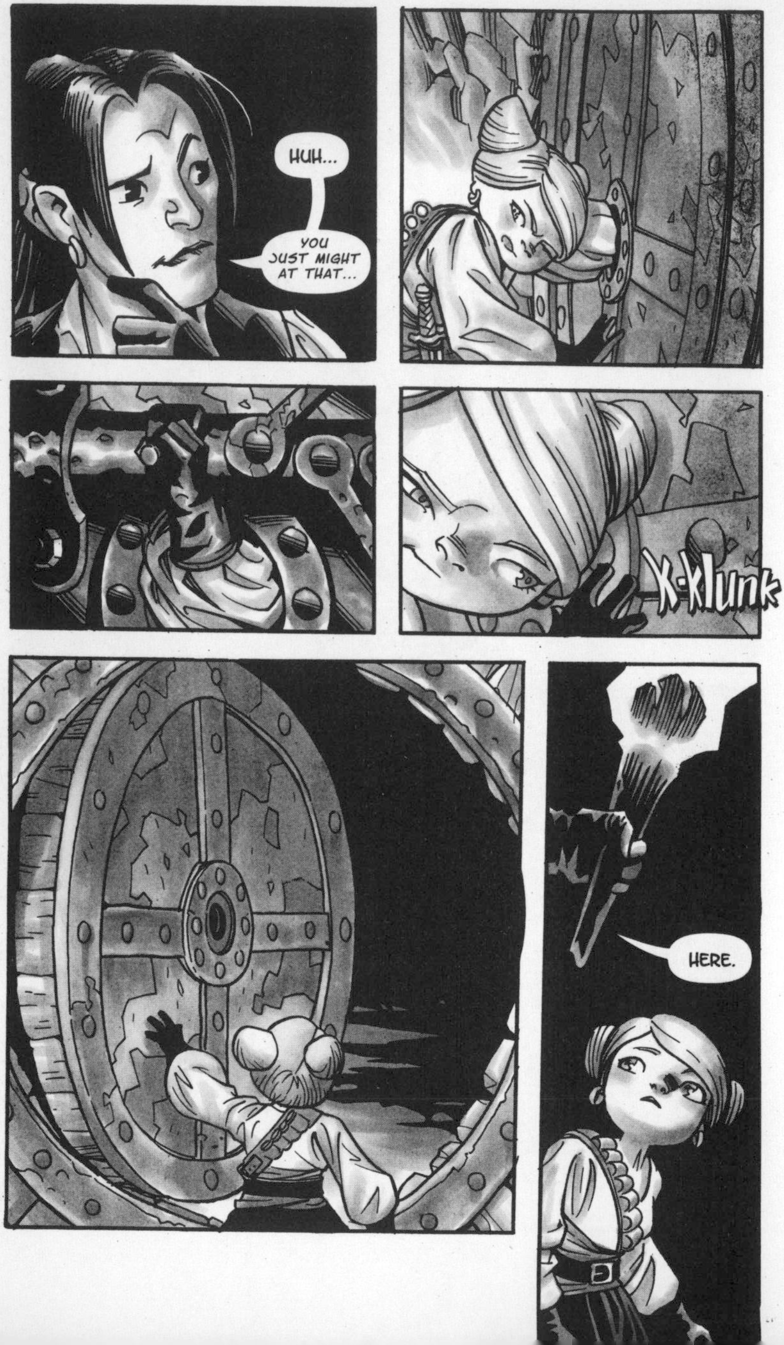
HUH...
YOU JUST MIGHT AT THAT...
K-KLUNK
HERE.

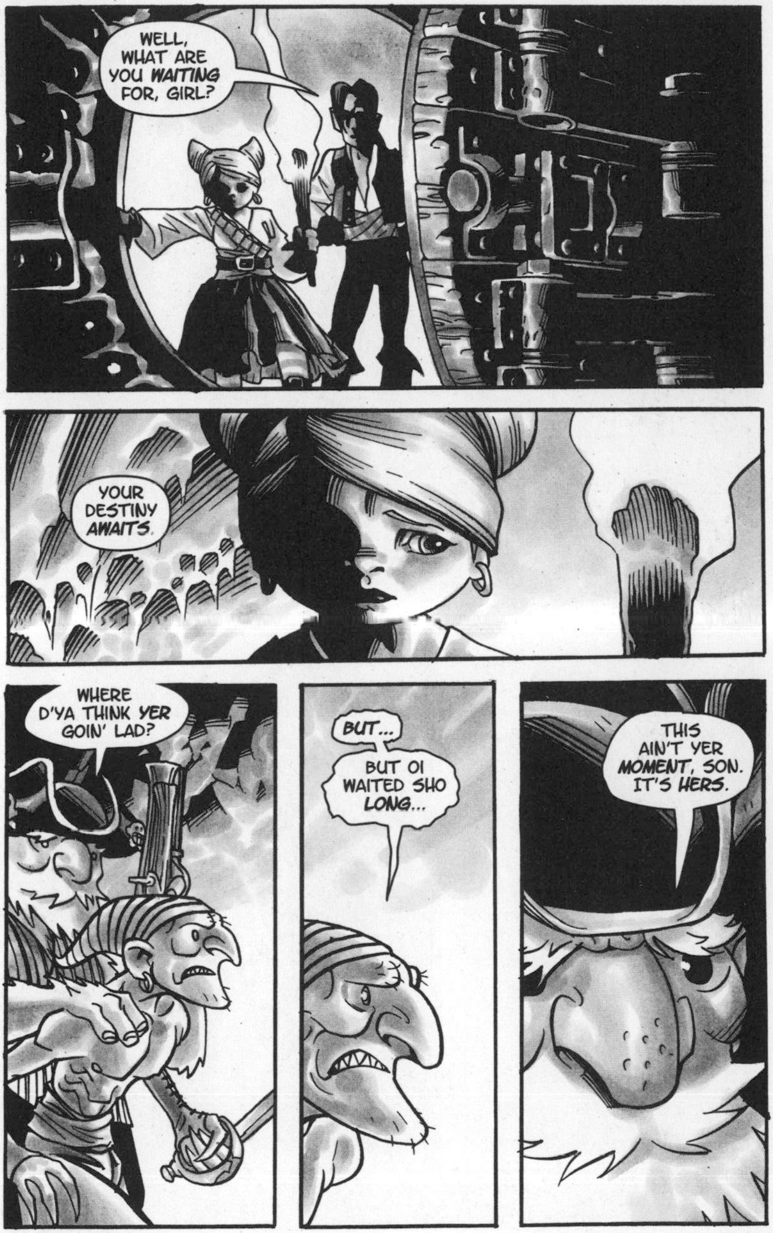
WELL, WHAT ARE YOU WAITING FOR, GIRL?
YOUR DESTINY AWAITS.
WHERE D'YA THINK YER GOIN' LAD?
BUT...
BUT OI WAITED SHO LONG...
THIS AIN'T YER MOMENT, SON. IT'S HERS.

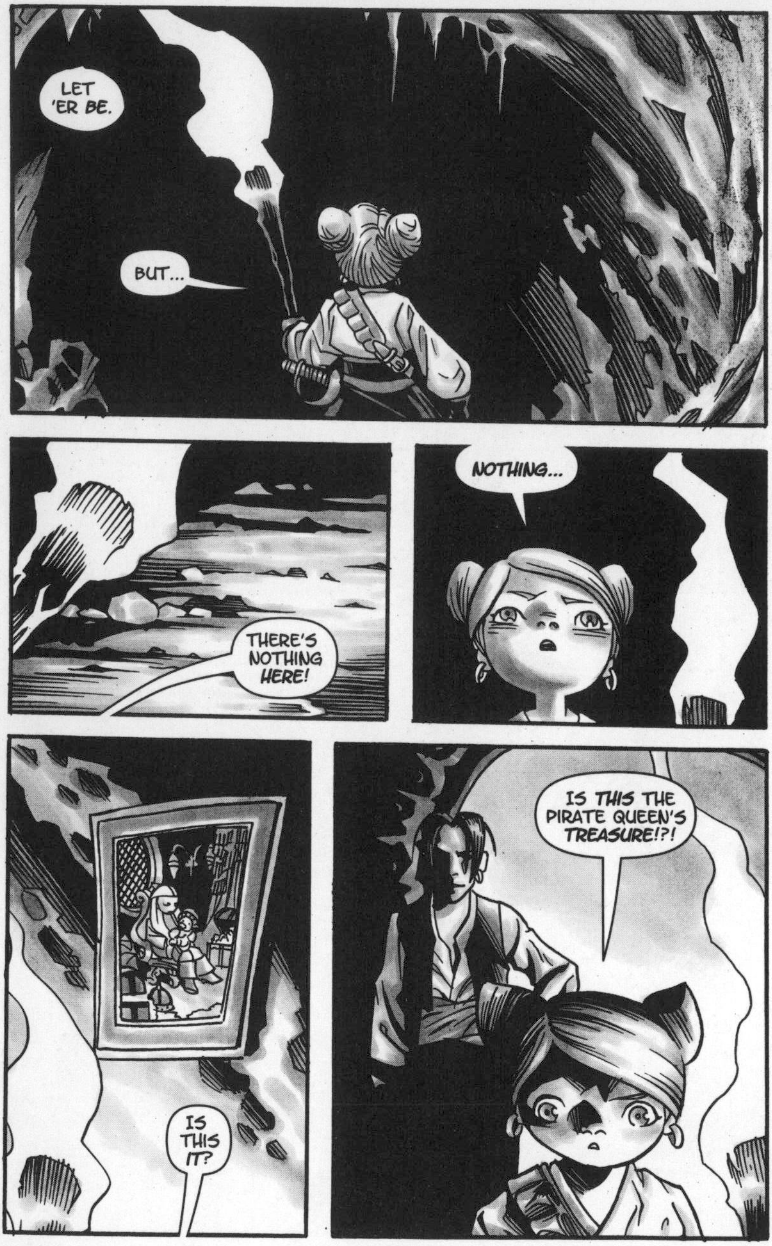
LET 'ER BE.
BUT...
THERE'S NOTHING HERE!
NOTHING...
IS THIS IT?
IS THIS THE PIRATE QUEEN'S TREASURE!?!

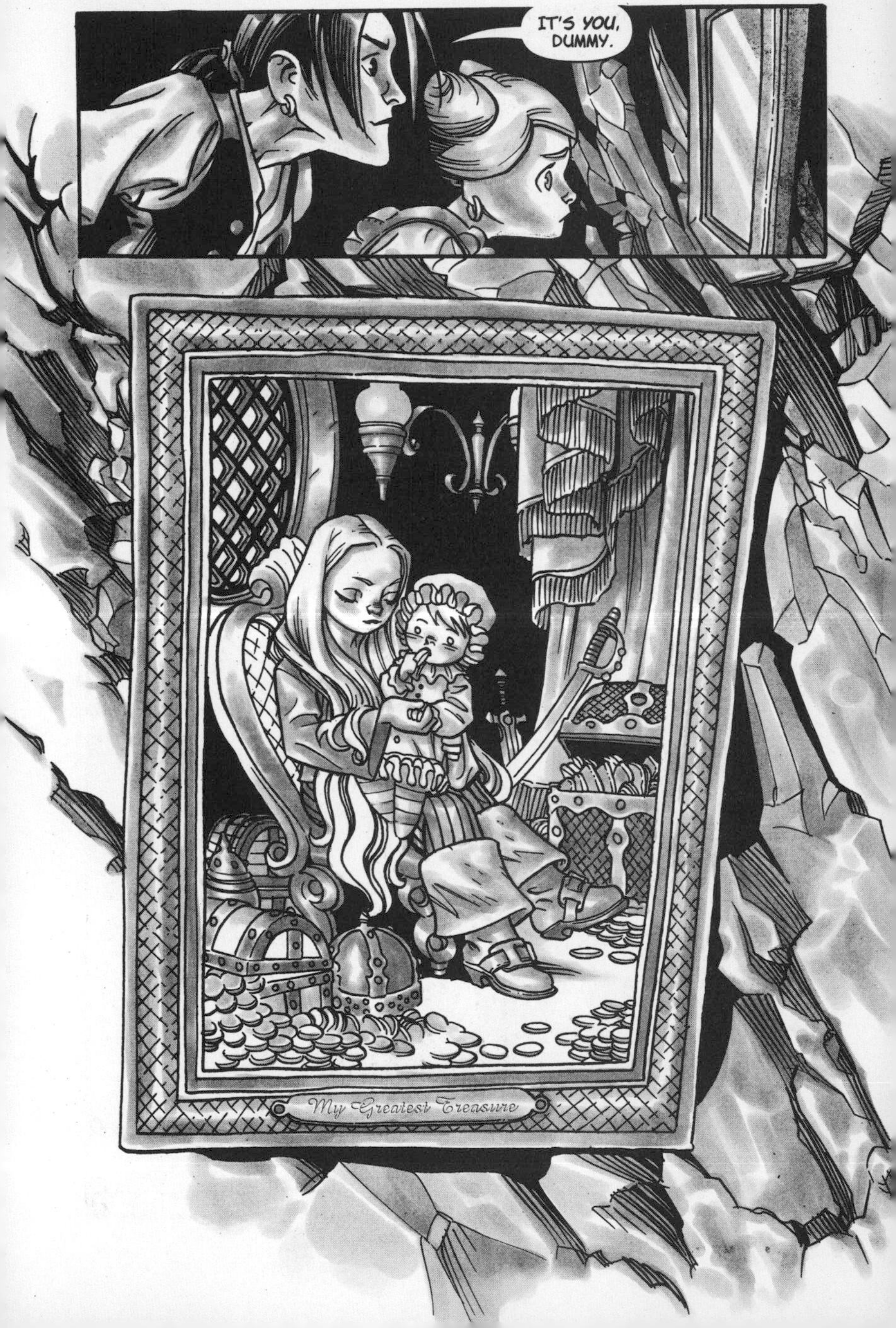
IT'S YOU, DUMMY.
My Greatest Treasure

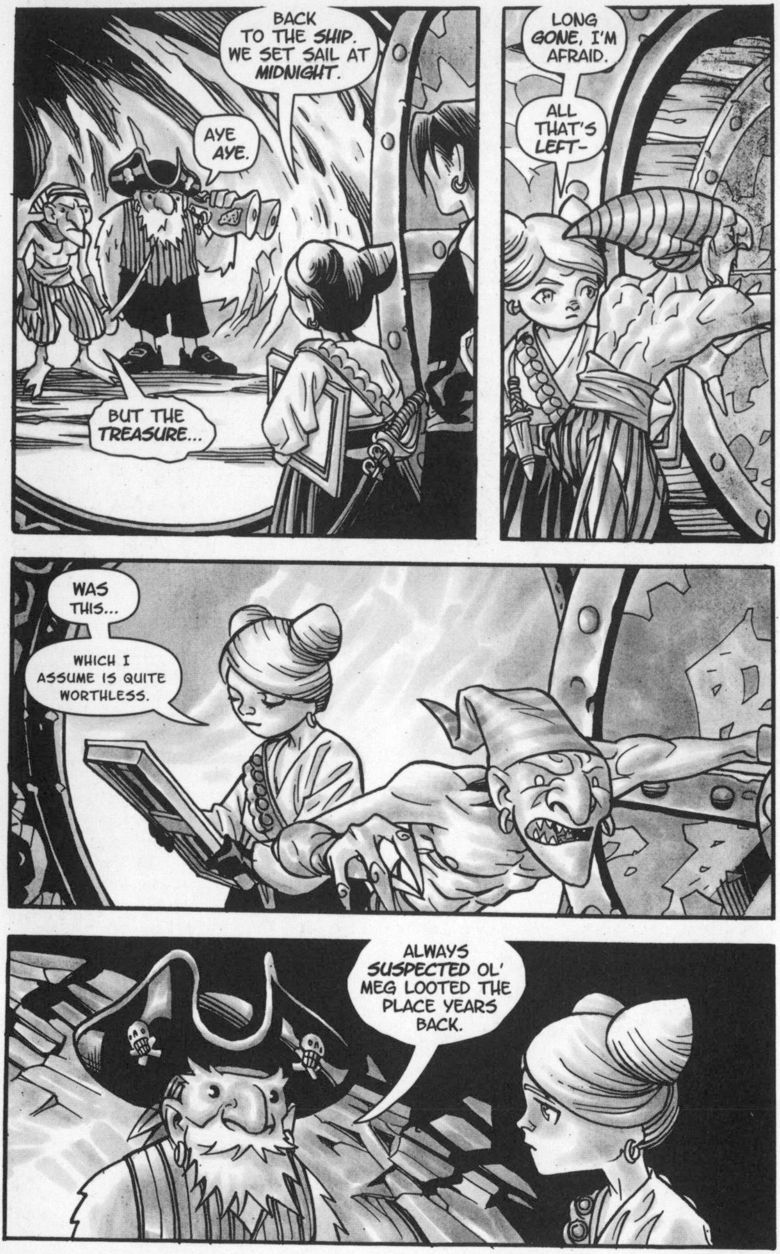
BACK TO THE SHIP. WE SET SAIL AT MIDNIGHT.
AYE AYE.
BUT THE TREASURE...
LONG GONE, I'M AFRAID.
ALL THAT'S LEFT-
WAS THIS...
WHICH I ASSUME IS QUITE WORTHLESS.
ALWAYS SUSPECTED OL' MEG LOOTED THE PLACE YEARS BACK.

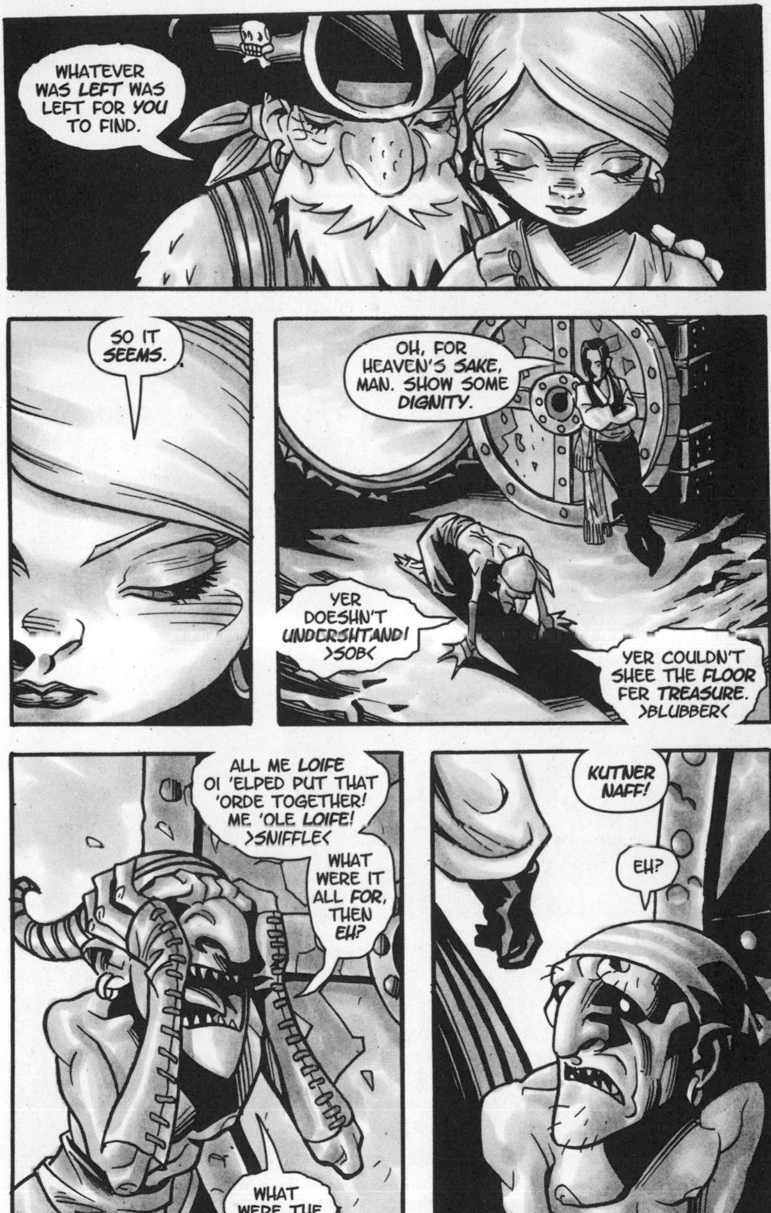
WHATEVER WAS LEFT WAS LEFT FOR YOU TO FIND.
SO IT SEEMS.
OH, FOR HEAVEN'S SAKE, MAN. SHOW SOME DIGNITY.
YER DOESHN'T UNDERSHTAND! >SOB<
YER COULDN'T SHEE THE FLOOR FER TREASURE. >BLUBBER<
ALL ME LOIFE OI 'ELPED PUT THAT 'ORDE TOGETHER! ME 'OLE LOIFE! >SNIFFLE<
WHAT WERE IT ALL FOR, THEN EH?
WHAT WERE THE POINT!?!
KUTNER NAFF!
EH?

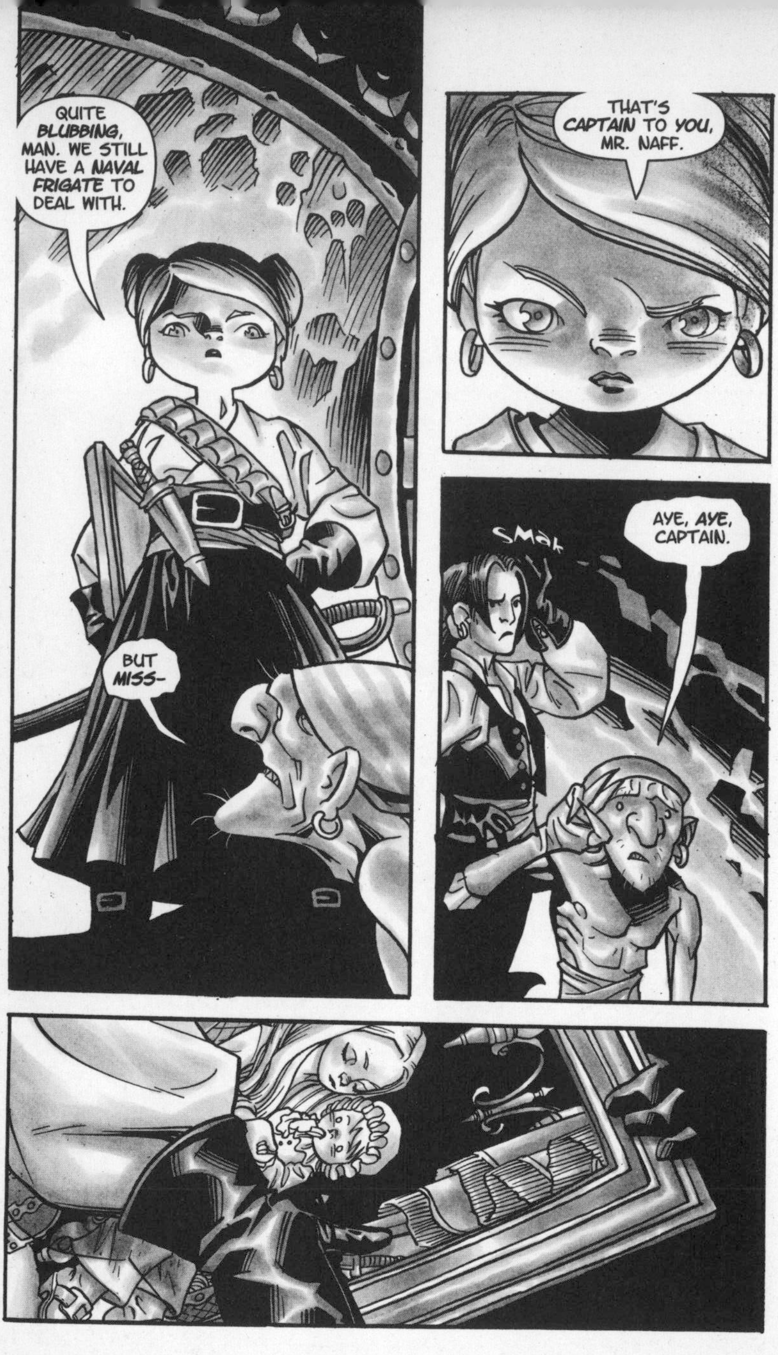
QUITE BLUBBING, MAN. WE STILL HAVE A NAVAL FRIGATE TO DEAL WITH.
BUT MISS-
THAT'S CAPTAIN TO YOU, MR. NAFF.
SMak
AYE, AYE, CAPTAIN.

Chapter 6

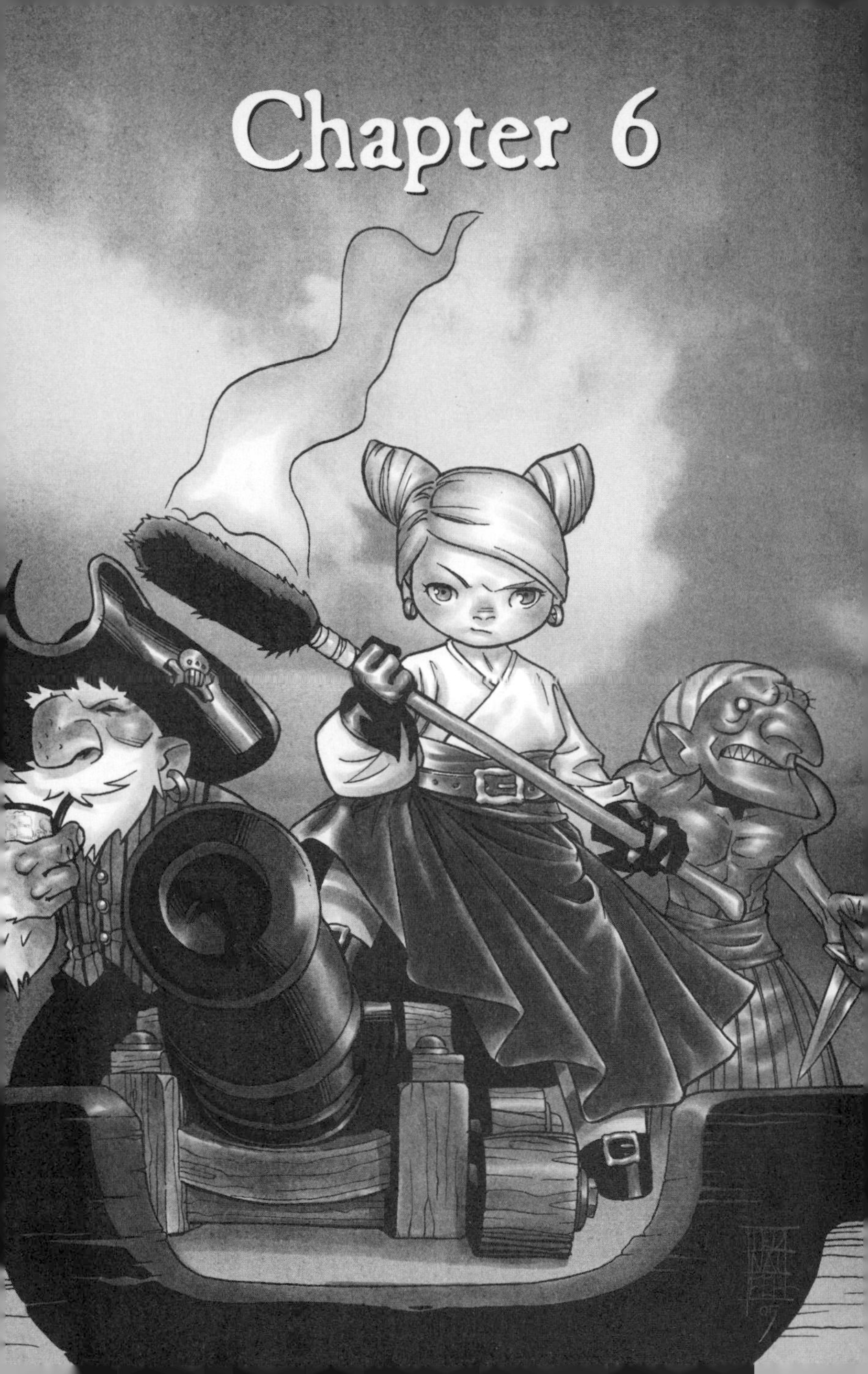

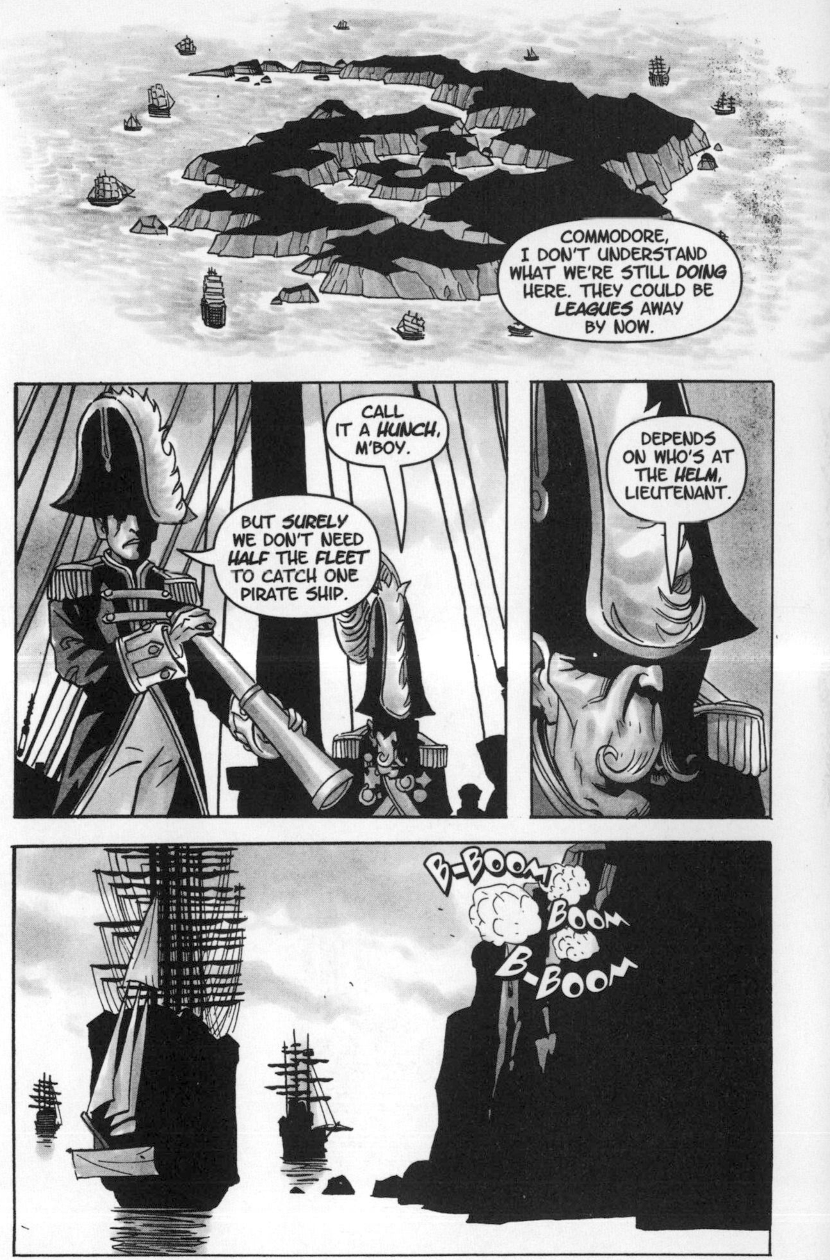
COMMODORE, I DON'T UNDERSTAND WHAT WE'RE STILL DOING HERE. THEY COULD BE LEAGUES AWAY BY NOW.
CALL IT A HUNCH, M'BOY.
BUT SURELY WE DON'T NEED HALF THE FLEET TO CATCH ONE PIRATE SHIP.
DEPENDS ON WHO'S AT THE HELM, LIEUTENANT.
B-BOOM
BOOM
B-BOOM

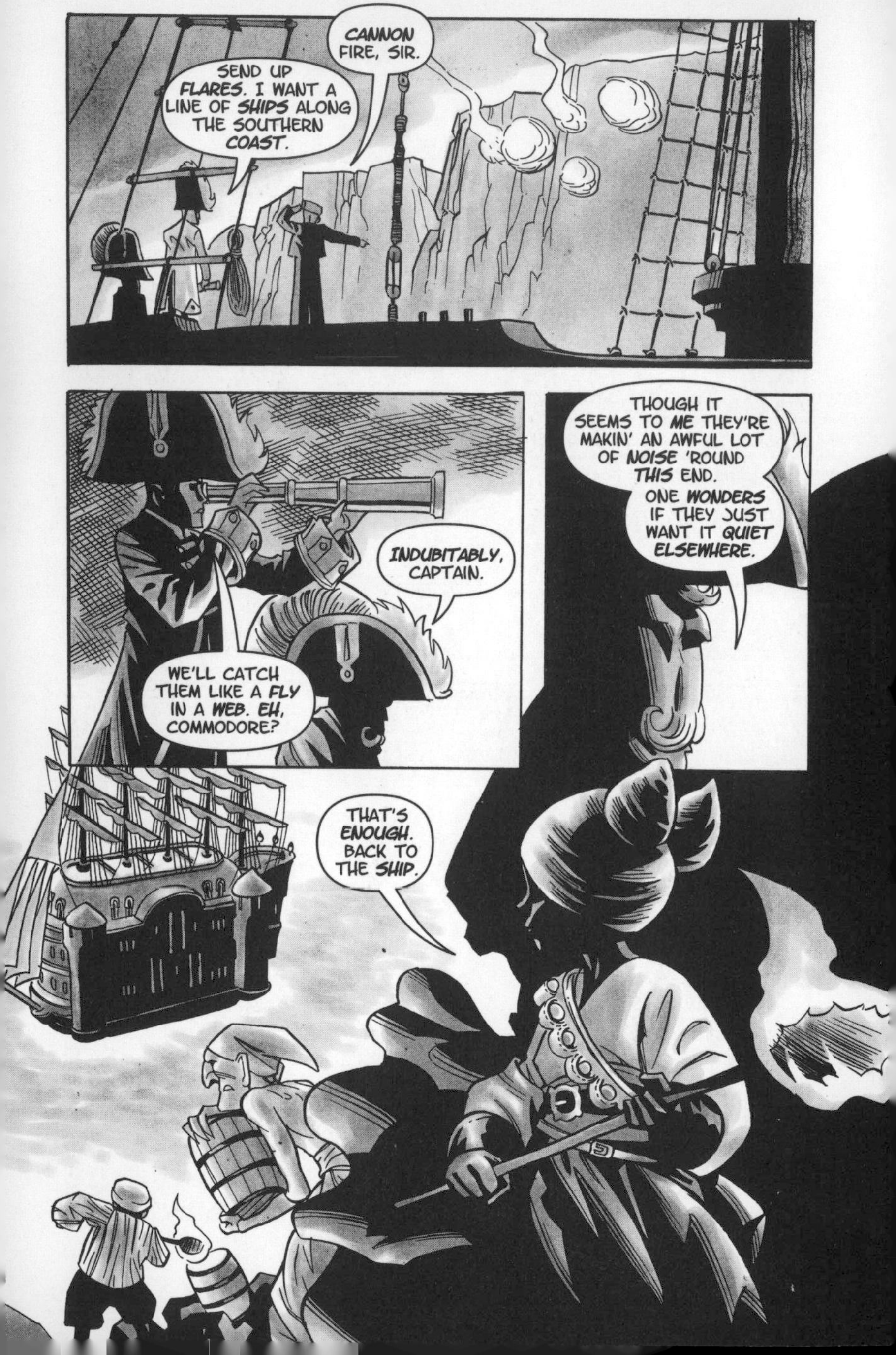
CANNON FIRE, SIR.
SEND UP FLARES. I WANT A LINE OF SHIPS ALONG THE SOUTHERN COAST.
WE'LL CATCH THEM LIKE A FLY IN A WEB. EH, COMMODORE?
INDUBITABLY, CAPTAIN.
THOUGH IT SEEMS TO ME THEY'RE MAKIN' AN AWFUL LOT OF NOISE 'ROUND THIS END.
ONE WONDERS IF THEY JUST WANT IT QUIET ELSEWHERE.
THAT'S ENOUGH. BACK TO THE SHIP.

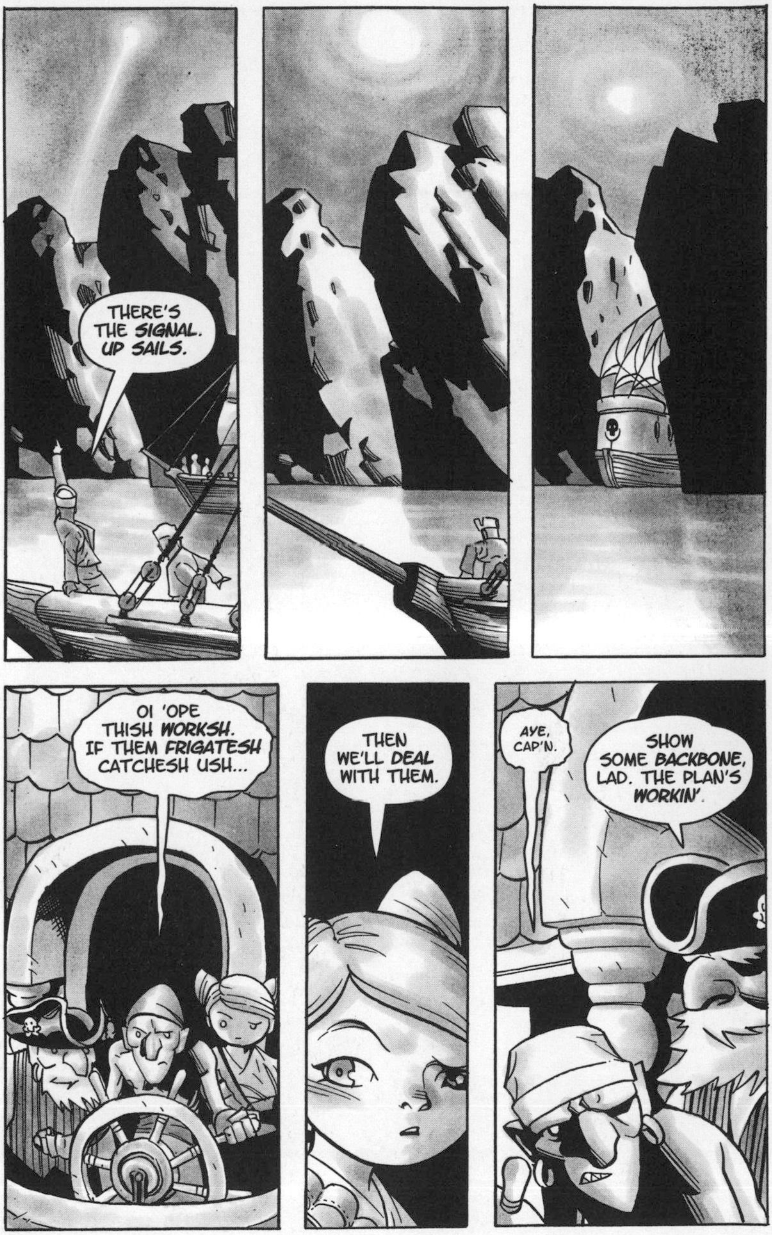
THERE'S THE SIGNAL. UP SAILS.
OI 'OPE THISH WORKSH. IF THEM FRIGATESH CATCHESH USH...
THEN WE'LL DEAL WITH THEM.
AYE, CAP'N.
SHOW SOME BACKBONE, LAD. THE PLAN'S WORKIN'.

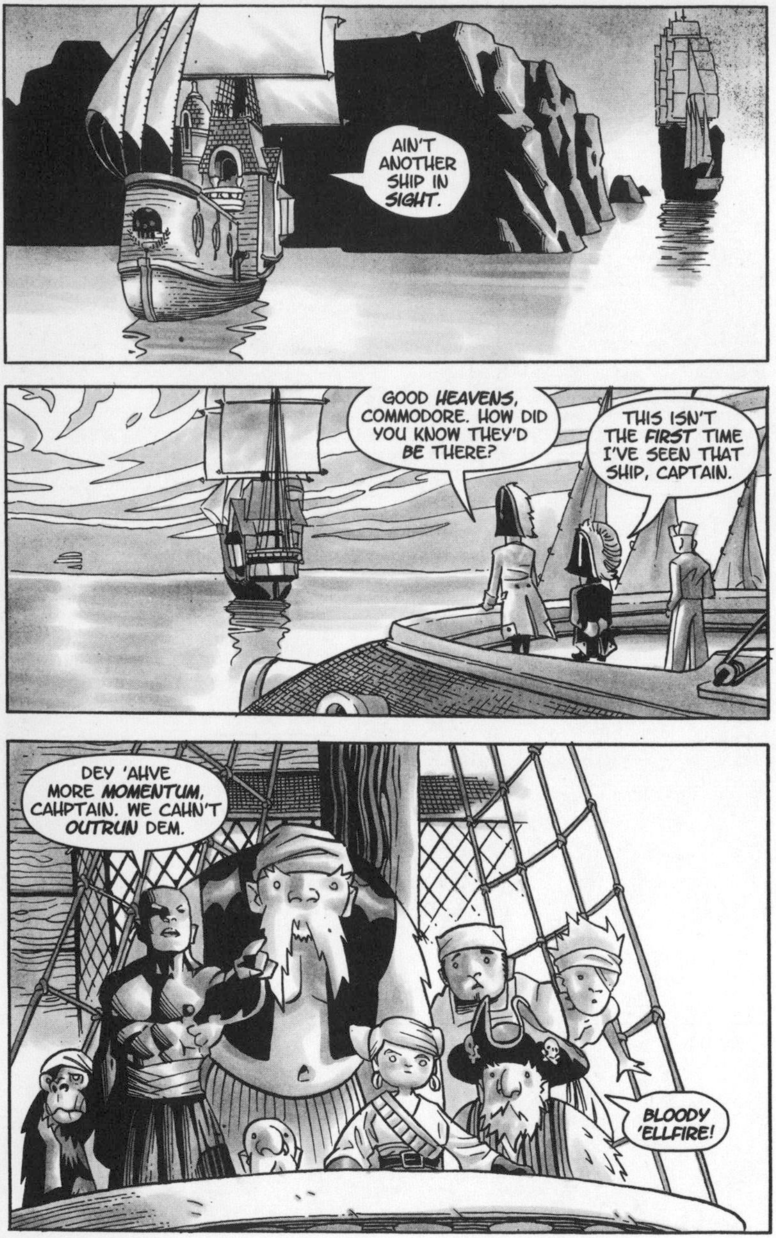
AIN'T ANOTHER SHIP IN SIGHT.
GOOD HEAVENS, COMMODORE. HOW DID YOU KNOW THEY'D BE THERE?
THIS ISN'T THE FIRST TIME I'VE SEEN THAT SHIP, CAPTAIN.
DEY 'AHVE MORE MOMENTUM, CAHPTAIN. WE CAHN'T OUTRUN DEM.
BLOODY 'ELLFIRE!

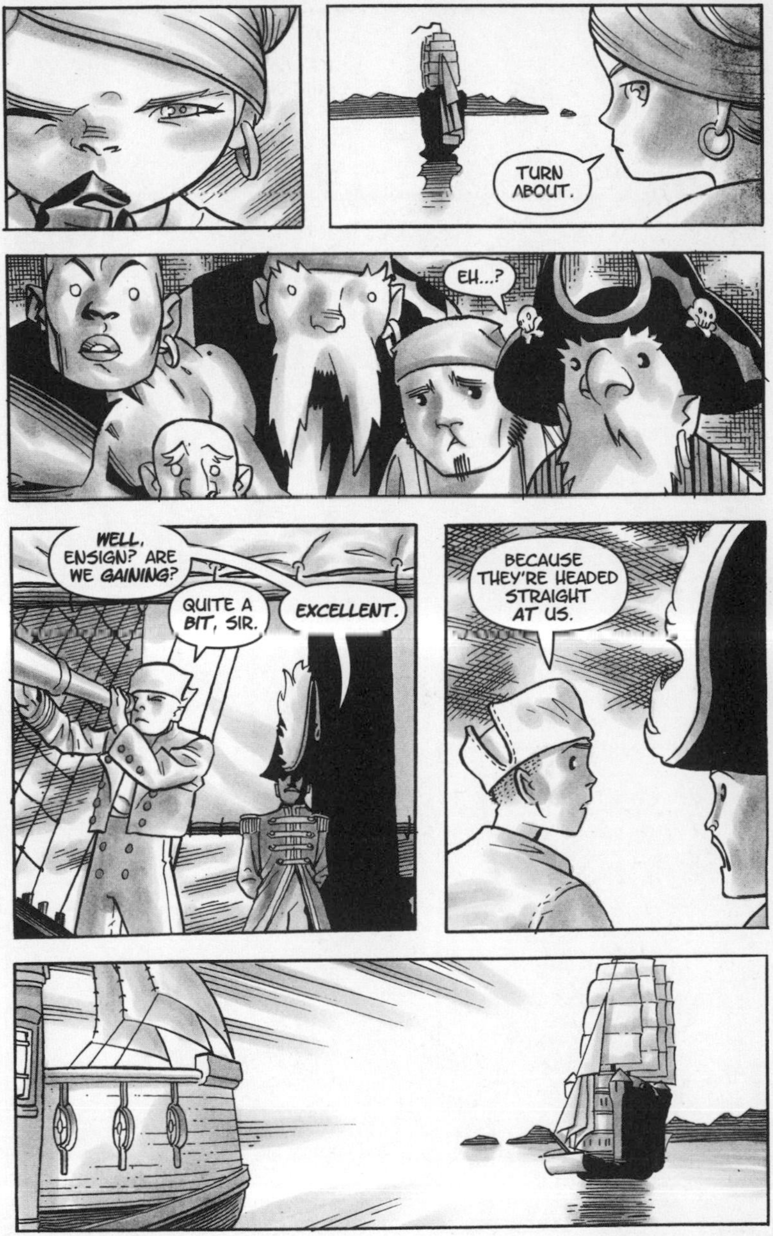
TURN ABOUT.
EH...?
WELL, ENSIGN? ARE WE GAINING?
QUITE A BIT, SIR.
EXCELLENT.
BECAUSE THEY'RE HEADED STRAIGHT AT US.

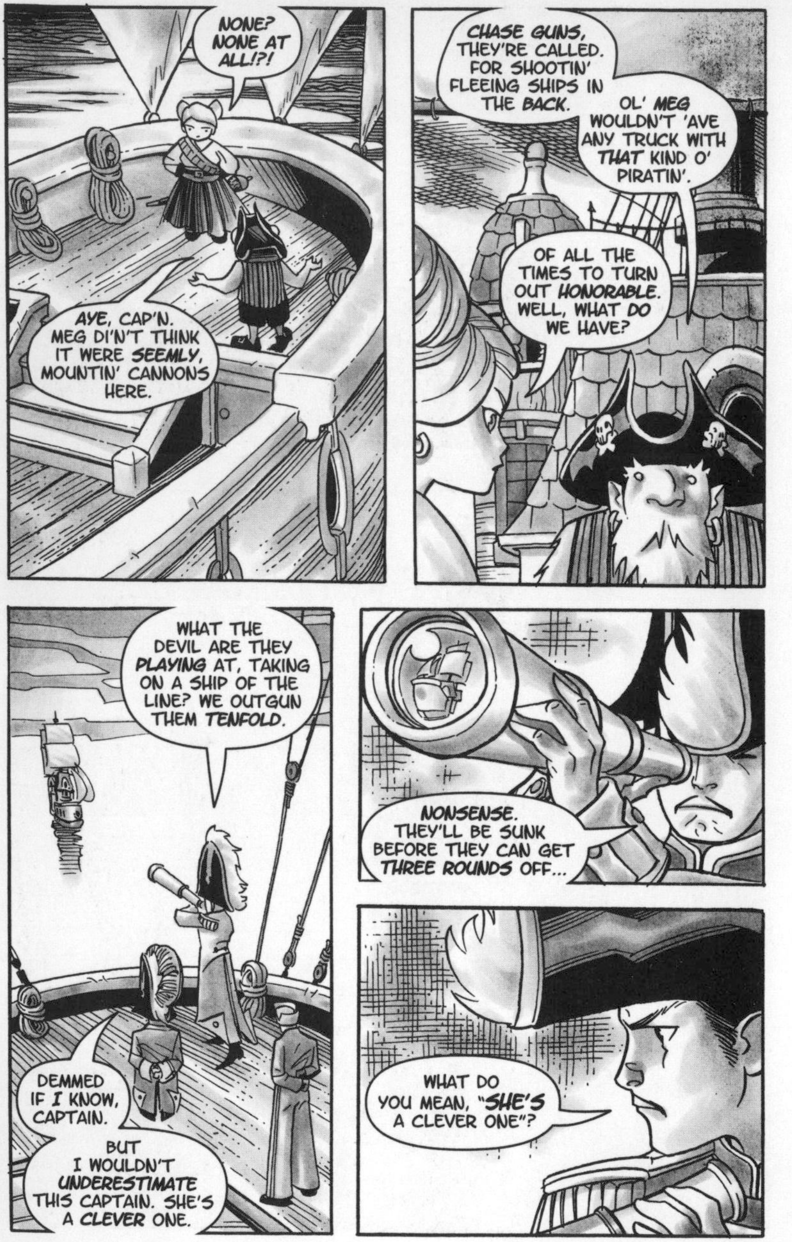
NONE? NONE AT ALL!?!
AYE, CAP'N. MEG DI'N'T THINK IT WERE SEEMLY, MOUNTIN' CANNONS HERE.
CHASE GUNS, THEY'RE CALLED. FOR SHOOTIN' FLEEING SHIPS IN THE BACK.
OL' MEG WOULDN'T 'AVE ANY TRUCK WITH THAT KIND O' PIRATIN'.
OF ALL THE TIMES TO TURN OUT HONORABLE. WELL, WHAT DO WE HAVE?
WHAT THE DEVIL ARE THEY PLAYING AT, TAKING ON A SHIP OF THE LINE? WE OUTGUN THEM TENFOLD.
DEMMED IF I KNOW, CAPTAIN.
BUT I WOULDN'T UNDERESTIMATE THIS CAPTAIN. SHE'S A CLEVER ONE.
NONSENSE. THEY'LL BE SUNK BEFORE THEY CAN GET THREE ROUNDS OFF...
WHAT DO YOU MEAN, "SHE'S A CLEVER ONE"?

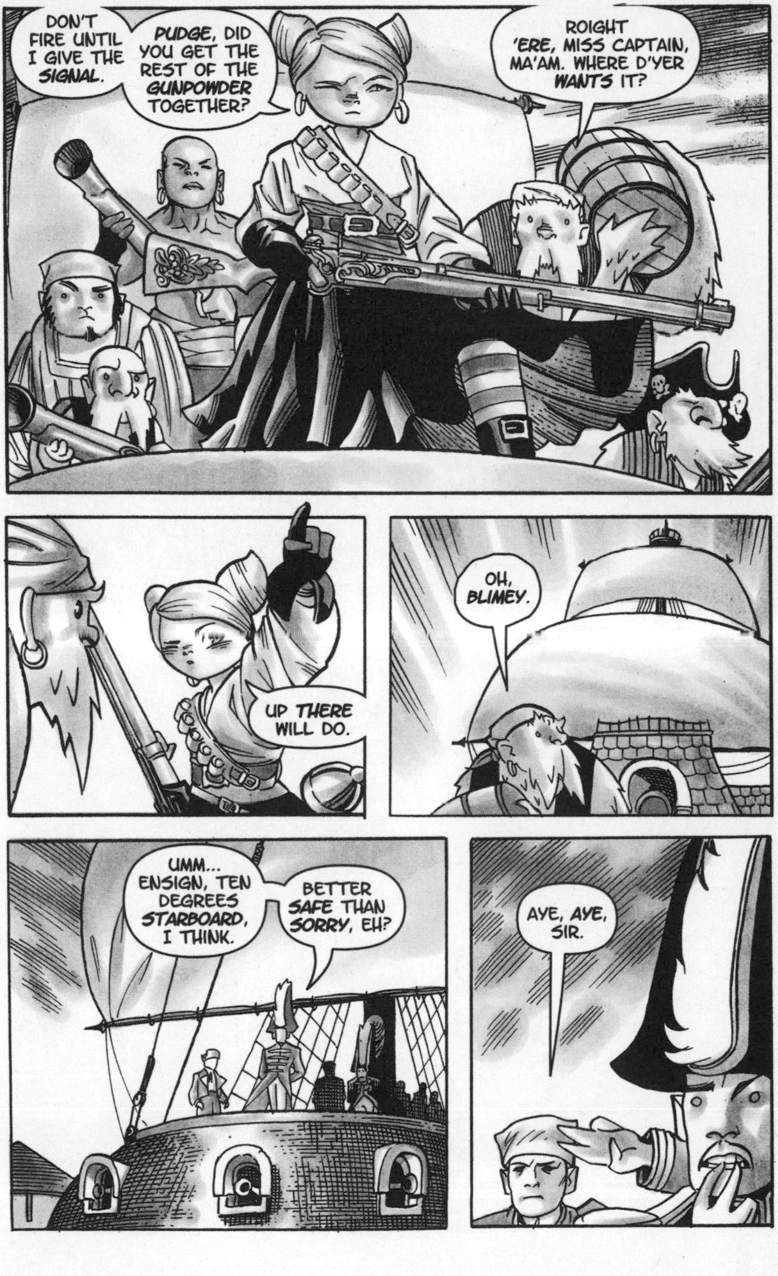
DON'T FIRE UNTIL I GIVE THE SIGNAL.
PUDGE, DID YOU GET THE REST OF THE GUNPOWDER TOGETHER?
ROIGHT 'ERE, MISS CAPTAIN, MA'AM. WHERE D'YER WANTS IT?
UP THERE WILL DO.
OH, BLIMEY.
UMM... ENSIGN, TEN DEGREES STARBOARD, I THINK.
BETTER SAFE THAN SORRY, EH?
AYE, AYE, SIR.

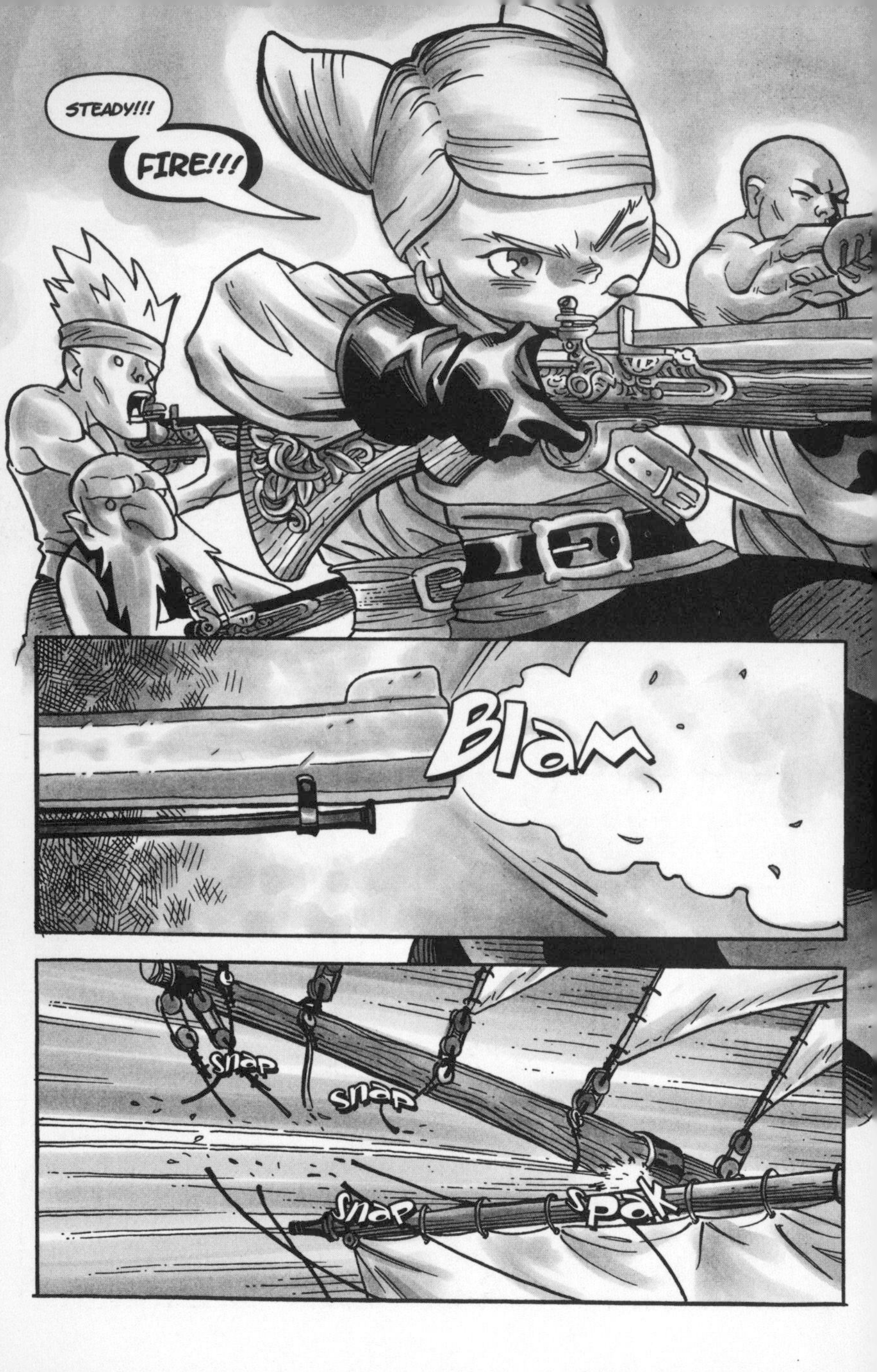
STEADY!!!
FIRE!!!
BLAM
SNAP
SNAP
SNAP
SPAK

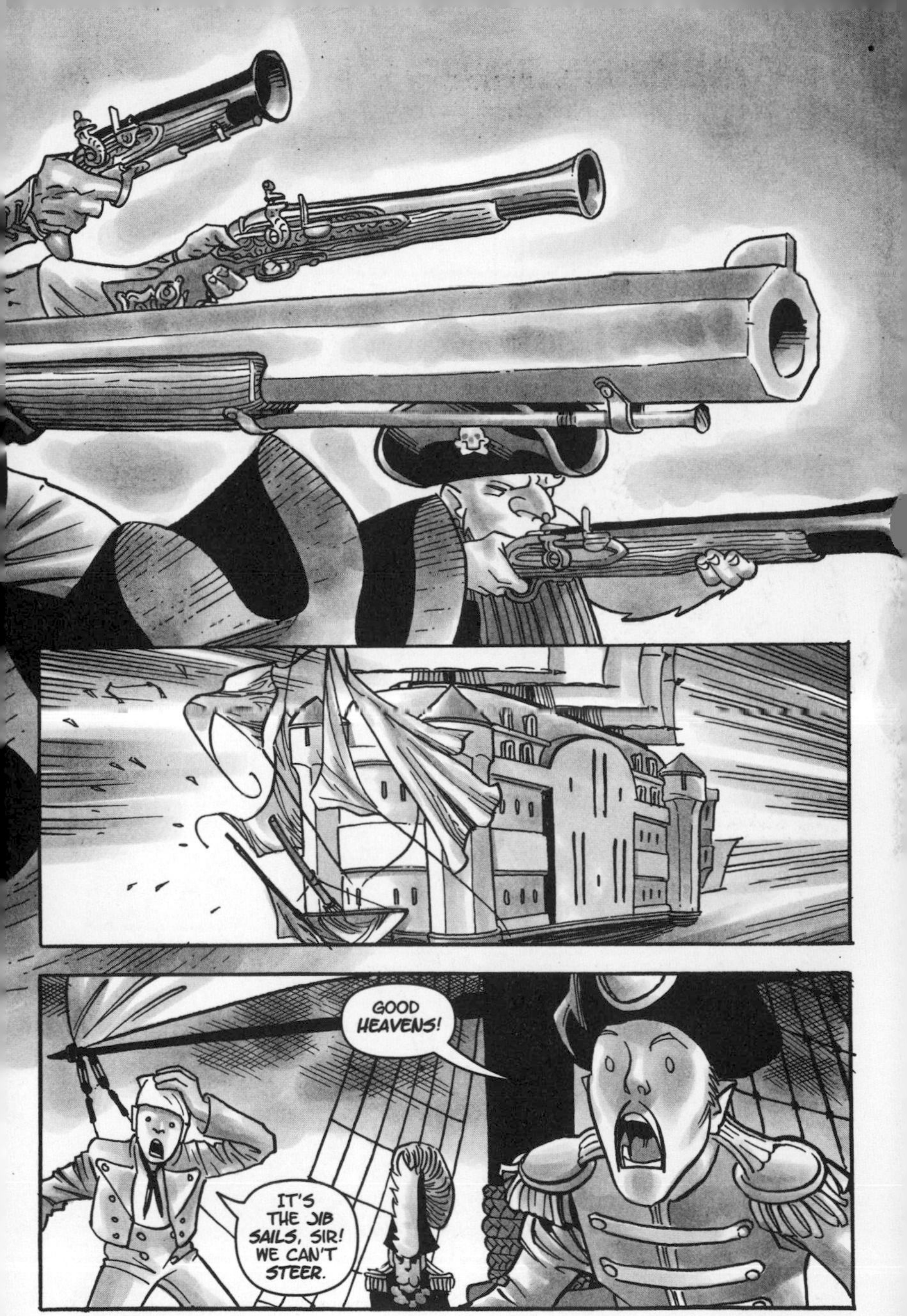
GOOD HEAVENS!
IT'S THE JIB SAILS, SIR! WE CAN'T STEER.

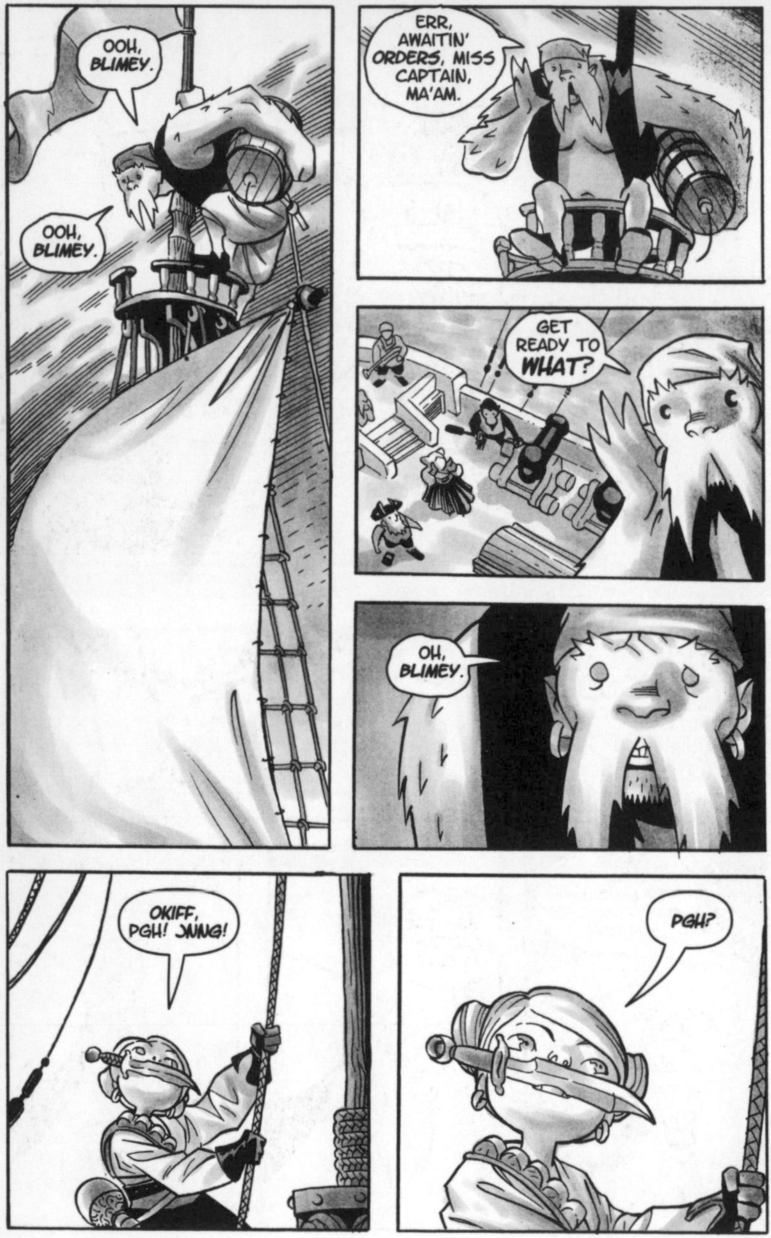
OOH, BLIMEY.
OOH, BLIMEY.
ERR, AWAITIN' ORDERS, MISS CAPTAIN, MA'AM.
GET READY TO WHAT?
OH, BLIMEY.
OKIFF, PGH! JNNG!
PGH?

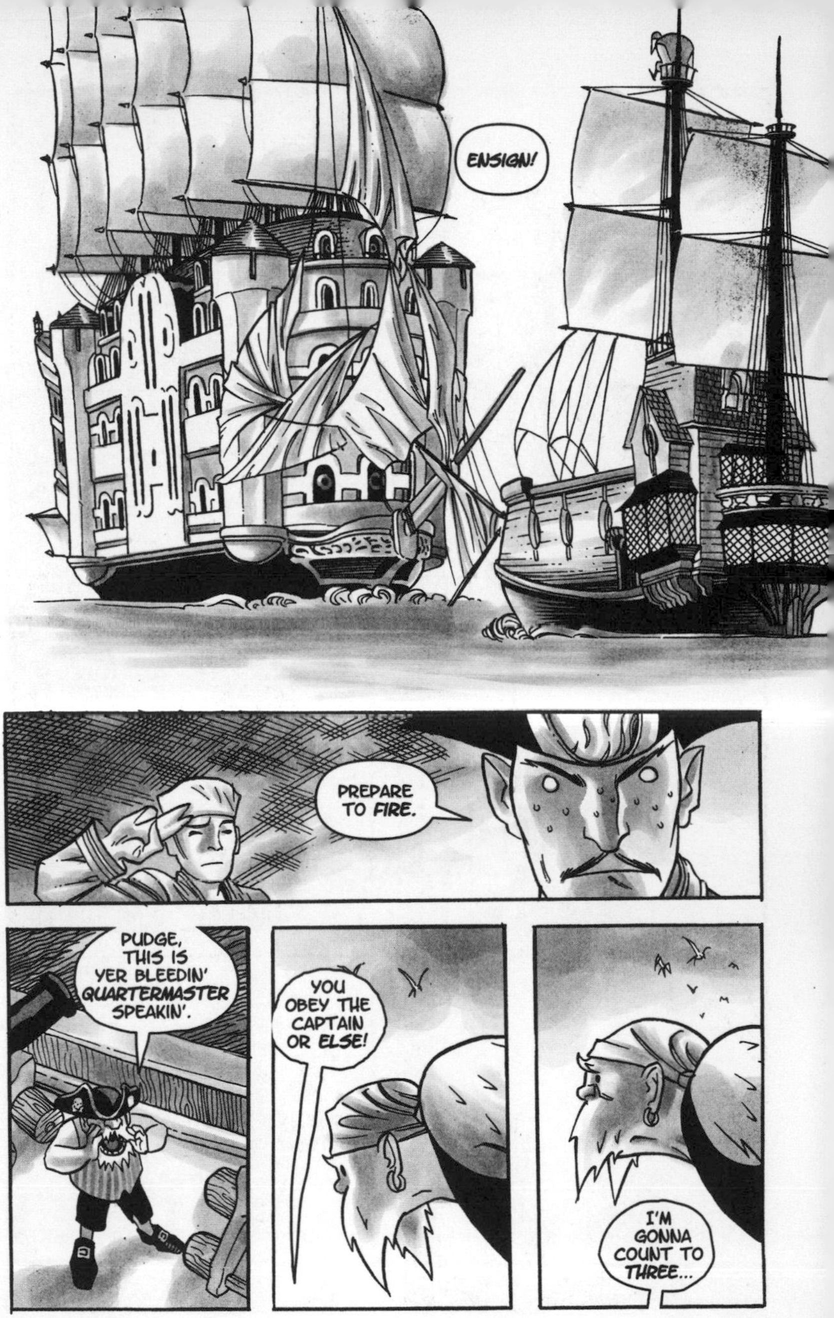
ENSIGN!
PREPARE TO FIRE.
PUDGE, THIS IS YER BLEEDIN' QUARTERMASTER SPEAKIN'.
YOU OBEY THE CAPTAIN OR ELSE!
I'M GONNA COUNT TO THREE...

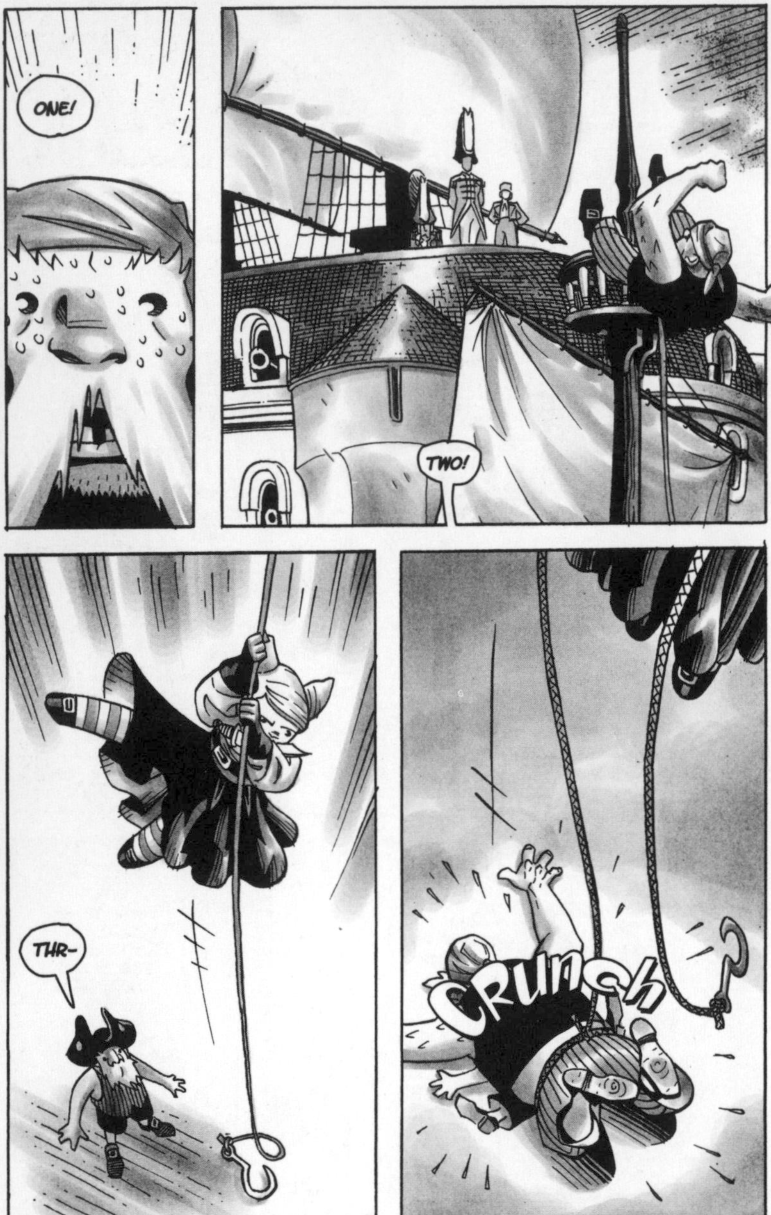
ONE!
TWO!
THR-
CRUNCH

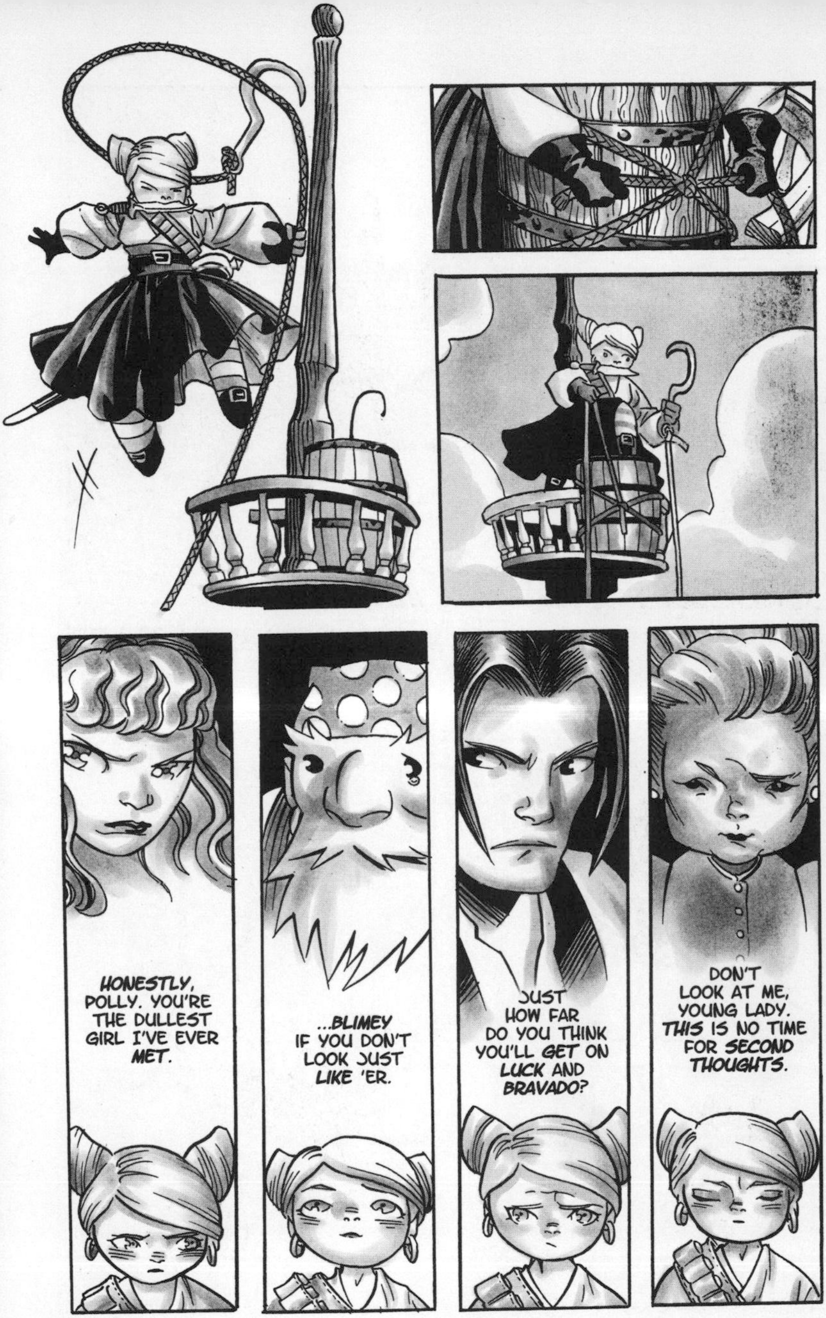
HONESTLY, POLLY. YOU'RE THE DULLEST GIRL I'VE EVER MET.
...BLIMEY IF YOU DON'T LOOK JUST LIKE 'ER.
JUST HOW FAR DO YOU THINK YOU'LL GET ON LUCK AND BRAVADO?
DON'T LOOK AT ME, YOUNG LADY. THIS IS NO TIME FOR SECOND THOUGHTS.

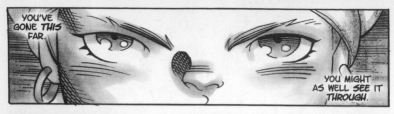

YOU'VE GONE *THIS* FAR.

YOU MIGHT AS WELL SEE IT *THROUGH.*

FIRE AT *WILL!*

SINK MEH!

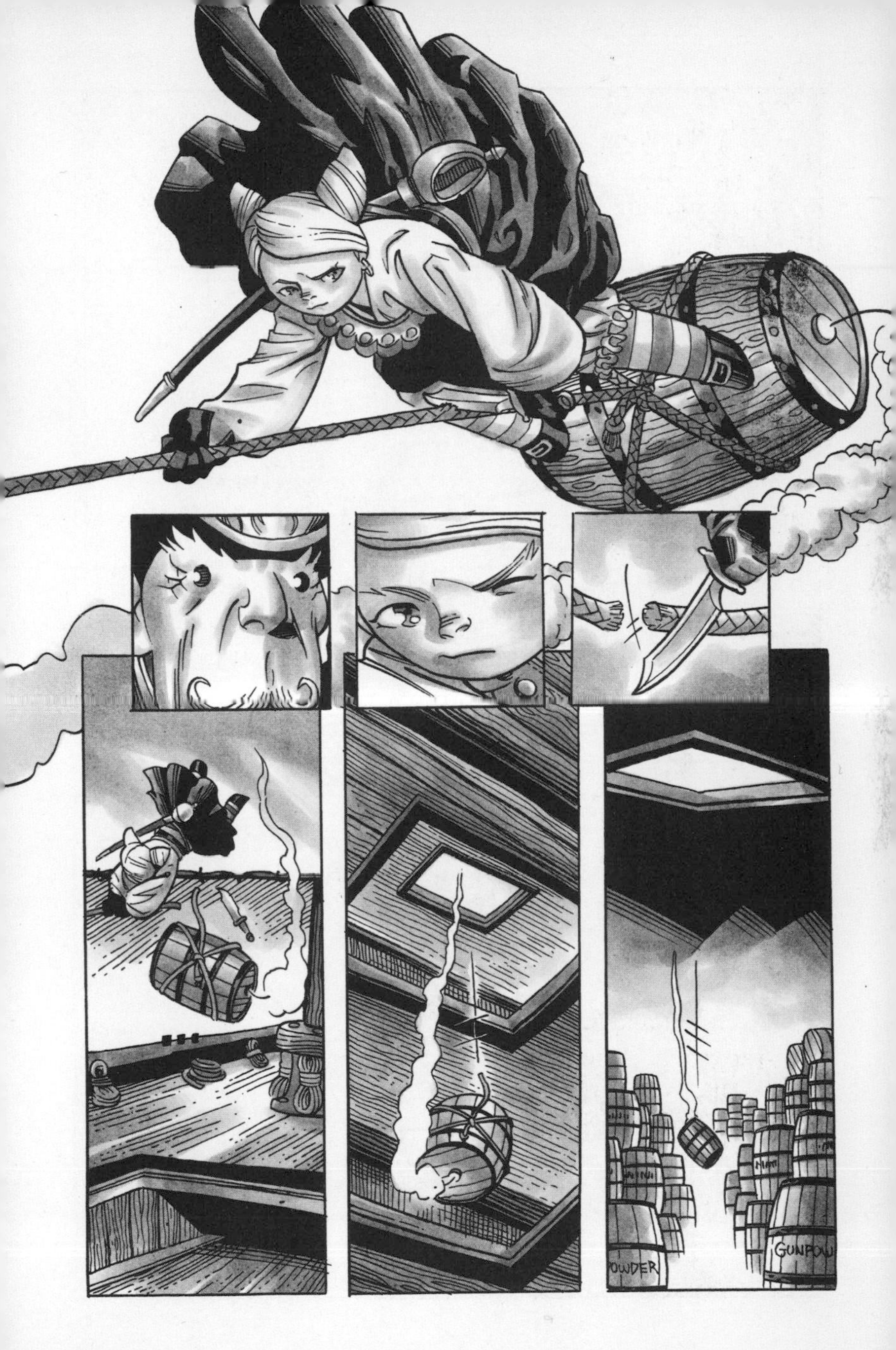
POWDER
GUNPOW

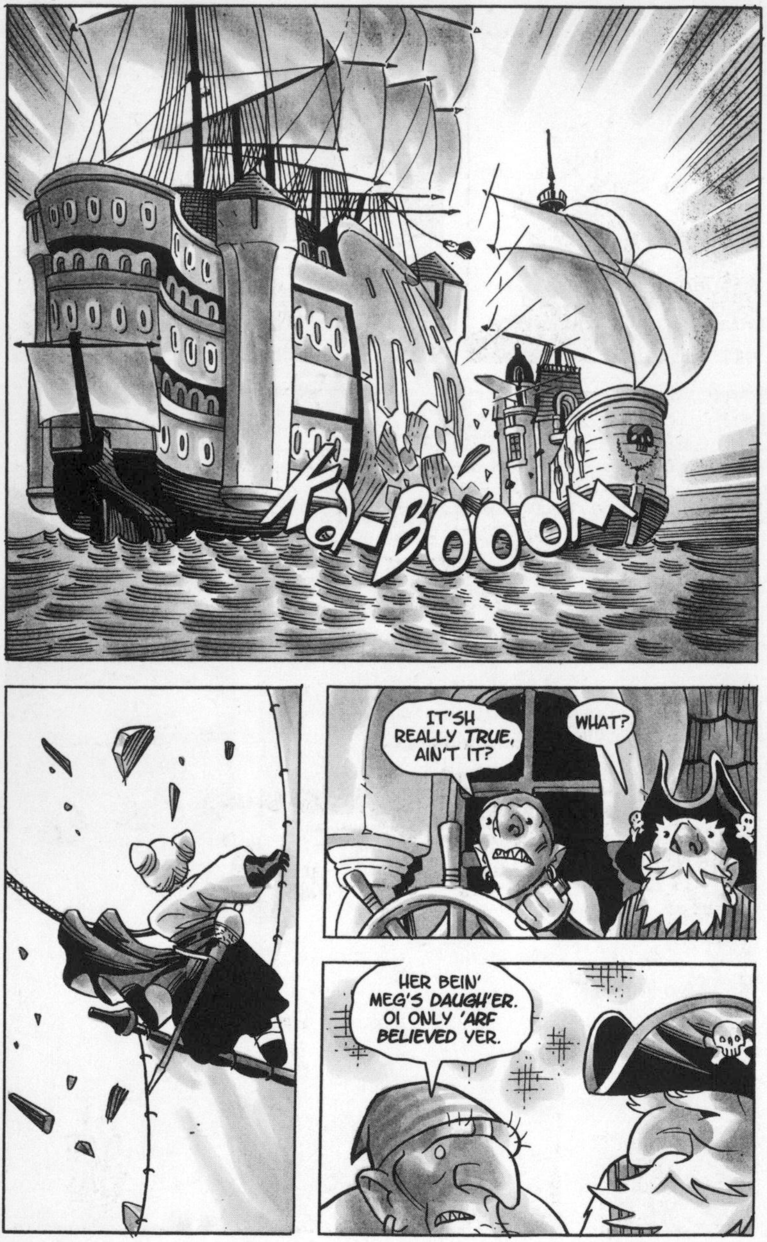
KA-BOOOM
IT'SH REALLY TRUE, AIN'T IT?
WHAT?
HER BEIN' MEG'S DAUGH'ER. OI ONLY 'ARF BELIEVED YER.

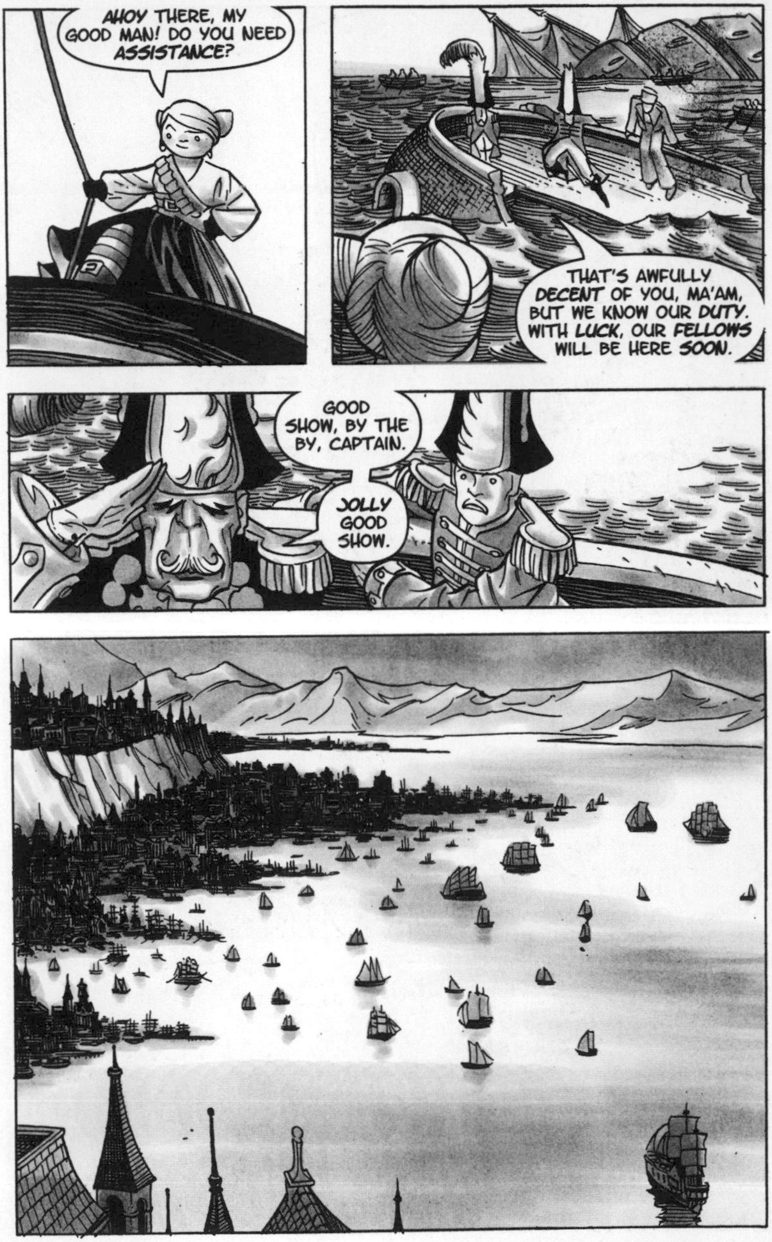
AHOY THERE, MY GOOD MAN! DO YOU NEED ASSISTANCE?
THAT'S AWFULLY DECENT OF YOU, MA'AM, BUT WE KNOW OUR DUTY. WITH LUCK, OUR FELLOWS WILL BE HERE SOON.
GOOD SHOW, BY THE BY, CAPTAIN.
JOLLY GOOD SHOW.

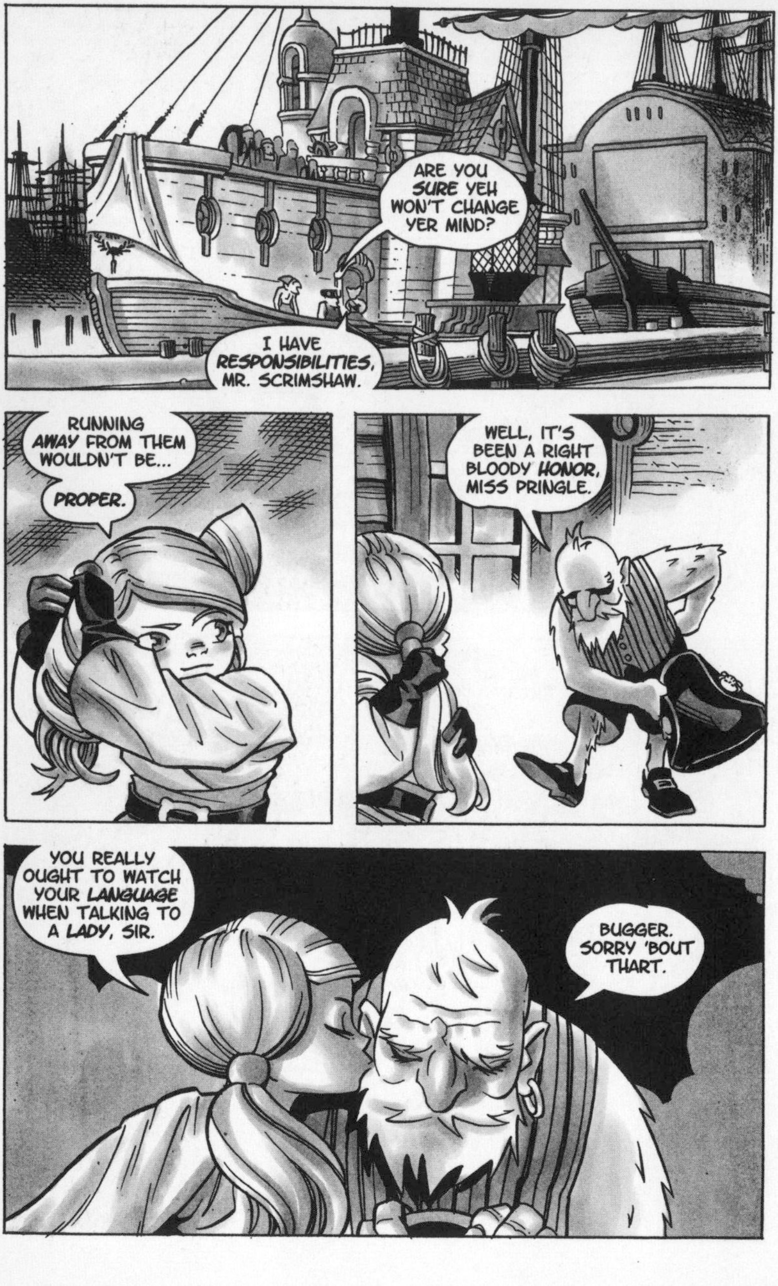
ARE YOU SURE YEH WON'T CHANGE YER MIND?
I HAVE RESPONSIBILITIES, MR. SCRIMSHAW.
RUNNING AWAY FROM THEM WOULDN'T BE...
PROPER.
WELL, IT'S BEEN A RIGHT BLOODY HONOR, MISS PRINGLE.
YOU REALLY OUGHT TO WATCH YOUR LANGUAGE WHEN TALKING TO A LADY, SIR.
BUGGER. SORRY 'BOUT THART.

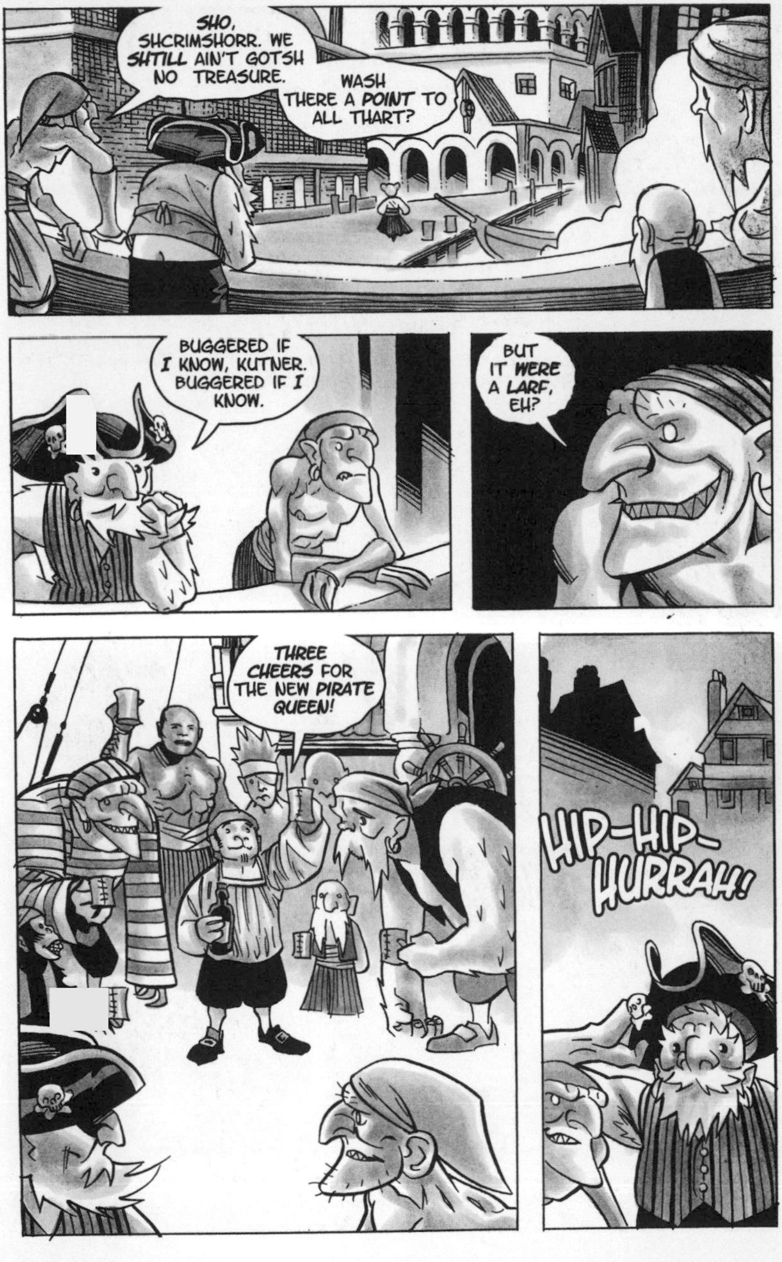
SHO, SHCRIMSHORR. WE SHTILL AIN'T GOTSH NO TREASURE.
WASH THERE A POINT TO ALL THART?
BUGGERED IF I KNOW, KUTNER. BUGGERED IF I KNOW.
BUT IT WERE A LARF, EH?
THREE CHEERS FOR THE NEW PIRATE QUEEN!
HIP-HIP-HURRAH!

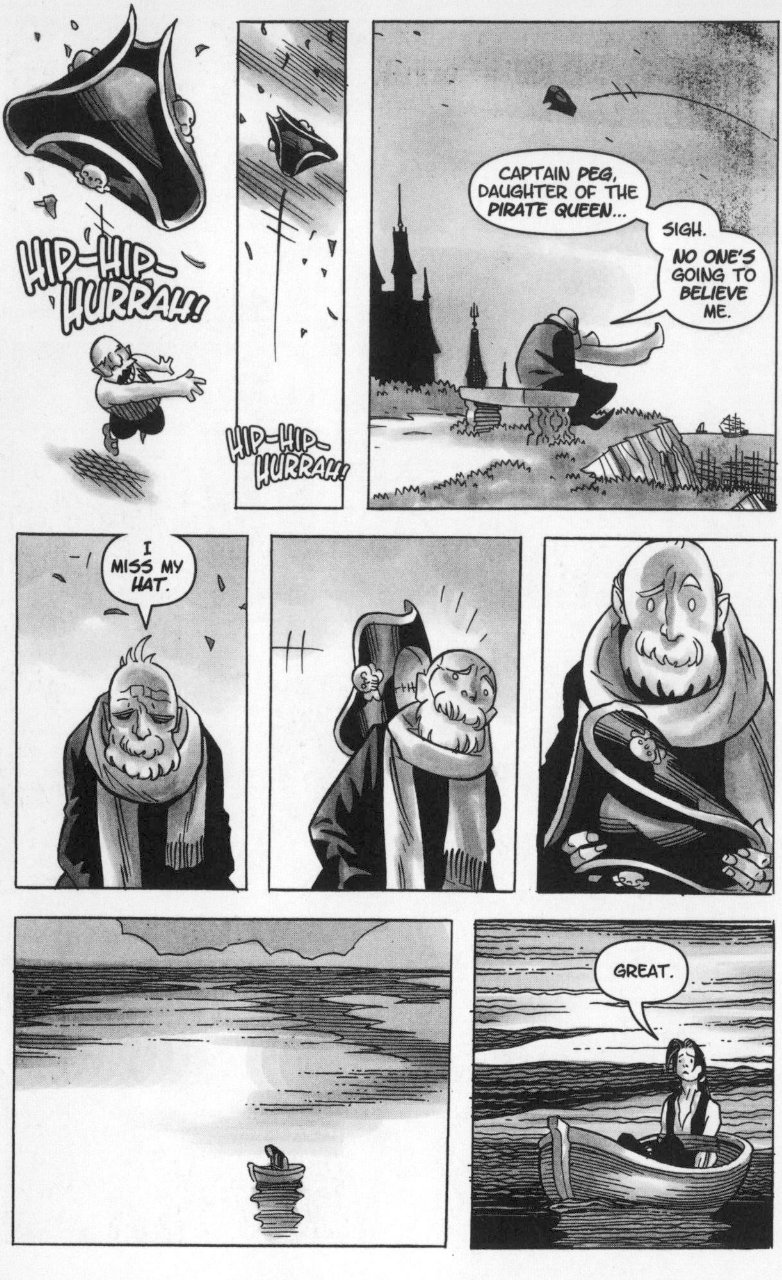
HIP-HIP-HURRAH!
HIP-HIP-HURRAH!
CAPTAIN PEG, DAUGHTER OF THE PIRATE QUEEN...
SIGH.
NO ONE'S GOING TO BELIEVE ME.
I MISS MY HAT.
GREAT.

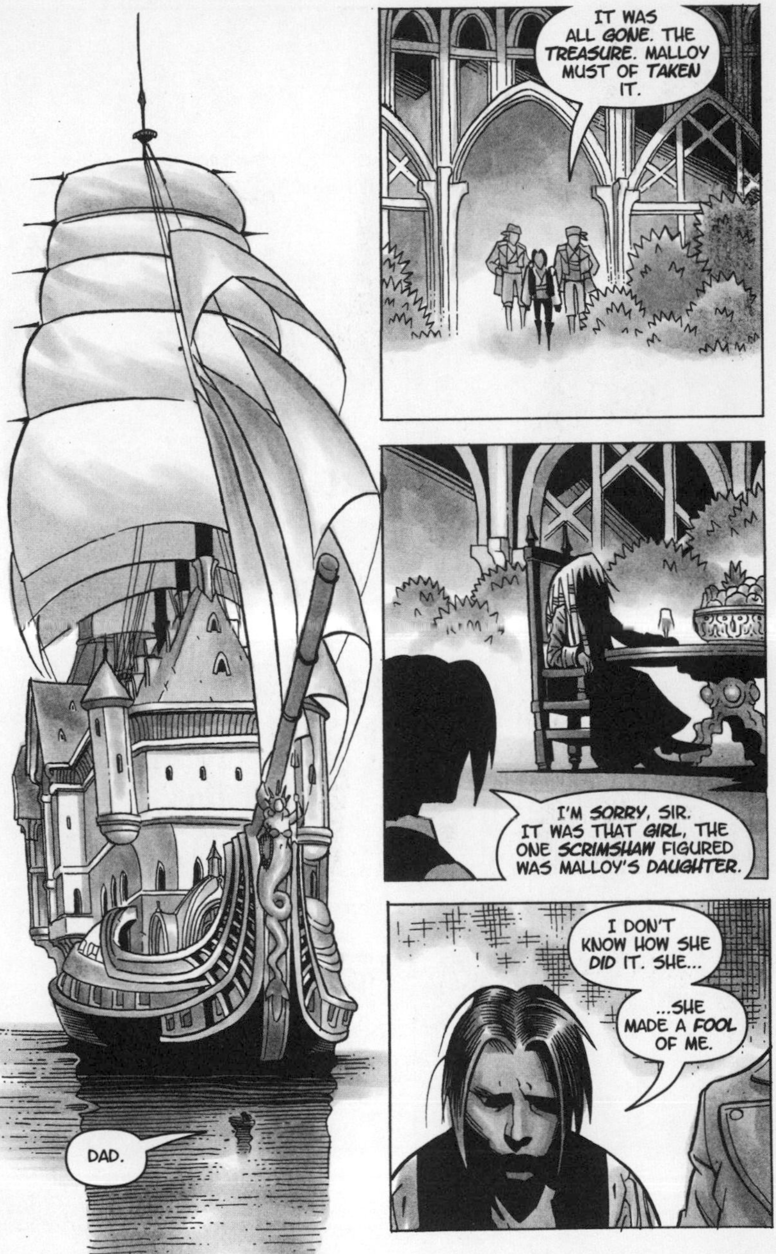
IT WAS ALL GONE. THE TREASURE. MALLOY MUST OF TAKEN IT.
I'M SORRY, SIR. IT WAS THAT GIRL, THE ONE SCRIMSHAW FIGURED WAS MALLOY'S DAUGHTER.
I DON'T KNOW HOW SHE DID IT. SHE...
...SHE MADE A FOOL OF ME.
DAD.

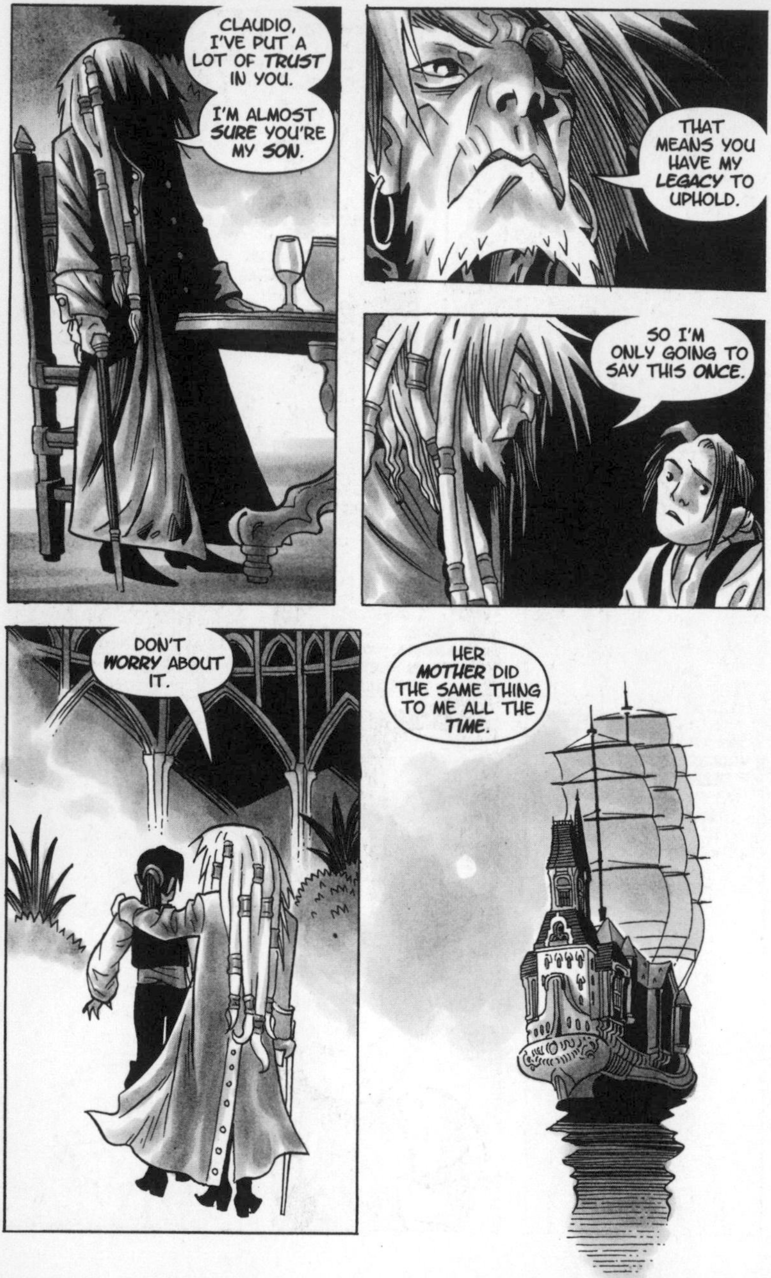
CLAUDIO, I'VE PUT A LOT OF TRUST IN YOU.
I'M ALMOST SURE YOU'RE MY SON.
THAT MEANS YOU HAVE MY LEGACY TO UPHOLD.
SO I'M ONLY GOING TO SAY THIS ONCE.
DON'T WORRY ABOUT IT.
HER MOTHER DID THE SAME THING TO ME ALL THE TIME.

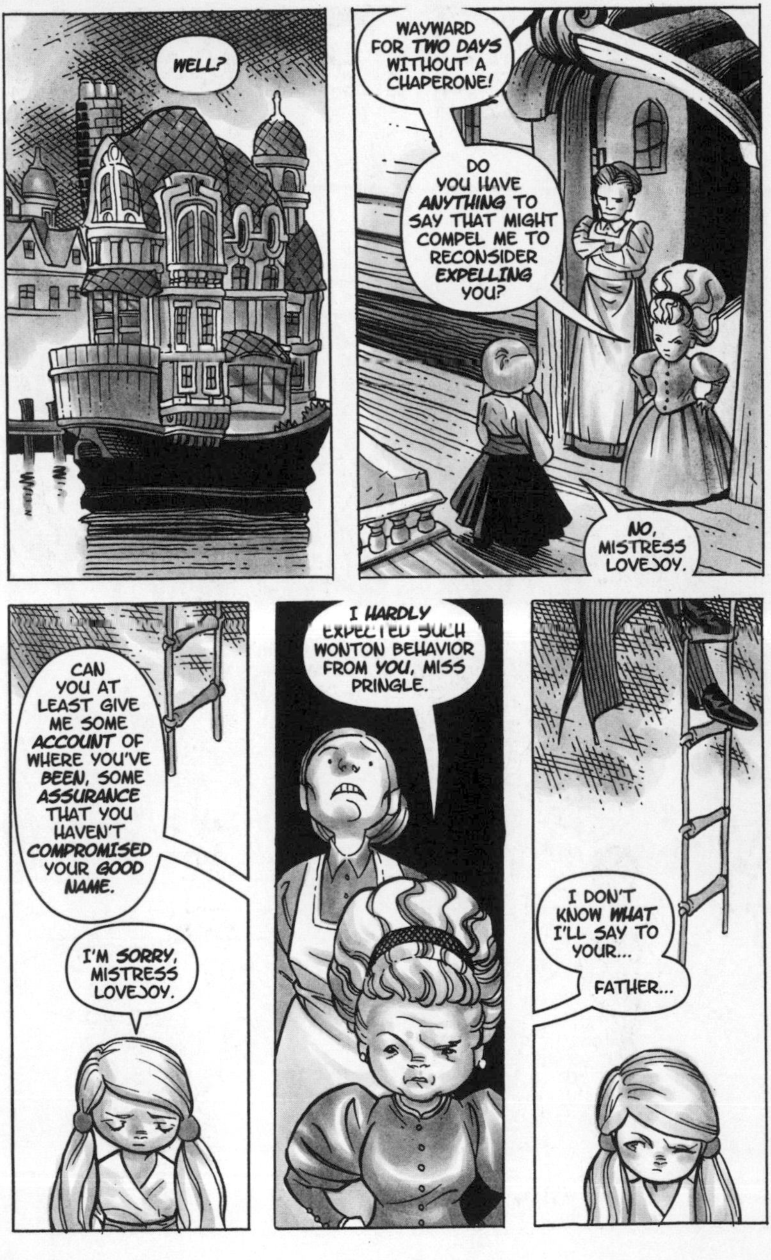
WELL?
WAYWARD FOR TWO DAYS WITHOUT A CHAPERONE!
DO YOU HAVE ANYTHING TO SAY THAT MIGHT COMPEL ME TO RECONSIDER EXPELLING YOU?
NO, MISTRESS LOVEJOY.
CAN YOU AT LEAST GIVE ME SOME ACCOUNT OF WHERE YOU'VE BEEN, SOME ASSURANCE THAT YOU HAVEN'T COMPROMISED YOUR GOOD NAME.
I'M SORRY, MISTRESS LOVEJOY.
I HARDLY EXPECTED SUCH WONTON BEHAVIOR FROM YOU, MISS PRINGLE.
I DON'T KNOW WHAT I'LL SAY TO YOUR...
FATHER...

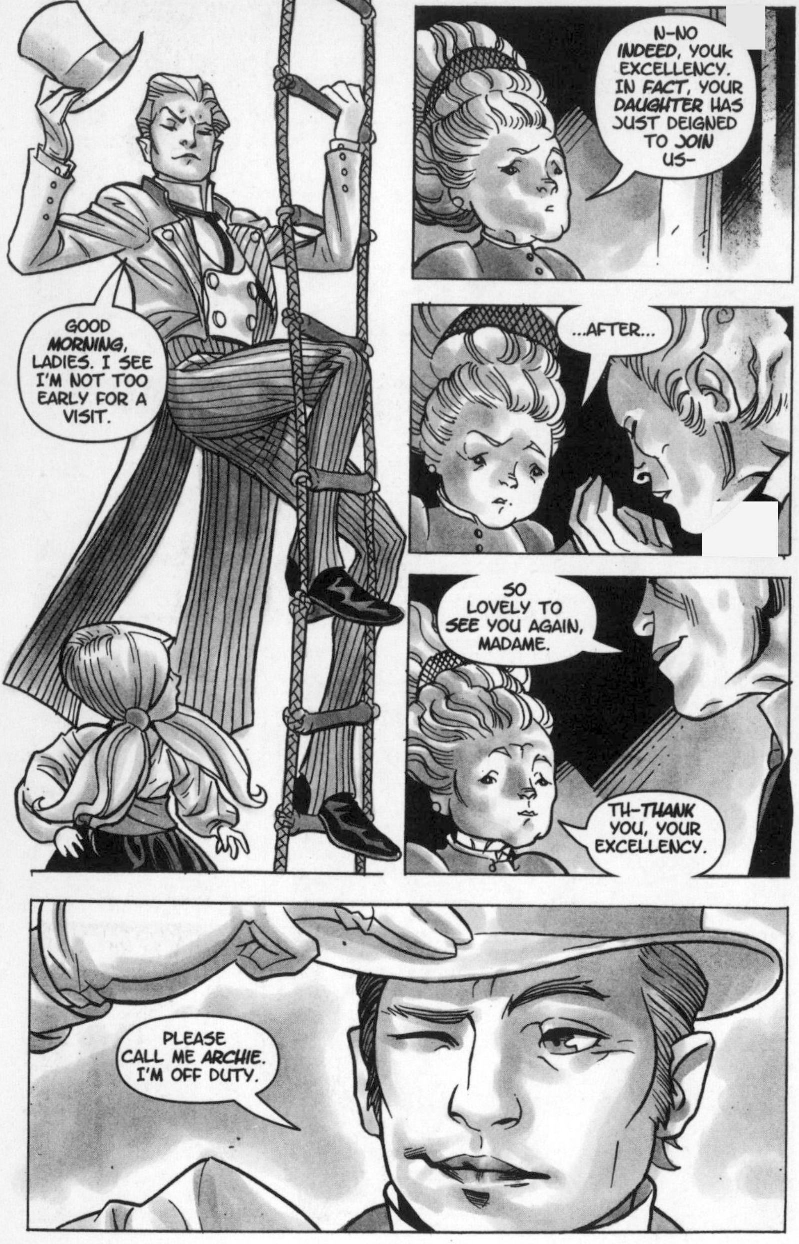
GOOD MORNING, LADIES. I SEE I'M NOT TOO EARLY FOR A VISIT.
N-NO INDEED, YOUR EXCELLENCY. IN FACT, YOUR DAUGHTER HAS JUST DEIGNED TO JOIN US-
...AFTER...
SO LOVELY TO SEE YOU AGAIN, MADAME.
TH-THANK YOU, YOUR EXCELLENCY.
PLEASE CALL ME ARCHIE. I'M OFF DUTY.

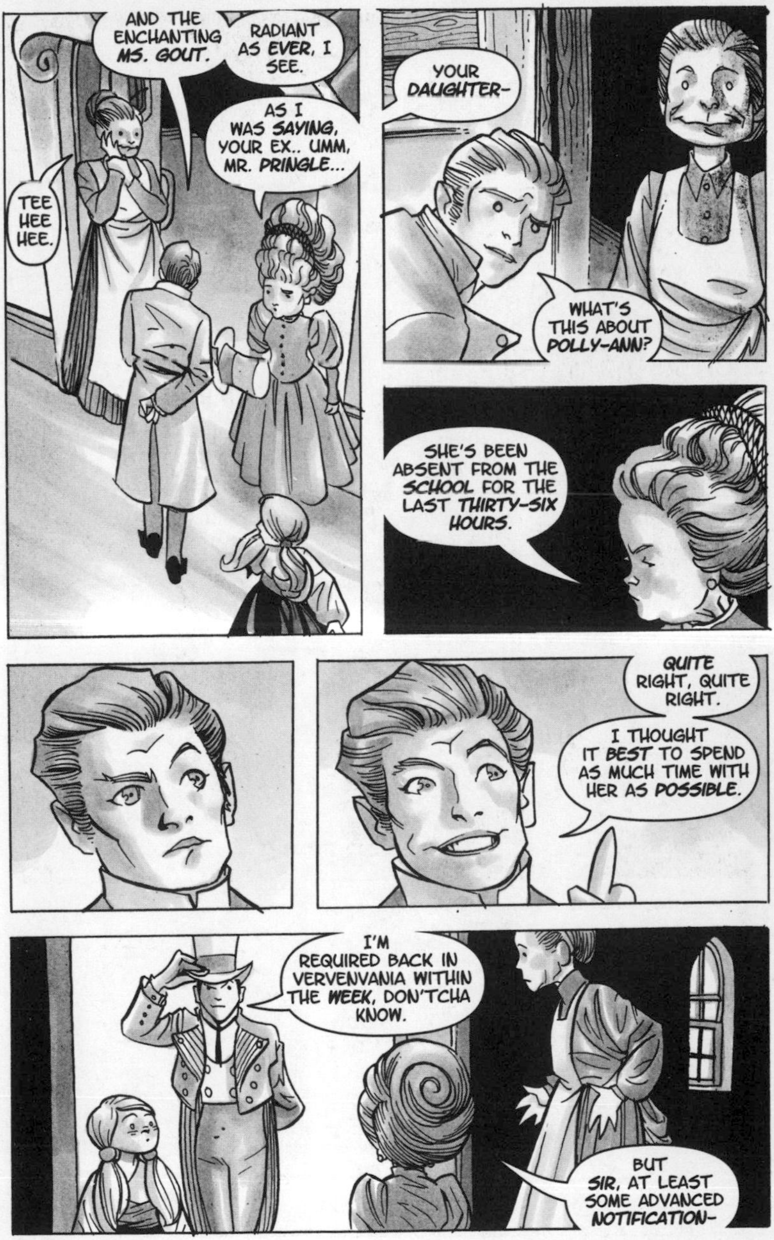
AND THE ENCHANTING MS. GOUT.
RADIANT AS EVER, I SEE.
TEE HEE HEE.
AS I WAS SAYING, YOUR EX.. UMM, MR. PRINGLE...
YOUR DAUGHTER-
WHAT'S THIS ABOUT POLLY-ANN?
SHE'S BEEN ABSENT FROM THE SCHOOL FOR THE LAST THIRTY-SIX HOURS.
QUITE RIGHT, QUITE RIGHT.
I THOUGHT IT BEST TO SPEND AS MUCH TIME WITH HER AS POSSIBLE.
I'M REQUIRED BACK IN VERVENVANIA WITHIN THE WEEK, DON'TCHA KNOW.
BUT SIR, AT LEAST SOME ADVANCED NOTIFICATION-

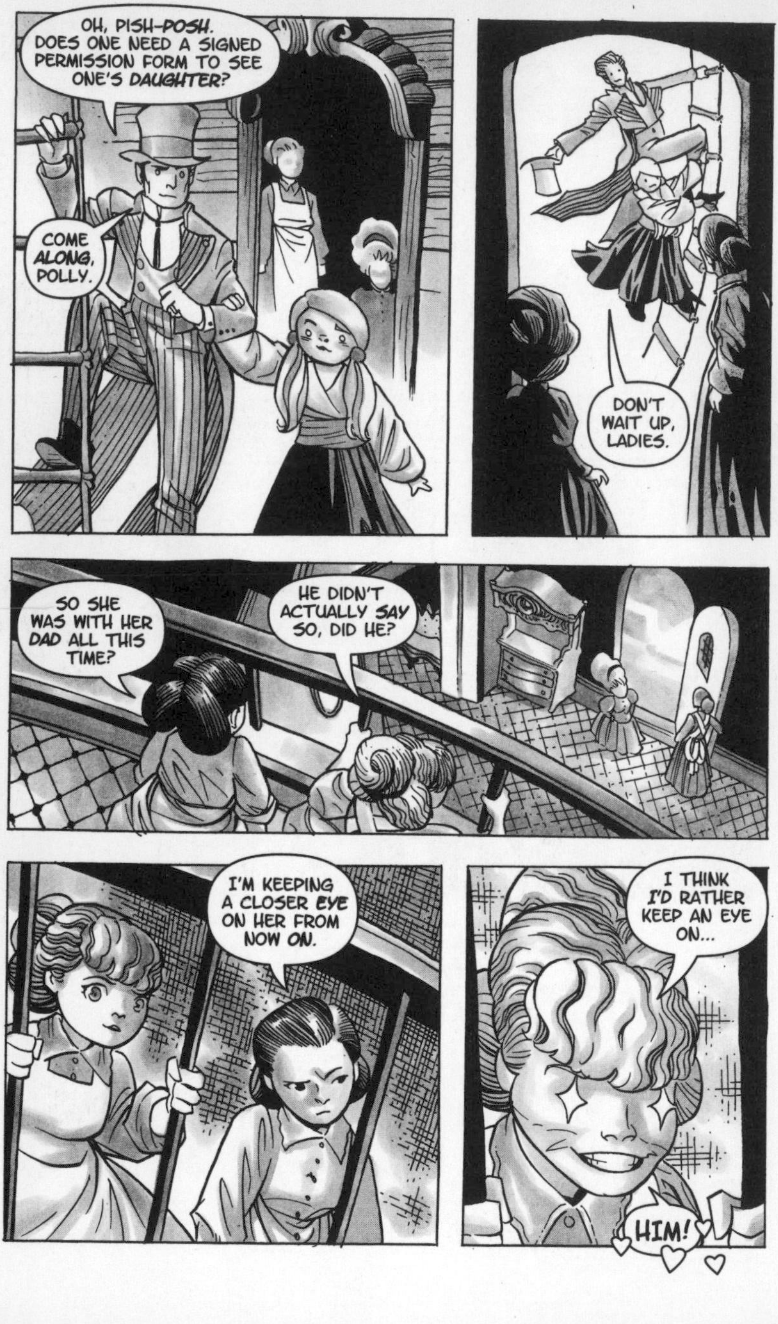
OH, PISH-POSH. DOES ONE NEED A SIGNED PERMISSION FORM TO SEE ONE'S DAUGHTER?
COME ALONG, POLLY.
DON'T WAIT UP, LADIES.
SO SHE WAS WITH HER DAD ALL THIS TIME?
HE DIDN'T ACTUALLY SAY SO, DID HE?
I'M KEEPING A CLOSER EYE ON HER FROM NOW ON.
I THINK I'D RATHER KEEP AN EYE ON...
HIM!

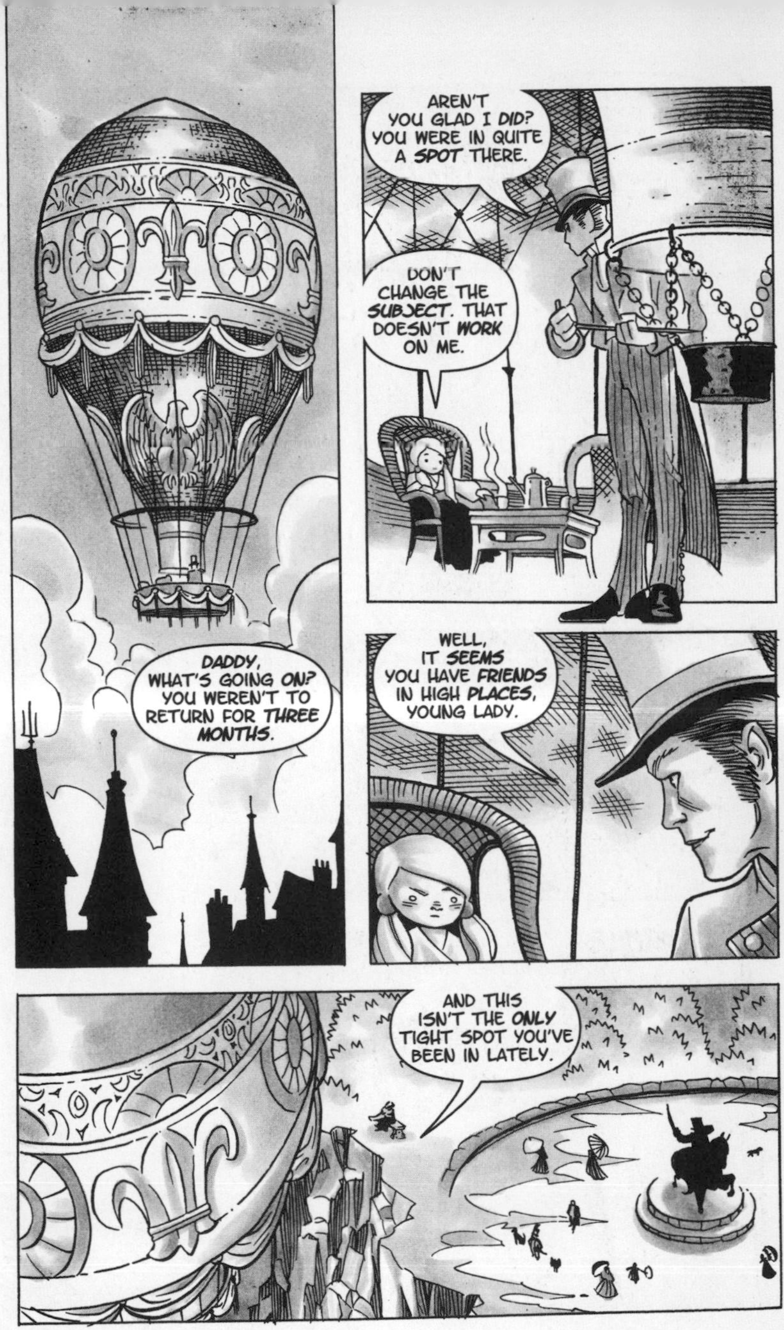
DADDY, WHAT'S GOING ON? YOU WEREN'T TO RETURN FOR THREE MONTHS.
AREN'T YOU GLAD I DID? YOU WERE IN QUITE A SPOT THERE.
DON'T CHANGE THE SUBJECT. THAT DOESN'T WORK ON ME.
WELL, IT SEEMS YOU HAVE FRIENDS IN HIGH PLACES, YOUNG LADY.
AND THIS ISN'T THE ONLY TIGHT SPOT YOU'VE BEEN IN LATELY.

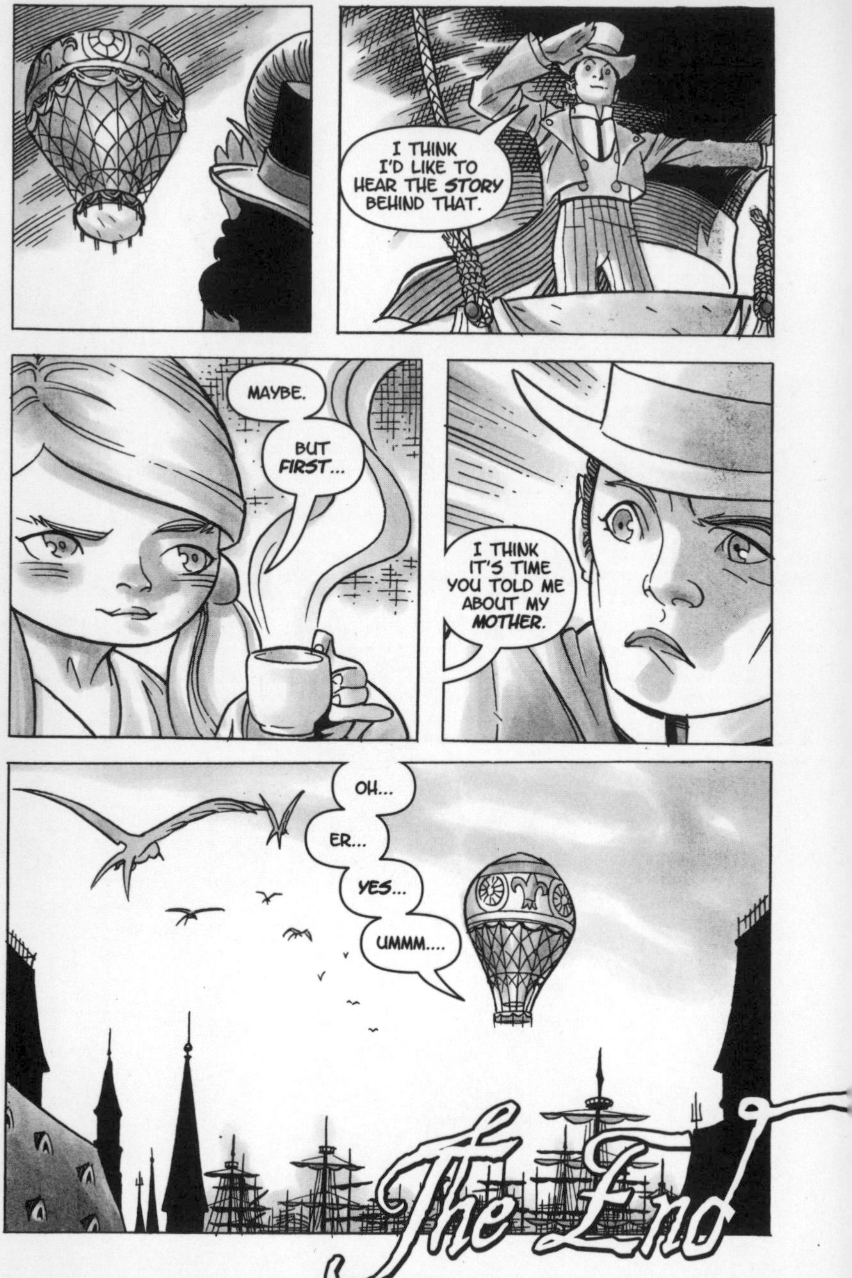
I THINK I'D LIKE TO HEAR THE STORY BEHIND THAT.
MAYBE.
BUT FIRST...
I THINK IT'S TIME YOU TOLD ME ABOUT MY MOTHER.
OH...
ER...
YES...
UMMM....
The End

Among readers of the spookier sorts of comics, Ted Naifeh is a fan favorite. Since the early nineties, he's done illustration work for a wide variety of publishers, ranging from Marvel to Dark Horse to Wizards of the Coast. He is best known for *Courtney Crumrin*, which represents his first published writing, and has been surprisingly well received. The original mini-series, *Courtney Crumrin and the Night Things*, was nominated for an Eisner award for best limited series in 2003. The third collection, *Courtney Crumrin in the Twilight Kingdom*, earned another Eisner nomination in 2005. To date, there are three volumes of Courtney Crumrin and a special prestige one-shot entitled *Courtney Crumrin Tales: A Portrait of the Warlock as a Young Man*.

Ted is also the co-creator of works such as the goth-romance *GloomCookie* and the groundbreaking *How Loathsome*, now collected at NBM. He was also the artist on books like *Death Jr.* and *The Gunwitch: Outskirts of Doom*.

Ted resides in San Francisco because he loves fog.